PERSPECTIVES OF TWO ISLAND NATIONS

Singapore–New Zealand

PERSPECTIVES OF
TWO ISLAND NATIONS

Singapore–New Zealand

Editor

Anne-Marie Schleich

S. Rajaratnam School of International Studies, NTU, Singapore

World Scientific

EW JERSEY · LONDON · SINGAPORE · BEIJING · SHANGHAI · HONG KONG · TAIPEI · CHENNAI · TOKYO

Published by

World Scientific Publishing Co. Pte. Ltd.
5 Toh Tuck Link, Singapore 596224
USA office: 27 Warren Street, Suite 401-402, Hackensack, NJ 07601
UK office: 57 Shelton Street, Covent Garden, London WC2H 9HE

British Library Cataloguing-in-Publication Data
A catalogue record for this book is available from the British Library.

PERSPECTIVES OF TWO ISLAND NATIONS
Singapore – New Zealand

ISBN 978-981-12-8753-4 (hardcover)
ISBN 978-981-12-8754-1 (ebook for institutions)
ISBN 978-981-12-8755-8 (ebook for individuals)

For any available supplementary material, please visit
https://www.worldscientific.com/worldscibooks/10.1142/13709#t=suppl

Desk Editor: Sandhya Venkatesh

For my husband, Tan Cheng Guan

Message

Singapore and New Zealand are natural partners.

We are both small and open economies that believe in trade liberalisation and economic integration. We share similar perspectives on the region, such as the importance of an open and inclusive regional architecture.

It is therefore no surprise that Singapore and New Zealand started several ground-breaking initiatives together. Singapore's first bilateral free trade agreement was with New Zealand, which then-Prime Minister Helen Clark and I signed in 2000. Our two countries were both part of the Trans Pacific Strategic Economic Partnership Agreement (P4) that eventually grew to become the Comprehensive and Progressive Agreement for Trans-Pacific Partnership (CPTPP). We were pioneers in the digital economy space, launching the Digital Economy Partnership Agreement with Chile, which several economies are now keen to join.

I congratulate Dr Anne-Marie Schleich for assembling a compilation of wide-ranging essays from thought leaders from Singapore and New Zealand. They showcase the excellent bilateral cooperation between Singapore and New Zealand, and offer insights into the foreign and trade policies, environmental and social issues, and creative industries of both countries.

Readers of this book will gain insights on how small states can survive and thrive in an increasingly uncertain world.

GOH CHOK TONG
Emeritus Senior Minister
Prime Minister of Singapore (1990–2004)

Foreword

The year 2025 will commemorate the sixtieth anniversary of the establishment of official diplomatic relations between New Zealand and Singapore. Over these six decades, the two nations have established close co-operation in many areas. New Zealand and Singapore maintain comparable stances on various critical policy concerns faced by small states.

Both countries have a strong belief in the importance of multilateralism and adherence to the rule of law. New Zealand and Singapore have similar positions on various critical policy issues that small states currently encounter. They actively co-operate with a diverse group of partner countries and with a number of international institutions. Presently, they are witness to geopolitical challenges, including those resulting from USA–China tensions, and share concerns about threats to the international legal regime upon which both rely. While maintaining a focus on their respective national interests, both countries carefully navigate their political, economic, and trade relations.

In 1971, the Five Power Defence Arrangements, comprising Singapore, New Zealand, Malaysia, the UK, and Australia, led to more substantial military co-operation between New Zealand and Singapore, a relationship that has grown further since. In 2019, the 'Singapore–New Zealand Enhanced Partnership' was established. This partnership has expanded and now focuses on five pillars of co-operation: trade and economy; defence and security; people-to-people contacts; science, technology, and innovation; and green economy.

New Zealand and Singapore hold a common stance on multilateral trade liberalisation. Both countries presently have six bilateral and multilateral trade agreements with each other. The New Zealand–Singapore Closer Economic Partnership (CEP), signed in 2000 by the then-Prime Minister Goh Chok Tong and me, was ground-breaking as it was Singapore's first-ever bilateral foreign trade agreement. Our co-operation on this led to the negotiation of the Trans-Pacific Partnership Agreement, a forerunner to the Comprehensive and Progressive Agreement for Trans-Pacific Partnership.

This book highlights the accomplishments of both countries working together, while also discussing the history, foreign policies, and economic challenges of each country. Other chapters cover topics such as environmental sustainability, social issues, and the arts sectors in both countries. During my time as Prime Minister and Minister for Arts, Culture, and Heritage, a bilateral agreement on film co-production was signed.

I am sure that this impressive book will educate readers about two island states that have made remarkable progress in a relatively short period. I extend my congratulations to the editor and authors.

Helen Clark

Hon Helen Clark
Former Prime Minister of New Zealand

Acknowledgements

In 2025, Singapore and New Zealand will celebrate 60 years of diplomatic relations. This anniversary marks a significant milestone in the relations between the two countries. They share a long history of close and trusted cooperation in politics, defence, trade, business, and people-to-people contacts.

Both countries also hold a special place in my heart. I started working in Singapore as a young German diplomat back in 1982 and am married to a Singaporean. Since 2016, we have been retired in Singapore. For the past few years, I have been attached as an Adjunct Senior Fellow to one of Singapore's prominent think tanks, the S. Rajaratnam Institute of International Affairs (RSIS). I got to know New Zealand and became friends with a number of New Zealanders while serving as the German Ambassador to New Zealand from 2012 to 2016. Having lived and worked in both countries, I was motivated to edit this volume in order to highlight the sixty-year anniversary of diplomatic relations and to uncover lesser-known aspects of each country's many facets.

I would like to thank all the contributors from Singapore and New Zealand for sharing their thoughts and analyses. I am most grateful for their valuable contributions.

My deep appreciation goes to Singapore's Ambassador-at-Large, Professor Tommy Koh, who first encouraged me to edit this volume and gave invaluable advice and support for this project.

My special thanks go to Helen Clark, former Prime Minister of New Zealand for writing a foreword and to ESM Goh Chok Tong, former Prime Minister of Singapore, for his message.

I wish to thank Ambassador-at-Large Ong Keng Yong, the Executive Deputy Chairman of the S. Rajaratnam School of International Studies (RSIS), Nanyang Technological University, for his continued support and sound advice. My friend Arun Mahizhnan, Special Research Advisor, Institute of Policy Studies, National University of Singapore, was most helpful in getting me in touch with some of the Singapore authors. Ambassador Lawrence Anderson, Senior Fellow at RSIS, provided valuable assistance.

I am grateful to my friends in New Zealand for their support and for helping me find the right experts. I want to especially mention Ian MacKinnon, former Deputy Mayor of Wellington; Malcolm McKinnon, historian and Professor at Victoria University of Wellington; Allan Bollard, former Governor of the Reserve Bank of New Zealand; Chris Seed, former Chief Executive and Secretary of the Ministry of Foreign Affairs; Hon Tim Groser, former Trade Minister for Trade; Peter Kiely, ONZM, Senior Partner at Kiely Thomson Caisley; Errol Clark, Chairman ICCNZ; Judith Geare, Goethe-Institut New Zealand; Peter Carter, Teaching Fellow at the New Zealand Defence Force Command and Staff College in Wellington Defence College; and Karim Dickie, President of the United Nations Association New Zealand.

Finally, I would like to thank my publisher Max Phua and my editors at World Scientific Publishing.

Anne-Marie Schleich

Introduction

Anne-Marie Schleich

The island nations of Singapore and New Zealand have much in common. Both are small countries with a population of just over five million. Notably, both countries share commonalities as former British colonies and young nations. New Zealand, also known as Aotearoa in Māori, attained full independence in 1947, while Singapore gained independence in 1965. New Zealand was one of the first countries to officially recognise Singapore when it became independent. Both countries share similar views on international geopolitics and are strong supporters of multilateral frameworks and the Rule of Law. Moreover, both nations are facing an increasingly-contested Indo-Pacific region. They are active participants in regional, United Nations, and other international organisations. Both Singapore and New Zealand face similar global challenges arising from overlapping international crises. Their economies have been adversely impacted, albeit to varying degrees, by the aftermath of the COVID-19 pandemic and disruptions of global supply chains. As small and open economies that rely heavily on trade, they share similar views on trade issues, believe in trade liberalisation, and are signatories to numerous multilateral free trade agreements.

Despite these similarities, the two nations have developed at different speeds and in different ways. New Zealand has a low population density of 20 people per square km, whereas Singapore has a much higher population density of 8,058 (2023) people. The two countries differ in terms of their economic foundations. New Zealand has a resource- and agriculture-based economy and also relies on tourism, manufacturing, and education as primary contributors to its GDP. It faces the challenge of geographical remoteness from major Asian markets, with only Australia and Pacific Island countries as its closest neighbours. New Zealand is the world's 12th largest agricultural exporter, with 81.4% of its exports being agricultural commodities, mainly dairy products and meat. Singapore, on the other hand, is a prosperous city-state situated on one of the world's most vital shipping and trading routes. It has become a major financial hub and is focused on advanced technology (manufacturing of electronics, biomedical products, and chemicals) and high-end science research. In 2022, Singapore's GDP per capita was approximately US$82,800 compared to New Zealand's US$ 48,400 (World Bank). Both countries have implemented tax and other incentives in order to attract foreign direct investment from around the world.

What connects New Zealand and Singapore? In 2025, Singapore and New Zealand will celebrate 60 years of diplomatic relations. In his essay, David Capie describes the longstanding defence relationship between the Armed Forces of Singapore and New Zealand. Until today, cooperation between the armed forces of both countries remains close. The two countries also share common interests across international trade and in political and strategic issues. In 2000, the New Zealand–Singapore Closer Economic Partnership was signed by then-Prime Minister of Singapore Goh Chok Tong and then-Prime Minister of New Zealand Helen Clark. It was significant as it was Singapore's first-ever bilateral free trade agreement and New Zealand's second. Singapore is now New Zealand's fourth-largest trading partner. In 2019, New Zealand and Singapore signed the 'Enhanced Partnership' which focuses on four pillars of cooperation in the areas of trade and economics, security and defence, science and innovation, and people-to-people links. A bilateral Arrangement on Science, Technology, and Innovation was signed in 2019 to support research collaboration in areas such as Data Science and Future Foods. In 2022, a climate and green economy pillar was established. Then, during the visit of New Zealand Prime Minister Christopher Luxon to Singapore in April 2024, a supply chain and connectivity pillar was added to further broaden the Enhanced partnership.

This volume is **a compilation of essays written by 27 prominent experts from Singapore and New Zealand**. The twenty-five essays highlight the similarities and differences between the two countries, covering a range of important topics, among them each country's history, foreign policy, economy, trade relations, sustainability policies, creative sectors, and policies regarding their ageing societies. Other authors discuss areas of close cooperation between the two nations, particularly in defence, trade, and business.

In the chapters on **History and Outlook**, eminent Singapore historian **Tan Tai Yong** tells the story of Singapore as a young nation and its remarkable transformation from a struggling former British colony to a successful global city-state. He provides excellent insights into the formidable challenges Singapore faced along the way and the key moments in Singapore's modern history. **Peter Carter**, a specialist in New Zealand's political and military history, presents a historical overview of diplomatic relations between New Zealand and Singapore from the 1950s to 1970, in the context of the emergence of both countries as independent states. He draws on New Zealand's archival records to provide a detailed account, including previously-unknown details, of the establishment of a diplomatic post in Singapore. **Hon. Christopher Finlayson KC,** a former New Zealand Attorney-General and Minister for Treaty of Waitangi Negotiations, analyses the New Zealand government's attempts over the last 50 years to address longstanding grievances between the Māori, the indigenous people of New Zealand, and the State. The process involved government apologies, returning land to the Māori people, and providing financial compensation. **William Tan**, Singapore's High Commissioner to New Zealand, and **Gabrielle Rush**, New Zealand's High Commissioner to the Republic of Singapore, jointly provide an overview of the strong relationship and trust between the two countries, and offer insights into future cooperation between Singapore and New Zealand.

The chapters on **Foreign Policy in a Changing Environment** illustrate how Singapore and New Zealand are delicately navigating ongoing geopolitical challenges. Despite their small populations, both nations play proactive roles in regional, UN, and other international agencies. Ambassador-at-Large **Tommy Koh**, a renowned Singaporean diplomat, discusses the challenges facing Singapore's foreign policy, the significance of ASEAN, and Singapore's relations with the two superpowers. He emphasises the importance of multilateralism, free trade, and adherence to the rule of law for small nations like Singapore and New Zealand which have a significant role to play. Distinguished New Zealand foreign policy expert **Nicholas Khoo** analyses the challenges faced by New Zealand's foreign policy between 2017 and 2023 under the administrations of Jacinda Ardern (2017–2023), Christopher Hipkins (2023), and Christopher Luxon (since 2023). The author discusses the country's response to various issues, including nuclear weapons, the environment, and New Zealand's management of relations with China, in the context of an increasingly-strained relationship between China and New Zealand's sole treaty ally, Australia, as well as its close partner, the US.

Former Singapore Ambassador **Lawrence Anderson** reflects on ASEAN, Southeast Asia's main regional institution, its achievements since its formation in 1967, and its limitations as well as the role of Singapore within it. He also discusses how ASEAN could address current regional challenges. Former New Zealand Ambassador **Michael Powles** and Singapore's Non-Resident Ambassador to the Pacific Island Forum, **Mary Seet-Cheng**, discuss their respective countries' relationships and engagement with Pacific Island nations. Michael Powles describes how Pacific Island countries are seeking solutions for the many problems they are facing including the difficulty of maintaining regional unity within the framework of the Pacific Island Forum and the impact of strategic competition between the US and China. He also discusses their right to self-determination and the role that New Zealand is playing in the Pacific region. Mary Seet-Cheng outlines Singapore's extensive cooperation with Pacific Island countries through various capacity-building programmes and close partnerships in international fora.

David Capie explores the longstanding and close **Defence and Security** cooperation between New Zealand and Singapore. He argues that despite this strong base of goodwill, New Zealand "needs to invest in the Singapore relationship to demonstrate ongoing value to an important security partner."

In the section on **Economic Challenges and Business Cooperation**, two renowned economists, **Brian Easton** of New Zealand and **Manu Bhaskaran** of Singapore, discuss the economic challenges their respective countries are facing. Brian Easton compares the structural differences and similarities between New Zealand and Singapore. The two countries have been able to work together in the international economic arena to their mutual benefit. This has been immensely beneficial to New Zealand in assisting its external diversification and derisking some of its exposures. He also analyses New Zealand's strong economic relations with China. Manu Bhaskaran identifies the economic challenges for Singapore amidst a turbulent global setting after a long period of impressive and strong economic performance and points out emerging weaknesses. **Siah Hwee Ang**, a leading New Zealand-based expert in international business strategy with a specialisation in Asian business affairs, focuses on key areas of bilateral business cooperation, such as agritech, logistics, green technology, and fintech-related services, and identifies potential areas of growth. **Ken Hickson**, an author and sustainability and communications consultant based in Singapore, shares his succinct observations on bilateral business ventures.

Free Trade Agreements (FTAs) which grant enhanced access to overseas markets have been instrumental in shaping New Zealand's and Singapore's global partnerships. The two countries are now connected through mutual membership in five plurilateral FTAs and one bilateral FTA. Singapore is presently New Zealand's biggest trading partner in Southeast Asia. **Tim Groser**, the former New Zealand Minister for Trade, provides a firsthand account of the early days of the Trans-Pacific Partnership Agreement

(TPP), the predecessor to the Comprehensive and Progressive Agreement for Trans-Pacific Partnership (CPTPP). Singapore's former Minister for Trade and Industry, **George Yeo**, contributes a perceptive commentary to Groser's observations. Both Groser and Yeo were the driving forces behind the TPP.

The chapters on **Climate Change, Environmental, and Sustainable Policies** discuss important aspects of our environment. The 2022 IPSOS Global Advisor Study revealed that 81% of New Zealanders were "very worried" about climate change. 43.7% of Singaporeans regard climate change as "either an immediate threat or an important issue" according to the 2023 Southeast Asia Climate Outlook survey conducted by the Institute of Southeast Asian Studies (ISEAS). **Dave Lowe** is a distinguished international atmospheric chemist, one of the lead authors of a 2007 United Nations IPCC report, and co-winner of the Nobel Peace Prize. He began atmospheric CO_2 measurements in New Zealand over 50 years ago. In his essay, he brings us to the very heart of climate science, outlines the shocking results of international climate change research, and discusses the various climate change agreements. Additionally, he analyses New Zealand's climate change policies. Complementing Dave Lowe's article, **Benjamin Horton**, Director of the Earth Observatory of Singapore (EOS) at Nanyang Technological University Singapore, and eleven members of his EOS team identify environmental threats that Southeast Asian countries are facing, such as climate change, rising sea levels, earthquakes, and volcanic eruptions. They also highlight the remarkable research and activities conducted by the Earth Observatory of Singapore. **Greg Severinsen** and **Raewyn Peart** of the Environmental Defence Society explore New Zealand's recent turbulent experience of environmental law reform. In 2023, the government of New Zealand enacted a rather innovative law that sought to better protect the environment while providing greater certainty for development. It briefly replaced the country's Resource Management Act.

Both New Zealand and Singapore have made significant progress in the **creative sectors**, as the next set of chapters demonstrate. **Sir Richard Taylor**, one of New Zealand's most prominent creators and innovators and an Oscar and BAFTA award winner, shares insights into the making of the country's successful film industry. He provides intriguing glimpses into the founding of the Wellington-based Wētā Workshop, his partnership with iconic film director Peter Jackson, and his passion for creating films. **Kennie Ting,** Director of Singapore's unique 'Asian Civilisations Museum', describes its recent transformation into a museum for modern times which presents ground-breaking perspectives on Asia's global connections, using its world-class collection of Asian art. **Hoe Su Fern,** a Singapore academic, examines the Singapore government's support of the emerging arts scene and explores key aspects of Singapore's drive to become a global creative hub.

The last section tackles the challenge of an **ageing population** which both Singapore and New Zealand face. In New Zealand, one in six people is presently over 65 years of age; in 2028, one in five — or over 1 million people — will be over 65. In Singapore, the number of people over 65 is more than the number of people under 15. Well-known former Singaporean Nominated Member of Parliament and vocal social advocate **Kanwaljit Soin** discusses the Singapore government's policies for ageing. The recent documentary series *Blue Zone* named Singapore a 'Blue Zone 2.0', "a place where the government has instituted policies designed explicitly to promote longevity." She argues that in order to be able to cope with this demographic challenge, the focus has to be on converting an ageing society into a longevity society. New Zealand's Retirement Commissioner **Jane Wrightson** analyses retirement income policies in New Zealand, with a focus on the situation of older women who are disadvantaged by the current system. She recommends an independent review to improve the situation.

I trust that our readers will have an enjoyable and informative journey through the many facets and perspectives of Singapore and New Zealand.

About the Editor

Anne-Marie Schleich served as a German career diplomat from 1979 to 2016. Most recently, she was the German Ambassador to New Zealand and seven Pacific Island countries from 2012 to 2016. She has also served in Singapore, Bangkok, Islamabad, London, and Melbourne. Dr Schleich holds a doctorate degree in Political Science from the University of Mannheim. Since her retirement, she has been a speaker at international conferences and has written numerous published articles on geopolitical developments in Asia and on climate security. Dr Schleich has been an Adjunct Senior Fellow at the S. Rajaratnam School of International Studies at Nanyang Technological University, Singapore since 2021 and is attached to the Institute for Strategic, Political, Security and Economic Consultancy (ISPSW), Berlin.

About the Contributors

Lawrence Anderson is a Senior Fellow at the S. Rajaratnam School of International Studies (RSIS). Before that, Mr Anderson enjoyed a distinguished 37-year career at the Singapore Ministry of Foreign Affairs. He served at the Singapore Permanent Mission to the United Nations in New York and at Singapore Embassies in the US and Thailand. He was appointed Ambassador to Cambodia (2004–2007) and later Ambassador to Saudi Arabia with concurrent accreditation as Ambassador to Bahrain (2013–2019). Ambassador Anderson is a Senior Fellow at MFA's Diplomatic Academy and Singapore's Representative on the Advisory Board of the ASEAN Institute for Peace and Reconciliation (ASEAN-IPR).

Siah Hwee Ang is Professor of Strategy and International Business and Professorial Chair of Business in Asia at Victoria University of Wellington. He is also Director of New Zealand's Southeast Asia Centre of Asia-Pacific Excellence. Siah Hwee's expertise centres on the connection between strategy, international business, and international trade. He is also currently the Reviewing Editor at a top international business journal, *Journal of World Business*, a panel member appointed by the New Zealand Tertiary Education Commission on the Business and Economics panel for the national assessment of research performance of New Zealand tertiary education organisations, and a member of OECD's Entrepreneurship Education Collaboration and Engagement Steering Committee.

As an active member of New Zealand's business community, Siah Hwee is a board member of Business Central New Zealand and the Wellington Chamber of Commerce and was, until recently, an executive board member of the ASEAN New Zealand Business Council. He has a PhD in Management from the National University of Singapore.

Manu Bhaskaran is a Partner of Centennial Group, a strategic advisory firm headquartered in Washington, DC. As founding CEO of its Singapore subsidiary Centennial Asia Advisors, he coordinates the Asian business of the Group, which provides independent economic research on Asian political and macroeconomic trends for investment institutions, government agencies, multilateral institutions, and companies with interests in Asia, leveraging 40 years of knowledge on Asia.

David Capie is Director of the Centre for Strategic Studies and Professor of International Relations at Victoria University of Wellington. His research focuses on conflict and security issues in the Indo-Pacific and New Zealand's foreign and defence policy. He has written widely on Asia's regional security institutions, defence diplomacy, arms control and disarmament, and peacekeeping. David was a member of the ASEAN Regional Forum Experts and Eminent Persons Group from 2012 to 2019. He is currently a member of the Ministerial Advisory Panel for the New Zealand government's Defence Policy Review.

Peter Carter is a Teaching Fellow at the New Zealand Defence Force Command and Staff College in Wellington. A graduate of Victoria University of Wellington, Peter completed a research master's degree on the New Zealand–Singapore bilateral relationship in 2007, which included extensive archival work and interviews with former New Zealand diplomats. Peter's work experience includes roles at the Department of the Prime Minister and Cabinet, the Ministry of Defence, and the Ministry of Foreign Affairs and Trade.

Rt Hon Helen Clark was Prime Minister of New Zealand from 1999–2008 and a Member of Parliament for 27 years. She advocated strongly for economic and social justice, sustainability, climate action, and multilateralism. Helen Clark served two terms as Administrator of the United Nations Development Programme (UNDP) and as Chair of the United Nations Development Group from 2009–2017. Earlier, she taught in the Political Studies Department of the University of Auckland, from where she graduated with BA and MA (Hons) degrees. Helen advocates for sustainable development, climate action, gender equality and women's leadership, peace and justice, and action on pressing global health issues. In July 2020, she was appointed by the Director-General of the World Health Organization as Co-Chair of the Independent Panel for Pandemic Preparedness and Response. She chairs the boards of the Extractive Industries Transparency Initiative, the Partnership for Maternal, Newborn, and Child Health, and other public good organisations and initiatives. In 2023, Helen Clark joined 'The Elders', a distinguished group of former world leaders.

Brian Easton is a senior New Zealand economist. A former director of the NZ Institute of Economic Research and holding honorary positions in six of New Zealand's eight universities, Dr Easton has worked on a wide range of New Zealand economic and developmental issues and published over 30 books and monographs including *Globalisation and the Wealth of Nations*. His most recent book is *Not in Narrow Seas: An Economic History of Aotearoa New Zealand*.

Goh Chok Tong was Singapore's Prime Minister from November 1990 to August 2004. Between 1979 and 1990, he served as Minister of Trade and Industry, Health, and Defence. He was appointed Deputy Prime Minister in 1985 and succeeded Mr Lee Kuan Yew as Prime Minister in November 1990. Mr Goh relinquished the premiership in August 2004 to pave the way for leadership renewal. He remained in the Cabinet as Senior Minister and was Chairman of the Monetary Authority of Singapore from August 2004 to May 2011. Upon leaving the Cabinet in May 2011, Mr Goh was given the honorary title of Emeritus Senior Minister. In April 2017, he was appointed Chairman of the Governing Board of the Lee Kuan Yew School of Public Policy at the National University of Singapore.

Hon. **Christopher Finlayson** KC is a barrister in practice in Wellington. Mr Finlayson was elected to Parliament in 2005, representing the National Party (the centre-right political party of New Zealand). After one term in opposition, Mr Finlayson entered the Ministry as Attorney-General, Minister of Treaty of Waitangi Negotiations, and Minister of Culture and Heritage. He remained Attorney-General and Minister for Treaty of Waitangi Negotiations until 2017. From 2014 to 2017, he was also the Minister in charge of the intelligence agencies during which time he undertook a major reform of the agencies. During his time as Minister for Waitangi Negotiations, he was responsible for 60 settlements with Māori tribes. As Attorney-General, he represented New Zealand in the International Court of Justice in 2013 in the case brought by Australia against Japan over commercial whaling in the southern oceans. New Zealand intervened and supported Australia in its case.

Hon. **Tim Groser** is one of the world's most experienced trade negotiators and strategists. Starting as a young economist in the NZ Treasury in the mid-1970s, he moved into trade policy as a member of the New Zealand team that negotiated NZ's first comprehensive FTA — the 'CER' (Closer Economic Relations' Agreement) — with Australia in the early 1980s. Tim was then appointed NZ's Chief Agriculture Negotiator and posted to the then GATT (now WTO) in 1985. In 1990, he became Chief Negotiator. He was Ambassador to Indonesia from 1994–1997, Principal Economic Adviser to the NZ Ministry of Foreign Affairs from 1997–1999, and CEO of the Asia New Zealand Foundation. In 2002, he was appointed the first NZ Ambassador to the WTO and immediately became Chair of the 'Rules' negotiations (subsidies and anti-dumping). After the collapse of the WTO negotiations in Cancun in 2003 over agriculture, Tim was asked to chair the Agriculture Negotiations. In that capacity, he produced the 2004 'Framework Agreement on Agriculture', widely considered at the time to be a breakthrough. In 2005, Tim stood for Parliament and became Opposition Spokesperson on Trade. In 2008, he was appointed by the Prime Minister to be Minister of Trade, Associate Minister of Foreign Affairs, and Minister of International Climate Change Negotiations. In that capacity, he proposed the 'NDC' (Nationally Determined Contribution) — the core commitment of the Paris Agreement of 2015 — and established the Global Research Alliance on Agriculture Emissions. Tim was appointed Ambassador to the United States in 2016. He is now an independent consultant and an Honorary Adviser to the Asia Society of New York.

Ken Hickson became a public affairs consultant to Singapore Airlines in 1983 after 21 years of experience in media and communications in New Zealand. He set up and managed Hickson PR from 1986 to the end of 2000. He has served as President of the Singapore–New Zealand Association, the NZ Chamber, and the Institute of Public Relations Singapore (IPRS). This was followed by ten years of teaching and consulting in Australia, after which he returned to Singapore in 2010 to establish Sustain Ability Showcase Asia (SASA), alongside ABC Carbon, and to produce content for media and clients. He is the author of seven books: Two of his books were published in NZ in 1980: *The Future South* and *Flight 901 to Erebus*. Four books were published in Singapore: *Mr SIA: Fly Past, Race for Sustainability* (both published by World Scientific), *Forty: Building a Future in Singapore*, and *Celebrating Forty Years of Transforming Lives. The ABC of Carbon* was published in Australia in 2009.

Hoe Su Fern is an arts researcher, educator, manager, and advocate. She is currently Assistant Professor and Lead Coordinator of the Arts and Culture Management Programme at Singapore

Management University. She is also a lecturer for the MA course in Arts and Cultural Management at Leuphana University of Luneburg (Germany). She has spoken, researched, and published on cultural policy, arts management, urban cultural economies, creative place-making, and the conditions of artistic production. She has a wealth of experience in developing, managing, and coordinating local, regional, and global projects in varying formats, all of which advocate for the value of arts and culture in urban environments. Her practice is informed by her pursuit of practice-oriented and engaged arts research and her interest in enabling better conditions for artistic production.

Benjamin Horton is Director of the Earth Observatory of Singapore at Nanyang Technological University (NTU), Singapore. His research concerns sea-level change. He aims to understand the mechanisms that have determined sea-level changes in the past, which will shape changes in the future. Professor Horton has won research awards from the European Geosciences Union, the American Geophysical Union, and the Geological Society of America. Professor Horton was an editor for the 6th Assessment Report of the Intergovernmental Panel on Climate Change (IPCC). Professor Horton has published over 240 articles in peer-reviewed journals, including *Science*, *Nature*, and *Proceedings of the National Academy of Sciences*. He has raised over $70m in research funding.

Nicholas Khoo is Associate Professor in the Politics Programme at the University of Otago. His research focuses on Chinese foreign policy, great power politics, Asian security, and international relations theory, with a focus on alliances and coercive diplomacy. Nicholas has a PhD and MPhil in Political Science from Columbia University, an MA in International Relations from Johns Hopkins University, and a BA in Economics from the University of California at Irvine. Nicholas has been a Visiting Fellow at the School of International Studies at Peking University and a Visiting Professor at the Foreign Affairs College (both in in Beijing, China). In addition, he has held positions at the Institute of Defence and Strategic

Studies (Singapore), the Council of Foreign Relations (Washington, DC), and the Center for Strategic and International Studies (Washington, DC). Nicholas's single-authored publications include *Collateral Damage: Sino-Soviet Rivalry and the Termination of the Sino-Vietnamese Alliance* (New York: Columbia University Press, 2011) and *Return to Power: China and East Asia Since 1978* (Edward Elgar, 2020). His co-authored publications include *Asian Security and the Rise of China: International Relations in an Age of Volatility* (Edward Elgar, 2013), *Security at a Price: The International Politics of U.S. Missile Defense* (Rowman & Littlefield, 2017), and *Chinese Foreign Policy Since 1949: The Emergence of a Great Power* (Routledge, 2022).

Tommy Koh is currently Emeritus Professor of Law at the National University of Singapore, Ambassador-At-Large at the Ministry of Foreign Affairs, and Chairman of the International Advisory Panel of the Centre for International Law at NUS. He had served as Dean of the Faculty of Law at NUS, Singapore's Permanent Representative to the United Nations in New York, Ambassador to the United States of America, High Commissioner to Canada, and Ambassador to Mexico. He was President of the Third UN Conference on the Law of the Sea. He was also the Chairman of the Preparatory Committee for and the Main Committee of the UN Conference on Environment and Development (Earth Summit). He was the UN Secretary-General's Special Envoy to Russia, Estonia, Latvia, and Lithuania. He was the founding Chairman of the National Arts Council, founding Executive Director of the Asia–Europe Foundation, and former Chairman of the National Heritage Board. He was Singapore's Chief Negotiator in negotiating an agreement to establish diplomatic relations between Singapore and China. He was also Singapore's Chief Negotiator for the US–Singapore Free Trade Agreement. He acted as Singapore's Agent in two legal disputes with Malaysia. He has chaired two dispute panels for the WTO. He is Co-Chairman of the China–Singapore Forum and the Japan–Singapore Symposium. Professor Koh has received awards from the governments of Singapore, Chile,

Finland, France, Japan, Netherlands, Spain, and the United States. Professor Koh has received the Champion of the Earth Award from the UNEP and the inaugural President's Award for the Environment from the government of Singapore. He was conferred honorary doctoral degrees in law by Yale University and Monash University. He was also conferred the Great Negotiator Award in 2014 by Harvard University.

Dave Lowe is Adjunct Professor of Atmospheric Chemistry, Antarctic Research Centre, Victoria University of Wellington, New Zealand, and Director of LOWENZ ltd, focusing on Climate Change and Sustainability Education. Dave, an atmospheric chemist, began the first continuous measurements of atmospheric CO_2 in the Southern Hemisphere midlatitudes over fifty years ago. Since then, CO_2, primarily from fossil fuel combustion, has increased by 30% in the atmosphere and dangerous climate change has become a stark reality. A researcher and educator, Lowe was one of the lead authors of a 2007 United Nations IPCC report that was awarded the Nobel Peace Prize. For his contribution to environmental science, he was presented with the 2020 Wellingtonian of the Year award, and his memoir *The Alarmist* won the EH McCormick Best Non-Fiction Title at the 2022 New Zealand Book Awards.

Raewyn Peart (MCom, LLB, BCom, BSocSc, MNZM) is Policy Director at the Environmental Defence Society. Raewyn heads EDS's environmental policy work. She has over 30 years of professional experience in environmental law and policy, having worked as a resource management lawyer and policy adviser to businesses, government, and the not-for-profit sector. Raewyn has published widely on coastal, marine, and other environmental issues.

Michael Powles, brought up partly in Samoa, is a former Aotearoa New Zealand diplomat. Overseas, he headed New Zealand posts in Fiji, Indonesia, and China, and was New Zealand's Permanent Representative to the United Nations in New York. In Wellington, he became Deputy Secretary of the Ministry of Foreign Affairs. After retirement, he spent time in China, founded the Pacific Cooperation Foundation, and worked as a Human Rights Commissioner and as a member of the Council of the National University of Samoa. He has spoken and published on foreign relations issues relating to New Zealand's role in the Pacific and its relations with China.

Gabrielle Rush has been New Zealand High Commissioner to Singapore since January 2023 and has worked on international law and foreign and trade policy issues since 1994. Most recently, she led the Consular Division of New Zealand's Foreign Ministry from 2020–2022, was Acting Divisional Manager of the Ministry's Legal Division in 2019, and earlier managed both the General International and Trade Law units. Ms Rush was New Zealand Consul-General to Hong Kong and Macao from 2014 to 2017 and has also served in the New Zealand Embassy in Beijing and High Commission in London. Ms Rush holds a Master of Laws degree in Public International Law from the London School of Economics.

Mary Seet-Cheng was a diplomat in the Ministry of Foreign Affairs of Singapore (MFA) from 1973 to 1997 and served in the Singapore Missions in Canberra, London, and Brussels. She was Ambassador to Belgium, Netherlands and Luxembourg, the European Commission, and the Holy See from 1993–1996. In 1997, she was seconded to the Maritime and Port Authority (MPA) of Singapore as Director (Policy). She remains MPA's Special Adviser. In 2006, Ambassador Mary Seet-Cheng returned to MFA as Senior Specialist Adviser (SSA) on maritime matters and was concurrently Singapore's non-resident Ambassador to the Republic of Panama and Cuba from 2007–2020. She has been Singapore's Non-Resident High Commissioner to the Republic of Fiji and Non-Resident Ambassador to the Pacific Islands Forum since 2020.

Greg Severinsen (PhD, LLB(Hons), BA) is Reform Director at the Environmental Defence Society. Greg provides the lead on EDS's environmental system reform projects. He has practised resource management law and worked on environmental policy in the central government. Greg has published, presented, and taught on a range of resource management and environmental law topics.

Kanwaljit Soin is an orthopaedic and hand surgeon who retired in 2022 after a 56-year career in medicine. She was Singapore's first female Nominated Member of Parliament (1992–1996). She was inducted into the Singapore Women's Hall of Fame in 2014. Dr Soin was a founding member of the Association of Women for Action and Research (AWARE) in 1985 and was AWARE's president between 1991 and 1993. She was the founding Chair of the Singapore chapter of the United Nations Development Fund for Women (UNIFEM) and the founding President of the Women's Initiative for Ageing Successfully (WINGS). She has received the Singapore Medical Association Merit Award, the International Women's Forum's *Women Who Make a Difference Award*, a UNIFEM Lifetime Achievement Award, and Singapore's *Woman of the Year* award. She is the author of *Silver Shades of Grey: Memos for Successful Ageing in the 21st Century.* She and Margaret Thomas are the editors of the book *Our Lives to Live — Putting a Woman's Face to Change in Singapore.*

Tan Tai Yong is Professor and President of the Singapore University of Social Sciences. He is Chairman of the Institute of South Asian Studies at the National University of Singapore, where he is Professor Emeritus. Professor Tan is Honorary Chairman of the National Museum of Singapore and serves on the National Heritage Board and National Library Board. He is a former Nominated Member of Parliament. He has authored and co-authored several books, including *700 Years: A History of Singapore* (2019), *The Idea of Singapore. Smallness Unconstrained* (2020), and *Freedom and Partition. Momentous Events of 14–17 August 1947 in India and Pakistan* (2023).

William Tan has been Singapore's High Commissioner to New Zealand since September 2023. Prior to that, he was Director-General of Technical Co-operation Directorate, Ministry of Foreign

Affairs. In that role, he was responsible for the Singapore Cooperation Programme which extends technical assistance to over 170 countries worldwide. Since joining the Ministry of Foreign Affairs in 1997, Mr Tan served in various capacities covering Northeast Asia, Southeast Asia, ASEAN, South Asia, and Africa. His overseas assignments have mainly been in the Asia-Pacific including Indonesia, Thailand, and Japan. Mr Tan is a graduate of Stanford University (Master's in International Policy Studies) and the University of Michigan, Ann Arbor (Bachelor of Science in Electrical Engineering).

Richard Taylor is the co-founder (alongside his wife and business partner Tania Rodger), co-CEO, and creative lead at Wētā Workshop. Wētā Workshop is a multi-award-winning concept design and manufacturing facility that services the world's entertainment and creative industries. This diverse and innovation-driven company also includes three tourism offerings, two retail experiences, a consumer products division making high end collectables, a digital gaming studio, a location-based experiences division, and a media production department servicing the emerging new media fields of the world. The studio also creates public sculptures and private commissions for clients all over the world. Richard focuses much of his creative time on the immersive experiences the workshop creates such as the Thea award winning exhibitions *Gallipoli: The scale of our War*, and *Wētā Workshop Unleashed*. Richard and his team are focused on creative excellence in everything they do.

Kennie Ting was the Director of the Asian Civilisations Museum and the Peranakan Museum from 2016 until 2024. He has overseen the shift in the museum's curatorial approach from a geographical focus to a thematic, cross-cultural focus, and from an ethnographic focus to a focus on aesthetics, craft, and design. He has helmed exhibitions on the arts of Myanmar, Korea, Cambodia, Indonesia, and Japan, and on the material culture of cosmopolitan Asian port cities. Most recently, the ACM under his direction presented exhibitions and experimental showcases on contemporary fashion and photography, spotlighting Asian masters such as

Andrew Gn, Russel Wong, Guo Pei, and BINhouse. Prior to the ACM, Kennie worked as a strategist and cultural policymaker at the National Heritage Board and the former Ministry of Information, Communications, and the Arts Singapore (MICA). He has played a key role in the development of arts and cultural masterplans, such as the Renaissance City Plan III (RCP III), Arts and Culture Strategic Review (ACSR), and the recent Our SG Heritage Plans 1.0 and 2.0. He is the author of the books *The Romance of the Grand Tour: 100 Years of Travel in South East Asia*, *Singapore Chronicles: HERITAGE*, *Singapore 1819: A Living Legacy*, and *The Great Port Cities of Asia: In History*.

George Yong-Boon Yeo is a Visiting Scholar at the Lee Kuan Yew School of Public Policy, the National University of Singapore, and Founding Patron of its Asia Competitiveness Institute. Mr Yeo was with Kerry Group in Hong Kong from 2012 to 2021. He was Chairman and Executive Director of Kerry Logistics Network from 2012 to 2019. From September 1988 to May 2011, he served in the Singapore government and was Minister for Information and the Arts, Minister for Health, Minister for Trade & Industry, and Minister for Foreign Affairs. Mr Yeo has a BA in Engineering (Double First) from Cambridge University and an MBA (Baker Scholar) from Harvard University. He began his military career as a Signals Officer in the Singapore Army, crossed over to the Air Force, and became Chief-of-Staff of the Air Staff and Director of Joint Operations and Planning in the Defence Ministry, attaining the rank of Brigadier-General. Mr Yeo was a Member of the Pontifical Commission for Reference on the Economic-Administrative Structure of the Holy See from 2013–2014 and the Vatican Council for the Economy from February 2014 to July 2020.

Mr. Yeo is a member of the Board of Trustees of Berggruen Institute on Governance, International Advisory Panel of Peking University, Senior Advisory Council of Beijing Forum, International Advisory Board of IESE Business School, International Advisory Council of China's Eco Forum Global Guiyang, International Advisory Board of Japan's National Graduate School for

International Policy Studies (GRIPS), International Advisory Committee of Mitsubishi Corporation, Global Advisory Board of MUFG, the External Advisory Board of the European University Institute's School of Transnational Governance, and the Board of Governors of the Singapore Manufacturing Federation. Mr Yeo is an Independent Non-Executive Director of AIA Group, listed on the Hong Kong Stock Exchange; Pinduoduo, listed on NASDAQ; and Creative Technology, listed on the Singapore Stock Exchange. He is an adviser to Brunswick for its Geopolitical Initiative, Singapore's V3 Group, Huawei International in Singapore, Winning International Group and Gurin Energy. Mr Yeo was the Conference Chairman of the Singapore Summit from 2012 to 2016.

Jane Wrightson was appointed New Zealand's Retirement Commissioner by the Minister of Commerce and Consumer Affairs in early 2020 and is now serving her second term. The role focuses on advocacy, financial education, and providing robust and independent advice to the government. Jane previously served as Chief Executive of government funder NZ On Air, allocating over NZ$140 million of contestable public media funds each year. She is also a former CEO of the Broadcasting Standards Authority, a regulator, and the Screen Producers' Association, an advocacy body. She was New Zealand's first woman chief film censor, after a decade in various programming and commissioning roles with TVNZ. Jane is currently the Chair of Experience Wellington, a regional organisation that oversees seven arts and heritage entities, and Director of RNZ, New Zealand's primary public media company. She holds an MBA with distinction, a BA in literature, and is a Distinguished Alumnus of Massey University. She was awarded the Sir Geoffrey Peren medal in 2018.

Contents

I

HISTORY AND OUTLOOK

Chapter 1

Singapore – From Colony to Global City-State

Tan Tai Yong

Introduction

Singapore gained independence in August 1965 in a most unexpected manner. The British colony had envisaged its post-colonial
future as a state in the Malaysian Federation, but within two years
of joining the Federation in 1963, fulfilling the long-held ambition of
the ruling People's Action Party (PAP), Singapore separated from
Malaysia to become an independent country in 1965. The conditions facing Singapore's unexpected birth as a nation-state were
daunting. There were doubts that the tiny, resource-scarce island
state could survive economically on its own. The situation in the
neighbourhood — the acrimonious break-up with Malaysia, strained
relations with Indonesia, and Cold war tensions in Southeast Asia
— made Singapore, a new state without proper defence capabilities, especially vulnerable. The new country also faced a whole
host of socio-economic problems — employment, housing, health,
and education — that needed urgent attention.

The circumstances in the immediate aftermath of separation
were indeed far from propitious. Nonetheless, having taken
Singapore out of Malaysia, the PAP government was determined
that the island state would have to make it on its own. The then

3

Prime Minister Lee Kuan Yew famously declared the ambition to make Singapore a metropolis, a multicultural and economically-vibrant nation-state (Lee, 1965). Navigating through the myriad of challenges and addressing these priorities required astute and determined leadership, strategic vision, and the collective efforts of the government and the people of Singapore. The story of Singapore in the decades after 1965 can be described as a remarkable transformation from a struggling former colony to a global city-state constantly punching about its weight. This essay narrates the strategic directions that guided Singapore's economic development after 1965, as well as the conditions that were created in the first decade after independence to position the city-state as a major player in international trade, finance, and technology, committed to and capable of embracing the full benefits of globalisation and an open global economy.

Economic Development

Throughout its history, Singapore's survival and growth depended on its economic relevance. From the 14th century, upswings in the cyclical fortunes of Singapore were brought about by its ability to and success in integrating with the regional trading networks of the times. The high points in Singapore's history over the *longue durée* coincided with its functions as a port city, serving maritime powers like the Srivijaya and Majapahit empires and the Melaka and Johore sultanates. In the 19th century, the British East India Company coveted Singapore as a strategic foothold in the Straits of Melaka to rival Dutch influence in the East Indies and control trade between India and China (Kwa *et al.*, 2019). This reality was no different in 1965. As an independent country, Singapore had to be economically relevant to survive. In the past, it had made its living as an entrepot and middleman for trade in the region. However, by the second half of the 20th century, both roles were rapidly becoming obsolete as new post-colonial nations in the region sought to build and protect their domestic industries. The separation from Malaysia meant the loss of a hinterland and market, with uncertainties, disruptions, and job loss. Singapore could no longer function as a staple port whose role was to support the primary economy of a large rural hinterland. Then, there was rampant unemployment, exacerbated by uncontrolled post-war population growth and limited job opportunities.

When Singapore attained self-governing status in 1959, it decided to turn towards industrialisation, alongside trade, as the panacea for its economic woes. The eagerness to join the Malaysian Federation was motivated by the promise of a Common Market and a much-needed economic hinterland. This belief was reinforced by the findings of a United Nations Industrialisation Team, which came to study Singapore in 1960. Led by Dutch economist Albert Winsemius, the study concluded that industrialisation was the only way to create sufficient jobs for an economy that could no longer be sustained by entrepot trade. But, the two years in Malaysia had been a setback in this endeavour. The Common Market did not materialise, capital was insufficient, and the federal government did not readily support the setting up of business and manufacturing facilities in Singapore.

After independence in 1965, Singapore re-modelled its economy from import substitution manufacturing for the local market to manufacturing for the global market. Albert Winsemius returned to serve as advisor to the Singapore government and advocated for the development of export-oriented industries. He encouraged Singapore to focus on manufacturing and trade, leveraging its strategic location and investing in industries that could compete on the global stage (Quah, 2022, pp. 228–231). This led to Singapore embarking on an accelerated export-oriented industrialisation programme from 1967 to 1979. Having decided on this economic strategy, conditions and systems had to be created to realise the plan. One key initiative was the transformation of a piece of swampy land in the west of Singapore into an industrial estate. The brainchild of Singapore's first finance minister, Goh Keng Swee, the Jurong Industrial Estate eventually became Singapore's largest industrial estate, hosting a diversity of industries. In addition to local factories producing simple and basic items like tyres, mosquito coils, and fertilisers, foreign multinational corporations such as ESSO and Texas Instruments were encouraged to set up local plants in the country (National Archives, 2008, pp. 70–73). Having built the infrastructure, the government sought to attract foreign investments. Incentives were introduced for local and overseas investors to establish enterprises in Singapore. The government adopted a pro-business approach to entice capital to the island, dangling attractions like pioneer certificates and tax-free status for five years. The Economic Development Bureau (EDB) was set up to invite the developed world — America, Europe, and Japan — to use Singapore as a manufacturing base and to export their products to these developed countries (Lee, 2000, pp. 77–78).

Fortunes favoured Singapore as it sought new markets beyond the region. A highly-favourable world economic environment, with booming economies in Germany, the United States, and Japan, presented many opportunities for Singapore. A further opportunity presented itself when China was convulsed by the Cultural Revolution. The proximity of Hong Kong and Taiwan to the mainland made them unattractive to investors. Singapore, at a safe distance from the upheaval, benefited from the disruptions. From the start, electronic goods were the leading sector of manufacturing for export, with a range of products including transistor radios, tape recorders, televisions, stereo sound systems, electronic computers, and satellite communications equipment. The EDB ran joint training programmes with them to ensure that workers would have the requisite technical skills in new-growth industries. In 1971, two training centres with Rollei and Philips were established to provide industrial training to local workers (Lee, 2008, pp. 265–280). The country strategically positioned itself as a manufacturing hub, focusing on electronics, petrochemicals, and precision engineering.

The concerted efforts of the Singapore government to re-position the country's economy, with its emphasis on industrialisation, export-oriented growth, and attraction of foreign investments, quickly yielded results. In the late 1960s, when the companies that were set up in Singapore went into full production, nearly 20,000 jobs were created, giving a timely boost to the weak labour market. Within 10 years, the impact of job creation was palpable; unemployment was halved from around 10% in 1965 to 4.5% by 1973, reduced further by subsequent growth periods (Krause, 1990, pp. 5–6). In 1965, the Singapore economy grew at about five per cent; between 1966 and 1970 annual growth rates had increased to 13% (Chew and Lee, 1991, pp. 194). Many new industries were established in the first decade following independence, leading to the construction of factories, oil refineries, shipyards, and infrastructural facilities. Within a decade, per capita income had grown five-fold from around US$500 in 1965 to nearly US$2500 in 1975. Strong governance, effective administration, and a low level of corruption contributed to political stability, while industrial peace, brought about by a cooperative relationship between government, employers, and trade unions, enhanced investor confidence in the country. The economic prosperity, in turn, generated widespread support for the government and the ruling party. The PAP government decisively returned to power in successive general elections. As economic success led to improved livelihoods for the people of Singapore, a positive social compact between government and society was formed, providing the political and social conditions for rapid development and continued economic growth.

Becoming Global City-State

Singapore's economic strategy was not predicated on industrial growth alone; it needed to operate in a global market and its full-hearted embrace of globalisation and international free trade became a key driver of its continued success. With competition intensifying and opportunities limited in Southeast Asia, Singapore had to search for new economic space and create the capacity to leverage an open worldwide trading system. Realising that globalisation and free trade would be the basis of sustained economic growth for a small trade-dependent city-state, the government sought to position Singapore as a global city-state and a global trading hub. In 1972, Foreign Minister S. Rajaratnam articulated his vision for Singapore to become a global city-state. He observed then that the demand for the traditional type of entrepot services that Singapore had rendered for over a century would become obsolete by the later part of the 20th century, and with that, its role as the trading city of Southeast Asia, the marketplace of the region, would become less important. In his view, Singapore could no longer hope to sustain its economic growth by serving the needs of Southeast Asia alone. It had to position itself as part of a supply chain of goods and services for a larger, global market (Rajaratnam, 1972).

The need to look beyond the region was prompted by political and geo-strategic realities. In an interview with the Time Bureau chief in 1969, Lee Kuan Yew expressed hopes that Southeast Asia would experience "constructive development" and that Singapore could act as a "spark plug" for the progress and development of the region. At the same time, he expressed concern that the region could go either way, towards chaos and destruction, in which case he hoped Singapore could play the role of Venice when the Dark Ages descended on Europe. In fact, Southeast Asia presented too many problems to become a bastion of stability and growth for Singapore during that period. Relations with Malaysia remained fraught following the Separation in 1965, and the race riots of 1969 in Kuala Lumpur were a stark reminder that the underlying tensions that led to separation a few years earlier had not wholly subsided. While *Konfrontasi* had ended, Indonesia was still finding its feet, emerging from the throes of domestic upheavals. The war in Vietnam was entering a critical stage with uncertain outcomes, and Indochina remained the cockpit of Cold War tensions in Southeast Asia. The formation of ASEAN in 1967 was an attempt to find political stability amidst these geostrategic challenges, but the economic possibilities in the region were not promising. Singapore had to find a way to leapfrog the region for economic growth (Tan, 2019, pp. 40–43).

Rajaratnam's vision was for Singapore to be a "world-embracing city, or as he called it an "Ecumenopolis." According to Rajaratnam, cities of the past had been "isolated centres of local civilisations and regional empires" and "somewhat parochial with an extremely limited range of influence." Thus, while Singapore's size and links to its region would remain part of its identity, it could connect with other cities in the world, and make "the world ... its hinterland" (Kwa, 2006, pp. 165–177).

Rajaratnam contended that the trend towards global cities would benefit Singapore. Many might have assumed that "an independent Singapore would be a self-contained city-state" or at most a "regional city ... [whose] fate and fortunes would depend wholly on the economic climate of the region." But, Singapore needed to realise its full potential which extended beyond the confines of its immediate neighbourhood. In Rajaratnam's vision, Singapore would draw sustenance from the international economic system, and its future would depend on how well it was able to integrate into this system (Kwa, 2006, pp. 165–177).

What did this shift towards a global city entail? Connectivity, both physical and technological, would be key. Singapore would need to leverage its traditional function as a port city to maintain its position as a global maritime hub. But, that alone would not be sufficient to turn Singapore into a global city; Singapore's air connectivity would have to be significantly enhanced if the city were to be closely connected to other global cities, like London, Tokyo, and New York. Connectivity was also viewed in terms of cable and satellite communications, the international financial network, and collaboration with multinational corporations. Investments in infrastructure were thus critical to Singapore's success. From the 1970s, the development of world-class ports, airports, telecommunications, and transportation networks facilitated efficient trade and business activities, further enhancing the nation's global competitiveness.

Enabling the Global City

Singapore's efforts in industrialisation and globalisation were aided by advancements in maritime and air connectivity. As part of the economic strategy to enhance Singapore's efforts to be a major manufacturing base, it was imperative that Singapore remain a nodal point in the international shipping network, so that Singapore would remain well connected with the rest of the world and the shipping of manufactured goods from their factories in Singapore to their end markets would be carried out with ease and with as low a cost as possible. To enable significant harbour traffic growth, plans were made to expand the port area to increase its capacity in 1965, and additional berths and godowns were planned at the Keppel Road port area to handle the anticipated rise in demand for cargo space. Accessibility to the port area was also enhanced with improved road systems.

Perhaps the most important enhancement to Singapore's maritime capacity was the addition of containerisation facilities. Goh Keng Swee revealed how a chance visit to the container ports in New York prompted him to initiate extensive studies on the feasibility of having the Singapore port containerised. Resources were then invested to build container wharfs. Containerised tonnage handled by the port rose from 60,954 tons in 1970 to 83,466 in 1971. By 1975, about 564 vessels had unloaded 2.6 million tons of cargo in the Container Terminal. By 1969, Singapore had outstripped London to become the busiest port in the Commonwealth and by 1975 it became the third-busiest port in the world after New York and Rotterdam (National Archives, 2008, pp. 86–88).

With Singapore's plans to increase air connectivity, the existing Paya Lebar Airport was facing a capacity crunch by 1970. Plans to expand the airport would have entailed acquiring large parcels of land in a central urban area. There was also concern about noise pollution with an enlarged airport located amidst a dense residential area. The British military withdrawal presented the government with an alternative option as the land formerly occupied by the Royal Air Force was now available for constructing an entirely new airport. Eventually, after extensive studies, the government decided, in 1975, to abandon the expansion of Paya Lebar in favour of Changi. Six years later, in July 1981, Changi Airport was opened as Asia's largest airport. With a focus on developing international routes, Singapore Airlines expanded its long-haul aircraft fleet to link Singapore to major cities in Europe, Australia, and Asia (National Archives, 2008, pp. 91–92).

The economy faced strong headwinds when, in 1968, the British Labour government announced that the military bases would be withdrawn from Singapore by the end of 1971 instead of the mid-1970s as originally planned. The economic impact of the withdrawal was considerable as the bases contributed about ten per cent of the national income and provided employment for 40,000 locals (Chew and Lee, 1991, p. 196). But, the government was able to turn adversity into economic opportunity. It was able to cushion the impact by converting some of the bases into commercial uses such as shipbuilding and repairing, and aerospace and electronic engineering. Gradually, with British aid, the Singapore government was able to overcome the worst effects of the withdrawal.

Alongside physical infrastructure, the Singaporean government recognised early on the importance of developing a robust financial sector. The strategic geographic location of Singapore, positioned at the crossroads of major trading routes, contributed to its status as a global financial hub. Located between Zurich and San Francisco, Singapore was well poised geographically to fill the gap in the 24-hour operating hours of the financial global financial markets (Lee, 2000, p. 89). Policies were crafted to attract financial institutions and foster an environment conducive to financial services. This included the lifting of foreign control restrictions on currency transactions between Singapore and the territories outside the sterling area. In 1968, Singapore became the headquarters of the Asian Dollar Market, when the Singapore branch of the Bank of America set up the first Asian Currency Unit with the approval of the Singapore government (Chew and Lee, 1991, pp. 195–196). In 1969, a free gold market was established. As in the case of industrialisation, a stable political environment, underpinned by effective governance, rule of law, and low corruption, reassured financial institutions and investors and made Singapore an attractive destination for their operations. Singapore designed a legal and regulatory framework to balance the need for investor protection with the promotion of business activities. To facilitate the manufacturing and shipping activities conducted in Singapore, international banks as well as insurance companies were encouraged to set up branches in Singapore. The Monetary Authority of Singapore (MAS), established in 1971 as a banker and financial agent to the government, played a key role in implementing prudent monetary policies and maintaining a stable currency. The Singapore dollar was managed carefully, and the country developed a reputation for having a strong and stable currency. Singapore invested heavily in building state-of-the-art infrastructure and adopting advanced technologies (Lee, 2000, pp. 93–97). The country developed a sophisticated telecommunications network and embraced financial technology (fintech) innovations, enhancing the efficiency and competitiveness of its financial sector.

The best-laid ideas for Singapore's transformation would not have been possible without a people committed and capable of delivering the goods. Singapore was able to achieve what it did in the decades after 1965 because it prioritised education and talent development, developing a skilled workforce and turning education into a key competitive advantage. Education played a pivotal role as an enabler in Singapore's economic transformation during the 1970s and 1980s. The government recognised the importance of a well-educated and skilled workforce in driving economic development and implemented strategic initiatives to enhance the education system, which underwent significant transformations from 1965 to 1980. In each phase of the transformation, the education system moved in tandem with the economic imperatives of the times. In the 1960s and 1970s, emphasis was placed on technical subjects and vocational training, with education, training, and skills upgrading being the key means of upgrading the economic productivity of the workforce. Polytechnics were established to provide practical, industry-relevant training in various fields, contributing to the development of a diverse and skilled labour pool (Goh and Gopinath, 2008, pp. 87–90).

The focus on a strong foundation in English, Mathematics, and Science was a strategic move that aligned with global trends. English became the medium of instruction, as the government believed that a strong command of English would aid Singapore's continued transformation as an open economy with international linkages. Proficiency in English became a significant advantage for Singapore in attracting international investments and business, as well as advancing its research and development ambitions. Subsequently, as the economy moved up the value chain, the government encouraged the pursuit of science and technology education, aligning educational priorities with the needs of a rapidly-industrialising economy. This focus on STEM (Science, Technology, Engineering, and Mathematics) disciplines laid the foundation for Singapore's emergence as a high-tech hub, preparing its workforce for the demands of the emerging knowledge-based economy.

Conclusion

Few thought that Singapore would survive as a viable nation-state when it left Malaysia in 1965. The challenges were formidable, but in the span of a few decades, Singapore has achieved unprecedented success in economic and social development. From a fledgling nation grappling with a whole host of challenges, Singapore has emerged as a successful global city-state with one of the highest standards of living in the world. The foundations were laid in the first 10 years of independence, when visionary leadership, sound economic policies, political stability, and a commitment to social cohesion set the conditions for Singapore to prosper.

Singapore chose to become a global city-state as a strategic response to its geographic limitations. Becoming a global city-state has not only driven economic success but has also contributed to an improved quality of life for Singapore's residents. Investments in infrastructure, education, and health care generated the conditions for further development. The convergence of historical legacies, economic diversification, education, governance, infrastructure development, and openness to globalisation has enabled Singapore to remain the only true and functioning city-state in the world today.

Bibliography

Chew, E. and Lee, E. (eds.). (1989). *A History of Singapore*. Oxford University Press, Singapore.

Goh, C. B. and Gopinathan, S. (2008). Education in Singapore: Development since 1965. In Fredriksen, B. and Tan, J. P. (eds.), *An African Exploration of the East Asian Education*. World Bank, Washington, DC .

Krause, L., Koh, A. T. and Tsao Y. L. (1990). *The Singapore Economy Reconsidered*. Institute of Southeast Asian Studies, Singapore.

Kwa, C. G. (ed.) (2006). *Rajaratnam on Singapore. From Ideas to Reality.* World Scientific, Singapore.

Kwa, C. G., Borshbergh, P., Heng, D., and Yong, T. T. (2019). *Seven Hundred Years. A History of Singapore*. Marshall Cavendish, Singapore.

Lee, E. (2008). Singapore: *The Unexpected Nation*. Institute of Southeast Asian Studies, Singapore.

Lee, S. A. (2019). *Singapore. From Place to Nation*, 4th edn. Singapore.

National Archives of Singapore (2008). *10 Years that Shaped a Nation.* Singapore.

Perry, J. C. (2017). *Singapore. Unlikely Power.* Oxford University Press, Oxford.

Quah, E. (2022). *Albert Winsemius and Singapore: Here It Is Going to Happen*. World Scientific, Singapore.

Rajaratnam, S. (1972). *World Scientific Singapore: Global City.* National Archives of Singapore, 6 February 1972.

Tan, T. Y. (2020). *The Idea of Singapore. Smallness Unconstrained*. World Scientific, Singapore.

Yew, L. K. (2000). *From Third World to First. The Singapore Story: 1965–2000*. Singapore Press Holdings, Singapore.

Yew, L. K. Speech on 12 September 1965. https://www.sg101.gov.sg.

Chapter 2

A Listening Place of Our Own: The Establishment of the New Zealand – Singapore Diplomatic Relationship

Peter Carter

Introduction

Acknowledging one of their country's strongest relationships, New Zealand officials finalised an enhanced partnership with their Singaporean counterparts in 2019. They updated the countries' free trade agreement and targeted contemporary areas like science and technology cooperation. Unlike other relationships, however, officials also reflected on longstanding defence and diplomatic linkages, which have endured despite New Zealand's forward military presence in Singapore being a distant memory. The ongoing strategic connection has drawn both countries' leaders to value each other's perspectives on international and regional issues.

This chapter traces the establishment of these linkages, from Wellington's interest in opening a diplomatic post in still-colonial Singapore in the 1950s onwards. It concludes in the early 1970s, following Singapore's separation from Malaysia and as the relationship's underpinnings shifted from a predominantly security focus to a broader economic one.

Evidenced is Wellington's increasing management of its own external affairs and interests. Assumptions that officials reached in establishing a diplomatic post in Singapore — orthodoxy today — were progressive for the time. Its establishment manifested progressive thinking, that New Zealand had to be politically present where it made security contributions and that those contributions needed to accord with New Zealand's national interests.

The study highlights other key themes, including increasing internationalism and the character of the New Zealand state. External matters were held tightly within the executive government and a small, highly-centralised bureaucracy. One British official noted, "New Zealand's policy on international political issues is as personal as that of any dictatorship."[1] The officials who influenced policy, however, had progressive views. Their blend of racial awareness, small-state identification, and personal skills helped develop the relationship. They believed that they had agency, particularly if present at key geographic locations.

In comparative terms, the Singapore relationship has been significant. The country's diplomatic post in Singapore was its second in Asia and first in Southeast Asia. It grew from a strategic interest into a trusted relationship in an era dominated by security concerns. Leaders believed that a forward defence presence was essential to regional security, both to support Commonwealth arrangements and to influence a US regional presence. Practically, Singapore's bases enabled this, and the city's internal stability underpinned access to these bases.

Certain national characteristics enhanced the relationship's appeal. For Singapore, while New Zealand could be viewed alongside Britain and Australia as part of an old colonial order, there was also a sense that it was different. Its perception of being better on racial issues, its smaller size, and its independent interests mattered. For New Zealand, the parsimonious nature of the state required the best return on a limited investment in external affairs, meaning the country's diplomats had to pick winners. Singapore

---

[1] Trotter (1990).

was one such winner. Wellington recognised the capabilities and non-communist credentials of Lee Kuan Yew and his senior ministers early on, and preferred their non-communal state-building approach to that in Malaya.

Prelude: Pre-World War II Engagement

New Zealand and Singapore shared limited links before World War II through both countries' inclusion in the British Empire. Common cultural cues and practices came through this shared experience. However, ships became the foremost link. Imperial shipping routes indirectly connected the territories from the mid-19th century, with initially small numbers of people and modest commerce flowing across these routes. As New Zealand's trade with Britain and dependence on its capital markets grew, so did the shipping links.

Protection from the Royal Navy (RN) was crucial. It guaranteed New Zealand's (and Australia's) security, safeguarding the trade routes and permitting these territories to avoid establishing significant militaries. This dependence continued after New Zealand attained Dominion status in 1907, but the RN faced increasing challenges in the Pacific from the Japanese and US navies.

Singapore became a strategic point where Britain could concentrate its regional naval power, providing New Zealand's first significant linkage to the city. Through the 'Singapore Strategy', Singapore became a key imperial naval base with Dominion help from 1918 onwards. Wellington contributed £1 million to the base's construction, supporting 'forward defence', which became a central concept in defence planning.[2] Although not fully completed until 1939, to New Zealanders, the pre-war Singapore base was to be an impregnable fortress.

The first Labour Government in 1935 significantly revised external and security policy. Despite economic reliance on Britain, the government adopted an independent position to Britain's, closely aligned with the League of Nations. The League's failures in the

---

[2] Carter (2007).

1930s necessitated reversion to collective security through the British Commonwealth, but Wellington maintained an independent and progressive voice.

World War II then forced Wellington to confront conflicting security interests abroad and nearer to home. In 1939, Wellington committed an expeditionary force to directly support Britain in Europe. Meanwhile, in the Pacific, the Singapore Strategy's flaws became increasingly apparent. No longer able to address concurrent threats across two oceans alone, the British predicated the strategy on naval cooperation with France and Italy, freeing resources for Singapore. By June 1940, the tide of the war proved untenable. While Churchill continued espousing the strategy, to Dominion leaders, the British position was increasingly one of "diplomacy and bluff."[3]

Aware of their exposure, Commonwealth nations reinforced Singapore and Malaya through 1941. New Zealand Prime Minister Fraser despatched limited forces, including an air force squadron and an aerodrome construction unit. Unable to send a full fleet, Churchill sent the small, advance 'Task Force Z' to Singapore, including the battleship HMS *Prince of Wales* and battlecruiser HMS *Repulse*.

Japan called Britain's bluff by launching the Pacific War in December 1941. Its rapid advance through Malaya, the sinking of Task Force Z off Malaya, and then the capture of Singapore on 15 February 1942 shocked Allied nations. For New Zealand, its airmen suffered heavy losses flying obsolete planes against modern Japanese fighters. Those captured joined British and other Allied forces in internment in Singapore.

The consequences from Singapore's loss reverberated regionally, including in New Zealand. For Singaporeans and others, it dispelled myths of the white man's superiority and advanced decolonisation. New Zealand personnel, while committed to the Commonwealth, also increasingly evinced their differences from the British. For leaders in Wellington, the loss was one of many

---

[3] Wright (2003).

wartime cases that illustrated the need for greater visibility of and the employment of their own forces. They had not been included in higher-level coalition planning and had limited opportunities to impress their national interests.

This growing independence was also evidenced by the creation of a Department of External Affairs (hereafter 'External Affairs') in June 1943. Fraser's government established the department with a small staff of internationally-focussed bureaucrats co-located within the Prime Minister's Department.[4] Fraser and External Affairs strived for a seat at the peace-making table to represent New Zealand's interests and those of other small states.

1945–1954: Post-War Insecurity and a Shift to Asia

Wellington initially returned to old security approaches in 1945, but wartime lessons and the country's security deficit post-war gradually forced change, meriting a presence in Singapore. Despite US power having displaced Britain's pre-eminence globally, British influence on Wellington remained 'virtually intact', and it only slowly reenvisaged the US relationship from providing a regional 'backstop' to the US being a critical security partner.[5] Analogous to wartime 'Europe-first' thinking, the government initially prioritised contributing to Commonwealth security in the Middle East to resist Soviet expansionism. The changing security environment, however, saw the country shift its contribution to Southeast Asia.

In Singapore, the British re-established control in 1945 with little resistance. With India's impending independence, London saw Singapore as a natural hub in Southeast Asia to consolidate trade and security interests. It separated Singapore from Malaya, returning it to direct colonial control and establishing a politico-military British Defence Coordination Committee (BDCC) in 1947.[6] The possibility of regional security issues was highlighted in Malaya

---

[4] McGibbon (2022).
[5] Wood (1956).
[6] Murfett (1999).

when the British proposal for a Malayan Union led to racial unrest and forced the move to a Malay Federation.

While External Affairs survived due to the skilful management of its first Secretary, Alister McIntosh, by 1946, Wellington had no direct diplomatic representation in Asia. The British handled diplomatic contact on its behalf in many places, while in others, a private company, New Zealand Insurance, provided this function. The Department of Industry and Commerce had international trade representatives but would not appoint one in Asia until the government approved a Bombay position in January 1947.[7]

Wellington had not yet prioritised the region strategically. When British Foreign Minister Bevan released a communique at the 1946 Commonwealth Conference calling for New Zealand to join others in a regional arrangement to replace Britain's Southeast Asia Command, Wellington's representative noted that it sought universal security agreements rather than regional ones.[8] External Affairs eventually supported representation on a defence council, but wished Britain to retain leadership.[9]

1949–1950: Limiting Change

Britain sought again to secure New Zealand assistance in Southeast Asia in 1948 as it bolstered its regional presence and as communist insurgency broke out in Malaya. This led to the Australia, New Zealand, and Malaya (ANZAM) defence arrangement in September 1949, under which Britain retained control of Malaya's internal security but the Dominions participated in regional security planning.[10]

All three countries saw ANZAM as a compromise. Britain, initially, had an interest in passing responsibility to Australia, which was keen to increase its regional presence. However, the British

---

[7] Industries and Commerce memo, 23 January 1947, EA62/455/1.
[8] Shanahan report, 7 August 1948, EA62/434/1.
[9] Corner memo, 27 May 1946, EA153/23/1.
[10] Murfett (1999).

Government later relented, considering its ongoing presence essential to defeating Malaya's insurgents. New Zealand suspected Australia's ambitions and did not regard the ANZAM region as vital in any future war.[11]

New Zealand's External Affairs Deputy Secretary, Foss Shanahan, figured prominently in this episode and the later establishment of a Singapore diplomatic post. Shanahan, known as 'Foss the boss' for his formidable intellect and organisational skills, had held top defence roles during the war.[12] Following British lobbying, Shanahan backed representation in Singapore but wanted it based on New Zealand's interests. He saw a post as essential for gaining independent reporting where Wellington's forces might be committed. While the British provided intelligence, only a New Zealand official "uncontaminated by the realities of life" and with the "right blend of economic and political knowledge" would be able to "appreciate this from the New Zealand point of view."[13]

Shanahan's effort was part of a broader External Affairs push for diplomatic representation in Asia. J.V. Wilson, the most experienced officer in External Affairs, wrote in January 1949 that "our future diplomacy should be guided by a keener strategical sense," with a greater focus on Asia, including India, China, and Japan. For a small state, Wilson argued for representation in "main international centres." He saw Singapore as an ideal location for "a listening place of our own" and favoured India, which he saw as "making a bid for the leadership of Asia" and able to bolster Commonwealth security against Japan and China.[14] Meanwhile, External Affairs also planned a joint diplomatic and trade post in Tokyo.

New Zealand politics, however, halted progress. Sidney Holland's National Party won the 1949 election, delivering a Prime Minister and Ministers of External Affairs poorly disposed towards officials. They jealously protected their primacy in managing External Affairs

---

[11] McKinnon (1993).
[12] McGibbon (1999).
[13] Shanahan report, 18 May 1948, EA62/434/1.
[14] Wilson memos, 19 May 1948 and 10 January 1949, EA62/434/1.

and thought that diplomatic representation "should be restricted as much as possible."[15] Also, British concerns about the Soviets in the Middle East swayed Holland to maintain the security contribution there. Holland did eventually consider sending a retired brigadier to Singapore, but this had little support, Shanahan thinking it would be a "catastrophe" to appoint a retired officer who "needed a job."[16]

The Calculus Changes

By late 1949, Wellington had entered a darker, more fragmented security environment. External Affairs, concerned should a resurgent Japan again threaten the region, pressured Washington for a hard peace treaty with Tokyo. In August, the Soviets tested their first atomic device and, in October, the revolutionary Chinese Communist Party won China's civil war, proclaiming the People's Republic of China (PRC). Then, in June 1950, the US became involved in Korea. The Malayan insurgency continued, while New Zealand, alongside Britain, resisted involvement in French Indochina.

Wellington initially sought security arrangements akin to those in World War II. It looked first to a renewed British Commonwealth, then to collective security through the UN, and finally to the US to 'bolt the back door' in the Pacific. ANZUS, although described by Foreign Minister Frederick Doidge as the country's "richest prize" on signing in 1951, was originally treated as a backup. Wellington wished to see the Commonwealth as a "third force" in the region. This involved assessing India's role in Commonwealth plans and strengthening arrangements in Malaya and Singapore, including by joining Britain and Australia in a Far Eastern Strategic Reserve.[17]

Wellington also engaged — although initially reticently — in Commonwealth economic development plans. Commonwealth leaders established the Colombo Plan for Economic and Technical

---

[15] "Next steps" minutes, 19 February 1954, EA62/434/1.
[16] Shanahan report, 7 August 1948, EA62/434/1.
[17] Smith (2005) and McKinnon (1993).

Assistance in January 1950. The plan aimed to openly counter communism by focussing on a shared development vision. Donor nations, including New Zealand, coordinated multilaterally and delivered aid through bilateral donor–recipient relationships.[18]

While External Affairs realised the magnitude of the change in the security environment, influencing the government to adapt took time. In 1951, McIntosh withdrew his recommendation that a Singapore post be established in order to focus on ensuring final approval for the Tokyo post from the cautious Holland.[19] It took until 1953 for the government to acknowledge the changing regional balance. When it did, it prioritised a perceived threat from the PRC, which had gained the attention of the media and domestic interest groups.

Holland accepted the shift from Middle East security arrangements to those in Southeast Asia in February 1955, as these arrangements further evolved. New Zealand joined the newly-formed SEATO, which External Affairs viewed positively: It drew Britain and the US into the same security framework and also included independent Asian nations, which could counter communism. Concurrently, Commonwealth arrangements in Singapore and Malaya coalesced. Britain's military commitment in Singapore deepened as imperial strategy assumed its importance in sustaining broader military capability. While committed to SEATO, the US left this area to the Commonwealth. Wellington's shift, therefore, aligned with great power dynamics, and its commitment extended to include participation in the Malayan Emergency.

Diplomatic Representation

What remained was for diplomatic representation to accompany the defence shift. Canberra had pressured Wellington since 1953 to establish representation in Singapore.[20] Holland's Cabinet had considered Australia representing New Zealand on Wellington's

---

[18] Carter (2007).

[19] Marshall and McIntosh to Doidge and Watts, 11 May 1951, EA62/434/1.

[20] Watt (1972).

behalf but had chosen to further review its own representation. The Australian precedent of establishing a post in a British colonial territory, however, provided Wellington with a useful example.[21]

The pivotal External Affairs engagement that progressed thinking towards a Singapore post was a 'next-steps' meeting on Asian representation in Wellington on 19 February 1954. McIntosh, Shanahan, and other key staff considered options for diplomatic posts across the region. Some key assumptions emerged: The cost of representation was "bound to be considerable" and only one post could be afforded. While staff preferred representation in India, they pragmatically accepted that Holland's views, including his dislike for India's position of non-alignment, meant that Singapore was a better bet.[22]

Despite increasing public pressure on Holland, he took his time, until May 1955, to decide. He already saw Singapore as a good place for representation as a geographical "clearing house for information." At the 1955 Commonwealth Conference, he acknowledged that alongside committing military forces, Wellington had to get its "own first-hand information" and appraise events "through New Zealand eyes."[23] However, he battled with External Affairs for three months on practicalities, including whether to appoint a politician or career diplomat. In the end, McIntosh doggedly drew a decision from Holland to appoint Shanahan over a retiring general, Bill Gentry.[24]

1955–1958: The first New Zealand Commission in Southeast Asia

Shanahan entered Singapore in 1955 as local politicians and colonial officials contested self-government. A new constitution provided Singaporeans with limited representation through a

---

[21] McIntosh memo, 12 July 1954, EA62/434/1; Craw report, 31 July 1954, EA62/455/1.

[22] "Next steps" minutes, 19 February 1954, EA62/434/1.

[23] 1955 Commonwealth Conference report, MS- Papers-6759-073.

[24] McIntosh to Larmour, 2 May 1955, EA62/455/1.

legislature headed by a Chief Minister. However, a British Governor had veto powers over this legislature, and policy initiatives relied on the British-dominated administration's acquiescence. Further, a 'Commissioner-General to Southeast Asia', Malcolm MacDonald, managed foreign affairs and defence matters across British Southeast Asia, from his 'miniature Whitehall' at Phoenix Park. MacDonald was accountable only to the British Prime Minister in London.[25]

External Affairs' announcement in June 1955 of Shanahan's appointment as a regional, roving Commissioner for Southeast Asia stated that the "outstanding success" of MacDonald's role and Australia's appointment of a regional commissioner, Alan Watt, had influenced the decision.[26] The colonial connotations of such positions, however, had somewhat tarnished their standing as Singapore and Malaya looked towards independence.

The colonial administration rebuffed New Zealand and Australian representation in Singapore. No precedent existed for Watt's and Shanahan's appointments. Watt reported being slighted by successive governors, who were used to "running their own show." British colonial officials based at Phoenix Park expected the Commonwealth nations to work through the Commonwealth Relations Office which had been the established diplomatic channel for engaging with British colonial territories.[27] As such, British authorities did not inform the Dominion representatives on crucial issues such as Singapore's future status.[28]

The post did provide an opportunity to join key security bodies, including the BDCC, for which the defence-focussed Shanahan was a good fit: For Shanahan, the post was to ensure the successful application of Wellington's regional security policy. His time was compromised by his holding a concurrent role as Wellington's

---

[25] Hack (2000).
[26] *External Affairs Review*, 5:6, June 1955, p. 4.
[27] Watt (1972).
[28] Shanahan memo, 16 February 1956, MS-Papers-6759-203.

representative to SEATO, but Singapore's proximity to Bangkok enabled this. Representation would otherwise have been difficult.

Shanahan rapidly grasped the important contribution Singapore's internal stability made to Commonwealth security, specifically the need to secure the city's bases from communist threats. However, this could not be baldly stated. In press comments, Shanahan "evaded the issue" of whether New Zealand forces would be used for internal security, particularly as, beyond a point, he *did* support the use of force against communist subversion.[29]

In his first radio message, Shanahan raised progressive views on decolonisation and the establishment of self-government in Singapore and the region. While a pre-briefed Watt questioned Shanahan's approach in case it impeded relations with the British or incited public response, Shanahan pressed on. Singaporeans received the broadcast well and Shanahan was pleased that the Chinese-language media positively covered New Zealand's good intentions through its military commitment.[30]

Shanahan's conclusions on internal security and trouble in engaging colonial officials prompted him to focus on Singaporean domestic politics. He assessed which leaders would outlast the colonial regime, laying an important base for future relations. He met Singapore's Chief Minister, David Marshall, on 30 July, three months after Marshall won the first legislative assembly elections. He judged Marshall an "impressive figure" and the "best bet" to take Singapore towards self-government, despite his limited experience and a tendency "to get carried away."[31]

In August 1955, Shanahan met Marshall's emerging opponent, the Straits Chinese, British-educated lawyer Lee Kuan Yew, who led the social-democratic People's Action Party (PAP). Shanahan recognised Lee's long-term political importance, despite British officials' concerns about Lee's position on communism. Shanahan concluded that Lee was "non-communist" and "the ablest man in

---

[29] Shanahan memo, 5 August 1955, MS-Papers-6759-202; Press notes, 1 and 23 July, PM 62/455/1.

[30] Shanahan memo, 16 February 1956, MS-Paper-6759-203.

[31] Shanahan memo, 30 July 1955, EA455/4/1.

the Assembly." While Lee likely regulated his comments, he high-lighted another aspect of New Zealand engagement; he claimed that Singapore's Chinese preferred relations with New Zealand due to its "excellent record" on racial policies. New Zealand got a better "psychological reception" than Australia, which was known for its "history of racial antagonism."[32]

Shanahan had to beware of policy contradictions. While committed to decolonisation, Wellington also had to reflect on its administration of Samoa. Further, tensions existed between Wellington's strong anti-communist position and decolonisation, where it committed forces to the Malayan Emergency while this, in turn, delayed Malayan and Singaporean independence.

Nevertheless, Wellington inserted itself as a small but useful intermediary in constitutional discussions. Before self-government talks in Britain in January 1956, the Foreign Office directly con-sulted Wellington and Canberra, and Minister of External Affairs Tom Macdonald then met David Marshall in Singapore. Wellington generally shared British positions, hoping talks could lead to non-communist self-government in both territories and their eventual merger. Shanahan also came to share British doubts over Marshall's continued suitability as a transitional leader. His insistence on con-trolling Singapore's internal security undermined negotiations, and Shanahan saw Marshall and his deputy, Lim Yew Hock, as strug-gling to grasp the implications of independence and the risks of increasing Chinese political involvement.[33]

Malaya's impending independence and the commission's resource pressures forced Wellington to review representation from 1956. It alleviated some pressure from SEATO duties by estab-lishing a Bangkok post, although Shanahan remained Wellington's SEATO representative. He also gained accreditation as High Commissioner to Malaya on its independence in 1957.[34] Maintaining the Singapore-based commission, however, remained the core

---

[32] Shanahan, 13 August 1955, EA455/4/1.
[33] Shanahan memos of 19 January, 15 February, 13 March 1956, MS-Papers-6759-203.
[34] McGibbon (2022).

focus, with External Affairs deciding not to shift resources to Malaya. Indicatively, the Singapore post's budget was second only to those of London and Washington.[35]

Wellington then unintentionally became embroiled in troubled self-governance discussions in 1956. Shanahan had minimised contact with the obdurate Marshall who, after returning from an unsuccessful London trip in May, proposed a plan for independence and threatened to resign by 6 June if not accepted.[36] However, Prime Minister Holland met Marshall in Singapore on 28 May, en route to the Commonwealth Conference. Intervening uncharacteristically and disregarding officials' advice, Holland asked Marshall not to resign and promised to take his concerns to London. The *Straits Times* quoted Holland as saying "Singapore's constitutional problems will have high priority" in London. He was "going … to help deal with the problems of other people." New Zealanders were "in full agreement with the aspirations of the people of Singapore." Marshall resigned anyway on 30 May, but the episode illustrated the diplomatic challenges in Singapore's volatile political environment.[37]

After Marshall's resignation, Singapore faced political unrest, including from communist opposition. Lim, as Marshall's replacement, vigorously suppressed disorder. He took a tough line with the Chinese population, adopting his "own peculiar methods" through his "bully boys." Whereas he did not have "the public appeal of Marshall," Shanahan commended his "capacity to keep his mouth shut" in public. Shanahan met him in September 1956, and they identified strongly in their anti-communist stances. Lim shared highly-indiscreet comments on political rivals, illustrating the "friendship and confidence" he placed in Shanahan.[38]

---

[35] Notes on representation, 1957, MS-Papers-6759-085.

[36] Chee (1974).

[37] Holland-Marshall notes, May 1956; Priority with the P.M.s. *Straits Times*, 29 May 1956 in MS-Papers-6759-078.

[38] Shanahan memo, 21 September 1956, MS-Papers-6759-203 and of 19 June 1956, MS-Papers- 6759-343.

The British convened further talks on Singapore's self-government in March 1957 as Malaya prepared for independence. An all-party delegation including Lim and Lee agreed on arrangements. A tripartite British, Singaporean, and Malayan body, the Internal Security Council, would oversee internal security. Britain accepted this as any communist threat would likely also concern right-wing Malayan members who, with the British, could outvote the Singaporeans. They were also convinced that Lim was "determined and capable," and that Lee's PAP may emerge as non-communist.[39]

While Shanahan's focus remained on defence and security, his post also became a focal point for discharging Wellington's Colombo Plan contributions. External Affairs had warmed to the plan as a crucial vehicle for forwarding New Zealand and Commonwealth interests and countering the spread of communism. The Colombo Plan aid became a second prong of Wellington's regional effort. McIntosh claimed it to be "as important — if not more important — than SEATO," particularly as the aid budget was seldom questioned and could be used outside of SEATO's area of focus.[40]

Changing of the Guard

By late 1957, the relationship between New Zealand and Singapore was at a turning point. External Affairs faced increased Malayan calls for direct diplomatic representation, while increasingly-strident anti-colonialism challenged representation in Singapore. Conversely, Singapore remained more important to New Zealand's interests due to ongoing defence commitments.

In Wellington, Labour won a tight election in November 1957 and the experienced Walter Nash became Prime Minister. The initial briefing to Nash highlighted the relative importance of Singapore and Malaya to Wellington and London, with a warning not to take for granted the fact that British interests were "necessarily identical

---

[39] Hack (2000).
[40] McIntosh to Macdonald, 22 May 1956, MS-Papers-6759-098.

with those of New Zealand." Both were parties to an Anglo-Malayan
Defence Agreement (AMDA) signed that September, but Wellington
had a long-term security interest, while for Britain, these countries
were "not ... so strategically vital." It was, rather, an "ex-Colonial
authority" that still had "a strong sense of responsibility" for these
territories.[41]

Nash showed an immediate interest in Colombo Plan aid. This
coincided usefully with New Zealand diplomat Hunter Wade serving as Colombo Plan Bureau Director. Nash's Government reor-
ganised aid into an effective technical assistance programme from
earlier, unsuccessful investments in capital projects. Notably, this
saw more Singaporean and other Southeast Asian students entering New Zealand universities.

By Shanahan's departure from Singapore in 1958, Nash had
reconfirmed New Zealand's interests there and gained reassur-
ances about Singapore's security directly from British Prime
Minister Macmillan. During a visit, both leaders agreed that Lim
would 'hopefully' win the elections, but Macmillan acknowledged
that Britain would step in should the communists win. During
Nash's subsequent Singapore visit that March, he backed Lim as a
"staunch friend of the British" and a "courageous and relentless
opponent of Communism."[42]

On 26 May 1958, Shanahan ended his term in the same way
that he began. He addressed the Singaporean people in a farewell
radio message, wishing for the city's stability through future independence. Despite being overburdened, Shanahan had shown
personal regard for the Singaporean people and created a sound
basis for future relations.

1958–1962: Supporting Singapore towards Merger

The relationship went through a dynamic period from the time of
Shanahan's departure until Singapore merged into 'Malaysia'.

---

[41] Briefing to incoming PM, 11 December 1957, MS-Papers-6759-104.

[42] Briefing to Nash, 31 March 1958, NYP3/22/4.

From a low after Shanahan's departure, when External Affairs looked to downgrade the Singapore-based commission in favour of relations with Malaya, the relationship survived and strengthened as links grew with Singapore's new Prime Minister, Lee Kuan Yew.

Nash accepted Alister McIntosh's recommendation in April 1958 that the Singapore-based commission be downsized in favour of a High Commission in Malaya.[43] This reallocation of limited diplomatic resources reflected what External Affairs saw as Malaya's pre-eminent role in merger arrangements. Wellington focussed on influencing, alongside Commonwealth partners, the political and economic aspects of the Federation of Malaya with the remaining British territories in the region, including Singapore, to complement the single ANZAM defence area. In doing so, Nash went out of his way to appoint Charles Moihi Bennett, a respected Māori leader and wartime commander of the 28th Māori Battalion, as High Commissioner in Malaya.

Prioritising Malaya likely appeared sound in early 1959 given the challenges Singapore faced before initial self-government elections in May. Reporting highlighted "gloomy prognostications" for the election and ambiguity over whether Singapore could be kept out of communist hands. Despite British and New Zealand support for Lim, his violent crackdowns on Chinese dissidents made him increasingly unpopular and the PAP's communist-leaning left wing appeared to be gaining support.[44]

External Affairs' position proved irreconcilable, however, with realities in both Southeast Asia and within the Wellington bureaucracy. Acting Commissioner to Singapore, Brian Lendrum, attended Malayan independence celebrations in August 1958. He reported that the discussions of Commonwealth representatives with Malayan leaders had been "rather futile" and that links in Singapore should not be abandoned.[45] Merger was unlikely in the short term

---

[43] McIntosh to Nash, 24 April 1958, PM 62/434/1; Cabinet paper, CP(58)45, 1 September 1958, EA62/455/4.

[44] PM's brief, May 1959, NYP3/22/4.

[45] Lendrum memo, 16 September 1958, EA62/455/1.

and defence linkages such as BDCC representation could not easily occur from Malaya. The Department of Industries and Commerce could also not be persuaded to cover political duties in Singapore in the event of it keeping trade representation there.

The retained commission in Singapore provided greater diplomatic value than Bennett's post. Bennett built a friendship — particularly over golf and poker — with Malayan Prime Minister Tunku Abdul Rahman (hereafter 'the Tunku') as one of his "closest friends and confidants and indisputably the closest diplomatic representative to him in Kuala Lumpur."[46] However, McIntosh noted the limited value as Bennett operated "in a vacuum" and failed to report key information.[47]

Alternately, successive career diplomats in Singapore built lasting, effectual links with Singaporean leaders and provided key insights on merger negotiations. When Lee became Prime Minister in June 1959, Lendrum's replacement, Reuel Lochore, supplied key reporting on Lee's political sympathies. He clarified that Lee's relationship with the PAP's left wing was one of convenience. Lee was non-communist, provided "dedicated, intelligent leadership," and was "a man with whom we could do business." Given this, Wellington assessed there was a "case for guarded optimism" about Singapore's immediate future.[48]

Lee's clear win rejuvenated Wellington's political interest in Singapore. Nash hurriedly reinstated a Commissioner in June 1959, appointing Cabinet Secretary Dick Hutchens. While Hutchens was accredited to the three British Borneo states, without Shanahan's other duties, he focused extensively on Singapore. Wellington instructed him to not pay "too much lip-service to formal British responsibility" for Singapore but instead to build close relations with Singaporean leaders.[49] The highly-legalistic approach the British initially took with Lee aided Hutchens' efforts, with him benefitting

---

[46] Caird (1970).

[47] McIntosh to Hutchens, 2 March 1960, MS-Papers-6759-285.

[48] Lochore memo, 2 June 1959, EA58/455/1; Memo, 26 May 1959, EA455/4/2.

[49] File note, 3 August 1959, EA58/455/1.

from greater freedom and New Zealand's good reputation. His staff effectively-built relationships and reported back to Nash in late 1959 that further "cultivation of personalities" would be a particularly "fruitful investment."[50] Wellington came to appreciate through these links, more than others, Singapore's distinct position and case for special status in a proposed federation.

Wellington also rapidly reversed aid restrictions in support of Lee and Finance Minister Goh Keng Swee's ambitious six-year industrialisation plan. When officials reconsidered representation, they had deprioritised aid as they considered Singapore more developed than other regional territories. Following the reversal, Wellington launched a targeted campaign of assistance through Colombo Plan channels. It recognised the PAP Government's exposed economic position due to Britain's equivocation over its bases and reduced foreign capital investment resulting from perceived communist threats.[51]

Colombo Plan aid provided small-state New Zealand with a means of influencing stability in a manner acceptable within Singapore's tense political environment. Singaporeans suspected British and Australian motives as donors while they regarded New Zealand as having no axe to grind.[52] Between 1950 and 1962, Australia provided the largest share of technical assistance to Singapore (69%), but New Zealand's was the second highest (13%), more than matching larger states such as Canada (12%).[53]

New Zealand could go further than many other states in supporting Singapore as Lee and Nash shared social democratic values. Nash speedily congratulated Lee on his election success, in response to which Lee praised New Zealand effusively as a "successful welfare state."[54] Nash instructed Hutchens to explore any possible avenues for New Zealand Labour Party and/or Colombo

---

[50] Memo, 7 October 1959, EA59/3/22.

[51] Memo, 25 November 1959, EA104/420/1.

[52] Hutchens memo, 16 November 1959, EA203/2/59.

[53] Singh (1963).

[54] Lee to Nash, 23 June 1959, EA62/455/2.

Plan assistance.[55] He also made the first visit to Singapore by a Commonwealth Prime Minister after Lee's Government came to power. On meeting, Lee pointedly recalled Nash's congratulations message and publicly proclaimed that he wished to "ferret out" Nash's "secret formula" for producing a successful welfare state.[56]

There *were* boundaries, which Wellington quickly learned. Lee inquired whether Wellington could help train 'tough' administrators through the Colombo Plan. Wellington offered instead to help renovate Singapore's trade union system. Not surprisingly, Lee turned down this offer.

Lee also adroitly exploited the situation. In what Hutchens considered a ploy to pressure Malaya to deepen economic links and extract further foreign assistance, in May 1960, Lee threatened to seek Soviet aid. In response, Hunter Wade, now Director of External Affairs' technical assistance programme, called for "a more positive programme" of aid to Singapore, "especially if we are to avoid leaving this important field open" to the Soviets. Hutchens had informed him that "a greater sense of urgency and degree of initiative" was needed and that Wellington needed to be "prepared to run a greater element of risk" in supporting Singapore.[57]

The successful 'ploy' led to a period of further significant support to Singapore. Wade rapidly approved telecommunications aid and lobbied for immediate expansion of technical training, even where New Zealand training facilities were stretched.[58] New Zealand also established an Industrial Research Unit (IRU) at Singapore Polytechnic to support commercial manufacturing. Most visible and important for people links was the increase in students studying in New Zealand universities. Between 1959 and 1962, 7% of Colombo Plan students in New Zealand came from Singapore.

---

[55] Brief, 1 July 1959, EA62/455/2.

[56] Hutchens memo, 22 March 1960, and Lee's speech of 8 April 1960 in MS-Papers-6759-285.

[57] Wade to Hutchens, 7 June 1960, EA118/13/44/7A.

[58] Colombo Plan report, UNZ10 K1-2.

Although fewer overall than from Indonesia and Malaya, this was far higher on a per capita basis.[59]

Singapore had taken strides by late 1960 thanks in part to the aid campaign's addressing of socio-economic problems. Singapore recognised the Nash Government's efforts during the June 1961 National Day celebrations. New Zealand was the only non-Asian country whose congratulatory message was included in the official programme and the cover included a picture of Nash with Singapore's Deputy Prime Minister, Toh Chin Chye.[60]

A Political Shock

While foreign aid assisted Singapore economically towards merger, the succeeding Holyoake Government faced a different challenge. Keith Holyoake, who had spent six weeks in Southeast Asia before the election, won the December 1960 vote and sought expanded regional involvement. Shortly into his term, however, PAP political losses seriously threatened Singapore's internal stability, bearing keenly on the proposed merger and regional security.

A by-election in Singapore in April 1961 precipitated a "seriously tangled skein of events" that endangered Lee's government.[61] The PAP lost the by-election to a former PAP member and city mayor, Ong Eng Guan. Lee had abolished Singapore's mayoral office from which Ong had cultivated a populist following. Not only did Ong then win the by-election as an independent but he also took with him two other PAP members. Lee's faction resisted the PAP's resurgent left wing, but their numbers were dangerously reduced. The Tunku, fearing a left-wing victory in Singapore, suddenly called for an advancement of the merger on 27 May, proposing that Singapore, North Borneo, Brunei, and Sarawak join Malaya in a 'Greater Malaysia' Federation.

---

[59] Colombo Plan Bureau, annual reports, Consultative Committee, 1951–67.

[60] Dunlop memo, 12 June 1961, EA58/455/1.

[61] Hutchens memo, 9 September 1961, EA455/4/1.

The Tunku's announcement caught Lee's government partway through its difficulties. Another by-election in July saw David Marshall's return and the loss of another PAP seat. The PAP's left wing and trade unions campaigned against Lee's candidate, fracturing the party. Thirteen left-wing members left to form the Barisan Socialis Party, taking much of the PAP's grassroots organisation. The Government's majority dropped to one, and with illnesses and defections among members, it required the now-independent Lim Yew Hock's support to keep a majority.

Wellington took unprecedented steps on what it saw as a deeply-serious situation. It supported the proposal for a rapid merger, with Lee's retention in Singapore as the only route to stability. External Affairs had been uncomfortable with Lee's increasingly-assertive style but saw his leadership in a stable, democratic Singapore government as essential. Therefore, for the first time, New Zealand's Malaya-based battalion trained openly for internal security operations.

Final Negotiations

The immediate crisis passed and, in August 1961, Lee and the Tunku agreed in principle to merge by June 1963. This prompted Wellington's reorganisation of both military arrangements and diplomatic representation. Pre-merger, Singapore's openness to SEATO operations had allowed Wellington to route its military forces through the city to circumvent Malaya's restrictions on these operations. The Tunku's pronouncement that, within a Greater Malaysia, the use of Singapore's bases would be similarly restricted required Singapore and the AMDA nations to renegotiate an extended AMDA in November 1961. Concurrently, Britain's replacement of the politico-military BDCC with a military-only Defence Council prompted Wellington to start developing its own logistics and command structures.[62]

---

[62] Murfett (1999).

Diplomatically, McIntosh advised Holyoake that while Singapore was "of more direct value to New Zealand," representation would need to reflect that the High Commission in Kuala Lumpur was technically senior to the Singapore Commission, being in a sovereign state.[63] McIntosh proposed that Hunter Wade replace Hutchens in Singapore in May 1962 before then succeeding Bennett as New Zealand's senior representative in Kuala Lumpur around the merger.

Wade rapidly discovered that merger plans rested on fraught personal relations between the Tunku and Lee and on economic challenges. Wade saw the Tunku's behaviour towards Lee as cynical, particularly when — to remove Lee "almost contemptuously" — the Tunku offered him the position of Malaysian permanent delegate to the UN.[64] On economics, Wade was well placed as a Colombo Plan expert to continue supporting Singapore's industrialisation and increase engagement on trade policy.

Wellington hosted a significant visit by Goh Keng Swee in November 1962. Lee advanced an economic vision of making Singapore a "New York of Asia," but it was Goh who had the technical background to deliver on it. A former member of Shanahan's staff strongly supported Goh's visit as he had a "pretty powerful interest in New Zealand," was the Singaporean minister "of most specific importance to" External Affairs, and took "a close personal interest" in Wellington's aid activities.[65] The visit highlighted that Wellington could benefit from Singapore's vision and the complementarity of the two countries' economies. Wellington could help address Singapore's high unemployment and build workforce expertise through continued scholarships and industrialisation support. It could also support joint manufacturing: Some companies had such plans and a joint venture dairy operation had already started.[66]

---

[63] PM's brief, 2 February 1962, EA62/455/2.
[64] Wade memo, 8 September 1962, EA59/3/22.
[65] Dunlop memo, 28 September 1962, EA59/3/22.
[66] Carter (2007).

While Wellington saw opportunity, pre-merger economic disputes erupted in early 1963. Lee ordered an extensive security
sweep against supposed communists and anti-merger activists,
which Malayan leaders saw as overly repressive and as a potential
justification for halting economic negotiations. Wade noted that the
"crushing blow" to opponents would allow negotiations to focus
beyond internal security.[67] However, bitter tensions arose between
Lee and Malayan Finance Minister Tan Siew Sin on the economic
terms of the federation. Wellington believed that Singapore's special economic position deserved recognition. Given the tension, it
accepted that Lee might have to increase brinkmanship, but, ultimately, he was expected to agree to the merger. Wellington saw
"more room for generosity on Kuala Lumpur's side."[68]

On Wade's last day in Singapore (16 May 1963), he addressed
Singaporean leaders at the IRU's opening, stressing the two countries' deepening relationship. The aid programme had fostered
"human relations and understanding" between the two countries.
From Wellington, Holyoake commented that the unit "should do
much to strengthen the goodwill that exists between Singapore and
New Zealand."[69]

This period influenced Wellington's comparative views of Kuala
Lumpur and Singapore, with External Affairs strongly backing Lee's
government over Malayan demands. Bennett, who McIntosh
believed "so closely identified with the Tunku" as to be "incapable
of doing the job," was gone. Wade had not played poker since university and had "rather rudimentary" golf skills, which reduced his
chances with the future federation Prime Minister.[70] He also took to
the Tunku a message that Wellington would see any federation
without Singapore as "not only unfortunate but unwise." He reported

---

[67] Wade memos of 4, 19 February 1963, NYP3/22/4.

[68] McIntosh memo, 7 May and Wade reply, 9 May 1963, EA104/420/1.

[69] Goh Keng Swee, Opening of the IRU, 16 May 1963, National Archives of Singapore, Ref:
1997109926; Opening of N.Z. Financed Research Unit in Singapore. *Evening Post*, 16 May
1963.

[70] Wade memo, 19 July 1963, MS-Papers-6759-362.

that Wellington should consider "very firm action" if Singapore was excluded.[71]

As predicted, Singapore and Malaya settled at the last minute, finalising economic terms as federation plans were agreed on 8 July. Singapore would lose free port status after two years and contribute 40% of state revenue to federal coffers, but Malayan leaders agreed to work towards a common market and facilitate Singapore's industrialisation.

1963–1965: The Malaysia Experiment

New Zealand's experience of Singapore's short, acrimonious time within the federation (16 September 1963–9 August 1965) profoundly influenced long-term relations. Malaysia faced a painful birth, with President Sukarno's Indonesia attacking a federation he viewed as a neo-colonialist plot. The conflict united Malaysia and its Commonwealth allies, with New Zealand forces joining in resisting the 'Confrontation' until Sukarno's overthrow. Malaysia could not, however, overcome internal, ethno-religious conflict. Wellington was not disposed to openly intervene, but its diplomats carefully played a supportive backroom role. In the federation-state tensions, Wellington gravitated towards closer relations with Singapore at the expense of relations with Kuala Lumpur.

The rapid merger and removal of colonial structures altered the form of New Zealand's relations. It enhanced direct relations with Malaysian leaders but also led to a reduction in the status of its post in Singapore. Wellington established a Deputy High Commissioner role that was senior enough to maintain relations with Singapore's leaders and deputise on Commonwealth committees.[72] Appointees also worked effectively with Wade to tactfully cover federation-state matters, although this upset Kuala Lumpur. It sought to reduce foreign missions in Singapore to consular status which, although procedurally correct, was assessed by

---

[71] PM to Wade, 22 May 1963 and Wade memo, 20 June 1963, EA104/420/1.
[72] McIntosh to PM, 8 March 1963, EA62/455/2.

Wellington's representatives as a deliberate attempt to "cut down the Singaporeans to size."[73]

Wellington's regional security involvement also evolved. The anti-communist focus reduced following Commonwealth success in the Malayan Emergency and Lee's outmanoeuvring of Singapore's communist opposition. However, concurrently, the US was pressuring Wellington to make a commitment in Vietnam. Officials tied the logic of a limited commitment there to Wellington's deeper contributions in Malaysia, and, indeed, Wellington was forced to bolster this Malaysian presence due to the Confrontation and Britain struggling to maintain its bases.[74] Irrespective of whether that convinced the US, Wellington's diplomatic presence in Malaysia became increasingly important following the BDCC's removal and as it built a separate logistics structure to support its regional defence presence.[75]

Successive Deputy High Commissioners provided essential reporting on federation-state relations and internal security. Bill Challis kept Wellington informed about Singapore's September 1963 state elections, providing awareness of a 'gentlemen's agreement' between the Tunku and Lee that the Tunku's United Malays National Organisation (UMNO) would avoid Singaporean state elections in return for Lee's PAP keeping out of non-Singaporean electorates in federal elections. Replacing Challis in January 1964, Brian Lendrum then enhanced relations with Lee's government, becoming close with key ministers, including Goh and Minister for Law Eddie Barker.

Lendrum observed the Tunku's breaking of the gentleman's agreement and Lee's response in contesting the April 1964 federal election.[76] Lee claimed not to be challenging the UMNO as he saw its leadership as vital to Malaysia's survival. Rather, he looked to displace the Malaysian Chinese Association (MCA), which allied with the UMNO. When Lee's campaign stuttered, winning only one

---

[73] NZC Singapore, telegram, 20 March 1964, EA62/455/1.
[74] RabelL (2013).
[75] McGibbon (2022).
[76] Report of 14 August 1963, EA455/4/1.

of eleven seats it contested outside of Singapore, the New Zealand representatives' prime concern was that Lee survive politically. To Wade, Lee's PAP would have provided "the only effective, responsible, non-communal, pro-Malaysia centre-to-left-wing alternative to the Alliance." Kuala Lumpur's actions and Malay views were more troubling than Lee's ambitious approach.[77]

1964: The Race Riots

By July 1964, Wade and Lendrum warned Wellington that the federal government's communal politics had brought relations with Singapore to 'a low ebb'. Malays opposed a policy Lee adopted on 19 July whereby Singaporean Malays would be rehoused, educated, and employed on equal terms with Chinese and Indian populations. Wade observed federal inaction in addressing these Malay attacks, complaining to Wellington about having to support a regime that showed itself "responsive to ... the most bigoted Malay nationalists."[78]

UMNO propaganda and speeches incited prejudice. Even moderates, including the Tunku, stoked Malay antipathy by labelling those who voted for the PAP in the 1963 election as 'traitors'. The UMNO, attempting to reclaim Singaporean Malay support, established a highly-communal Singapore Malay National Action Committee, which called for them to "unite and sweep away the Chinese from the face of Singapore."[79]

The racial tensions peaked in Singapore on 21 July when, during a street parade, a UMNO-linked group attacked a Chinese police officer. This triggered an eleven-day riot that took 23 lives. A second riot then ensued on 3 September after local Chinese murdered a Malay trishaw driver. In riots that authorities believed were inflamed by Indonesian insurgents, 13 more people died.

---

[77] Wade memo, 7 May 1964, NYP3/22/3; Lendrum memo, 13 March 1964, EA104/253/1.
[78] Wade memo, 20 July 1964, NYP3/22/3.
[79] Committee speech, 21 July 1964, NYP3/22/4.

While Britain and Australia unsuccessfully mediated, Wellington took a restrained approach, allowing continued relations with both sides. Holyoake prevented the Terendak-based regiment from intervening but he allowed it to assume additional anti-Confrontation tasks, which freed federal forces to police Singapore. Privately, Wade was clear: Lee's policies of 19 July had "lit the fuse that exploded in racial violence," but Malay radicals had "supplied the gunpowder."[80] Lendrum reported unequivocally that the riots were "sparked off by militant Malays attacking Chinese."[81]

The federal and state governments sought a modus vivendi in the aftermath. Wellington saw it as Kuala Lumpur's responsibility to de-escalate the conflict through this process. Holyoake and McIntosh clarified the conditions that they believed a successful modus vivendi needed to address. Malaysia depended "in large measure upon the willingness and determination of the politically dominant Malays to work towards a genuinely multi-racial society." Malaysia was "a Federation, not an Empire." It would take a trans-formation of the Malay leaders' communal views to save the fed-eration, which would involve the "controlled erosion of the special advantages the Malays enjoy."[82]

A limited modus vivendi agreed in September 1964 rapidly frayed as the underlying issues went unresolved. Malaysian Finance Minister Tan (also MCA Leader), in particular, undermined it. He provoked Lee by asserting that Singapore could not secede from the federation even if it wanted to and avoided consulting on major tax proposals that would affect Singapore. With excellent access to Lee and senior ministers, Lendrum concluded that it was federal leaders who had "something of an inferiority complex" towards the "more politically mature Singapore Government" that really threat-ened Malaysia. It was "highly probable" that Lee had thought of secession, yet Lendrum found it "hard to believe" that he "would seriously espouse such a course for he still ... supports Malaysia."[83]

---

[80] Wade memo, 6 August 1964, NYP3/22/4.
[81] Lendrum memo, 24 August 1964, NYP3/22/4.
[82] PM cable, 21 August 1964, NYP3/22/3.
[83] Carter (2007).

Lee Kuan Yew's New Zealand Visit in 1965

In March 1965, Lee travelled to New Zealand and Australia on what he described as "a working holiday with golf included."[84] This was far from reality. External Affairs judged that "Lee sought to make domestic political capital," to persuade both governments to pressure Kuala Lumpur, and "to prepare public opinion ... for the worst should it happen."[85] McIntosh cautioned Holyoake and ensured that Lee's visit invitation was extended through the federal government rather than directly. No matter how "one might deplore the Tunku's attitude," McIntosh noted, Wellington did not wish to offend him by assisting Lee to "make a splash in the Malaysian press."[86]

Lee had raised with Lendrum before the visit that he intended to discuss constitutional arrangements. The Tunku had broached Singapore's 'disengagement', which would involve the PAP avoiding Malayan politics while Singapore would receive greater autonomy, particularly over state finance and internal security. Britain, Australia, and New Zealand reached a shared position before the visit that disengagement would be highly undesirable, and by early 1965 the Tunku had gone off the idea.[87]

Lee still raised disengagement with Holyoake, to which he later recounted that leaders in Wellington gave him "a thorough-going over." He had emphasised the need for "a few years breathing space" as the Tunku had sought the federation's 'Malay-isation' and only after prompting "did he accept [the] need to minimise the nature of changes."[88] Lee's account reinforced Wellington's concerns with the Tunku's attitudes. However, his disengagement proposal was seen as "somewhat dogmatic, over-simplified and emotional." Holyoake warned that it would require constitutional change that would potentially dismantle the federation, open it to Indonesian control, or bring about an inherently-unstable government, as in South Vietnam. If so, the New Zealand public might

---

[84] Lendrum memo, 17 December 1964, EA59/3/22.

[85] External Affairs guidance 19/65, 1 June 1965, NYP3/22/3.

[86] McIntosh memo, 19 February 1965, EA59/3/22.

[87] Carter (2007).

[88] McIntosh to Wade, 15 March 1965, EA59/3/22.

not continue supporting a defence commitment. Malaysia was "a bargain," which was "not lightly to be broken."[89]

Wellington's frank response did not undermine what had become a trusting, robust relationship. Lee saw that disengagement would not be supported and rethought a potentially-risky approach. Further, outside of these discussions, Lee had a successful trip. His engagements confirmed McIntosh's views that Lee deserved Wellington's support. He and Holyoake could not "fail to be impressed" by Lee's "capacity and by the soundness of the arguments he put forth."[90]

Lee engaged the New Zealand public, touring for ten days and attending civic audiences. He struck a conciliatory tone, talking inclusively of the federation and his vision of a multiracial "Malaysian Malaysia" where all peoples had a right to equal citizenship. Lee also recognised New Zealand's defence commitment. As federal ministers had feared, in places like Invercargill, the focus was on Singapore, not the federation. The mayor talked specifically of the "bonds between Singapore and New Zealand."[91]

Wellington faced Malay blowback, with some UMNO leaders voicing displeasure. Melaka's Chief Minister, Enche Ghaffar, claimed that Lee made "evil" remarks, and "reminded" New Zealand and Australia that although they provided defence support, they were not to become involved in Malaysian politics: "We do not want this country to become a second Vietnam." It took Wade's intervention with federal ministers to ensure that there was "nothing aimed at" New Zealand.[92]

The Denouement

With disengagement unworkable, federation-state battle lines were drawn. Lee organised a federation-wide Malaysian Solidarity

---

[89] Memo, 15 April 1965, EA420/2/1.

[90] McIntosh to PM, 9 January 1965, and McIntosh to Governor-General, 11 March 1965, EA59/3/22.

[91] Press clippings, 13 March 1965, EA59/3/22.

[92] Wade memo, 21 May 1965, NYP3/22/3.

Convention for a non-communal "Malaysian Malaysia" in May 1965. This directly challenged the UMNO-led Alliance Party coalition that dominated federal politics, heightening tensions across all areas. External Affairs increasingly concluded that dissolution might be the only choice and informed Holyoake's government that its "tendency" was "to see a great deal of merit" in Lee's views and "a great deal to deplore in the attitude of Kuala Lumpur."[93]

Following a deceptive calm through July, federation-state leaders announced on 8 August 1965 that Singapore would leave the Malaysian Federation the following day. The separation arrangements and the Tunku's ultimatum of the previous day had been a well-kept secret.[94] Newly-independent Singapore faced both potential Malaysian reprisals and ongoing Indonesian Confrontation. With barriers to accessing traditional Indonesian and Malaysian markets, Singapore's entrepot economy faced upheaval.

Over the first months of separation, New Zealand, alongside Commonwealth partners, recognised the new Singaporean state and protected the city's interests. Among the turbulence, the New Zealand–Singapore relationship emerged fully from under the umbrella. Wellington appointed a high commissioner to Singapore, which (along with Singapore's reciprocity) capped a relationship in development since 1955. No longer was it overshadowed by British or Malaysian sovereignty over Singapore.

The separation's immediate aftermath determined the conditions under which the new relationship would operate. With other Commonwealth leaders, Holyoake had tried at the last minute, but unsuccessfully, to halt separation on 8 August. He told the Tunku how appalled he was "at any suggestion that Malaysia should be broken up or truncated." His concerns were that separation could isolate Singapore and could also trigger a break in defence arrangements. He stressed possible repercussions including the encouragement of Indonesian insurgents, the

---

[93] External Affairs guidance 19/65, 1 June 1965, NYP3/22/3.
[94] US Embassy Kuala Lumpur to Dept. State, 9 August 1965, FRUS, 1964–68, Vol. 26, Doc. 267; Holyoake to Tunku, 8 August 1965, EA455/4/2.

disheartening of Malaysia's supporters, and the prospect of New Zealanders questioning "how effectively we can maintain our support" of Malaysia.[95]

But, preventing Singapore's isolation required rapid recognition of its independence. Lee appealed to his closest friends, sending cables to Britain, Australia, and New Zealand on 9 August ciphered according to the pages of the Little Oxford English Dictionary. In this, Lee mentioned that the only reason Singapore could leave Malaysia quietly was that they had the "warm support" of friends such as New Zealand. Lee assured Holyoake that "you can rely on my colleagues and I to ensure that Singapore will remain a non-Communist nation so long as we are in authority and whatever the sacrifices we have to make."[96]

Wellington — while recognising Singapore — took a "tactfully bland" approach as it still had to engage Malaysian leaders.[97] New Zealand's recognition was second only to Britain. However, the ever-parsimonious government did not follow British and Australian examples of immediately appointing a Singapore-based high commissioner. Instead, it considered dual accreditation from Malaysia. Alongside challenges in gaining Holyoake's approval, Wade also convinced Wellington that, tactically, dual accreditation could slow down political separation.

Aside from his reluctance to address diplomatic appointments, Holyoake was optimistic. Reporting indicated that the single AMDA defence area was not immediately threatened. Further, both the Tunku and Singapore's finance minister, Lim Kim San, played down the risks of economic conflict. The chair of the Malaysian Tariff Advisory Board, a New Zealander, claimed that separation would not necessarily rule out a common market.[98] Wellington supplied Singapore with symbolic support by extending Commonwealth preferential trade treatment.[99]

---

[95] Holyoake to Tunku, 8 August 1965, EA455/4/2.

[96] Lee to Holyoake, 9 August 1965, EA455/4/2; Yew (1998).

[97] Wade memo, 10 August 1965, EA62/455/1.

[98] Special meeting minutes, 11 August 1965; Common market: it needn't 'die. *Malay Mail*, 10 August 1965 in EA455/4/2.

[99] Lendrum telegram, 19 August 1965, EA104/420/200/2.

However, both Singapore and Malaysia placed quota restrictions on each other's goods, the unmoved exports jamming the southern Malay Peninsula. Amidst this, Wade met the Tunku on 27 August. He pushed the Tunku and federal ministers to recognise the grave consequences of their actions, to which the Tunku tartly told him to keep out of internal matters. Wade retorted that Wellington had, not without misgiving, "gone out on a limb" to defend Malaysia against Indonesia, and the Tunku was "now sawing off the limb, at the same time telling" them not to "worry, it was none ... of our business" if they "hit the ground." Afterwards, he recommended that External Affairs "lay off" the angry Malaysian leader "for some time" and accepted that separation could not be checked.[100]

The separation experience influenced Wellington to focus first on supporting independent Singapore and to limit engagement with Malaysia generally to economic grounds. In the new climate, a healthy economic relationship was essential. Wade concluded that if the countries' economies could be held together and progress made towards a common market, the "sectors that concern us most deeply — defence and external affairs — will fall naturally into place." If they, conversely, "split hopelessly apart," then Wellington could not safeguard its regional defence interests.

With continued concerns for collective defence, Wellington objected to any Malaysian–Singaporean frictions that could undermine it. External Affairs noted that "if the marriage was one of convenience, the divorce can only at best be one of inconvenience: the divorced couple ... are to continue living in the same house."[101] Both countries noted, however, that they would consider defence support from outside the Commonwealth. With bases still central to Singapore's economy, Lee indicated that he might canvas the use of the bases by non-aligned states if the British withdrew. He announced (on 30 August) that he was "not prepared to go on with the Americans" in place of the British but would go on with Australia and New Zealand.[102] The threat from the Indonesian Confrontation

---

[100] Wade telegrams, 26, 27 August 1965, NYP3/22/3.
[101] Paper for discussion, EA455/4/2.
[102] Department of External Affairs, Wellington 15:8, p. 48.

ultimately ensured that the commitments held, but the incident highlighted that further tensions could undermine Wellington's interests.

The following few months highlighted that Wellington's representatives could achieve more through relations with Singaporean leaders than with their federal counterparts. Malaysian Finance Minister Tan took a vindictive approach to economic discussions, whereas Goh, Lee, and Lim entrusted Lendrum with key details on proposed accords. Lendrum could get Lee to even acknowledge when he "kicked over the traces a bit," such as when he upset Malaysia by resuming barter trade with Indonesia. He also identified where Lee showed restraint in keeping joint ventures that could help relations, such as with Malaysian Airways.[103]

External Affairs' final challenge in the aftermath of the separation — that of gaining approval for a High Commissioner — became a focus after hope faded of limiting separation. As previously, officials struggled to convince the government. Holyoake prevaricated, despite his valuing the relationship and its support to New Zealand's defence presence. Wade informed that Lendrum's efforts had gained Wellington "close and trusting relationships with the more important Singapore Ministers." His progress had been "much better" than his Australian and British counterparts and his close relationship with Lee enabled frank discussions.[104] Even then, Holyoake took two more months before appointing a career officer, Jim Weir, on 26 October.

Two final achievements crowned the 1965 year. Lee reciprocated Weir's appointment in late November and appointed Singapore's first High Commissioner to New Zealand, former senior Cabinet Minister and PAP founding member, Kenny Byrnes. Then, in December, Dr. Phay Seng What, Chairperson of Singapore's Public Service Commission, visited Wellington. Lee charged Phay with developing an external affairs department and

---

[103] Lendrum telegram, 17 November 1965, EA104/420/100/2.
[104] Wade to McIntosh, 11 October 1965, MS-Papers-6759-363.

overseeing Colombo Plan aid. External Affairs provided Phay with an important precedent for Singapore's department.[105]

Supporting Independent Singapore

Jim Weir arrived in Singapore in March 1966 to oversee what had developed into a mature diplomatic relationship. Weir's tenure would involve maintaining trusted links with leaders, supporting the young Singaporean state, and broadening relations. He quickly established a rapport with Lee and his ministers, noting a week after arriving that Lee's government was increasingly "casting out lines in various directions which could be useful."

External Affairs aided political stabilisation and economic development from 1966 in what it described as "not so much a state as a location."[106] However, it was guardedly optimistic about Singapore's future. It was in New Zealand's interests to assist Lee's government, which it saw as "the best possible" in the circumstances: efficient, non-corrupt, and progressive. It focussed intently on internal security and on forging social cohesion, which supported New Zealand's ongoing defence presence. Wellington was concerned, however, that the regional exposure of Singapore would require it to go "somewhat more than half-way in meeting the more reasonable demands of its neighbours."[107]

Malaysia's attitude to relations continued to be problematic, as did Indonesia's, with it only ceasing the Confrontation in mid-1966. There was also a triangular dimension to relations. From December 1965, Singapore pursued improved relations with Indonesia by re-establishing barter trade through its offshore island, Palau Senang. This prompted further tensions with Malaysia, which the British failed to mediate. When the Tunku considered blockading Palau Senang, Wellington prevented further escalation by clarifying

---

[105] Cochrane and Asbridge report, 8 December 1965, EA59/3/22.

[106] Brief, 29 March 1967, EA455/1/1.

[107] Brief, September 1966, EA123/1/1.

that its personnel, who partially staffed Malaysia's infant navy, could not be involved in such an action.[108]

When it came, the end of the Confrontation both coincided with deepening US commitments in Vietnam and the British withdrawal, forcing Wellington to review its defence presence. The Confrontation had delayed a British decision on the bases. Once Confrontation finished, decisions came rapidly. Harold Wilson's Cabinet, prompted by economic pressures, announced in 1967 its intent to halve its Singapore-based forces by 1971 and remove the rest by the mid-1970s. The pound's devaluation that November then brought full withdrawal plans forward to 1971.[109] As this occurred, the US sought further support in Vietnam.

Wellington's interests remained firm and its partners' changes influenced it to shift how it deployed its forces. The 1966 Defence Review upheld forward defence, particularly to address a perceived threat from the PRC. However, where previously New Zealand forces in Malaysia and Singapore had served solely in a Commonwealth context, from 1967 onwards rotations were made through Singapore to Vietnam as Wellington committed further forces there. Further, Wellington stepped up defence aid to Singapore.[110]

With New Zealand's underlying diplomatic and security commitments to Singapore reaffirmed, relations also started deepening and broadening. Weir continued to build on political relationships, often being included as the only outsider on trips with senior Singaporean ministers.[111] External Affairs lauded in 1967 a relationship of "longstanding" linkages in a "wide variety of fields" including trade and aid as well as defence.[112] Notably, in April 1966, the first direct air link to Singapore had been launched by Air New Zealand. External Affairs saw this as key in realising the

---

[108] Carter (2007).

[109] Murfett (1999).

[110] Smith (2005).

[111] Weir memo, 25 January 1967, EA455/1/1.

[112] Brief, 12 July 1967, EA455/1/1.

"conjunction of interests in the area" and opening up economic opportunities, particularly for high-value agricultural items.[113] Singapore was becoming a key entry point for New Zealanders to the rest of East and Southeast Asia. Wellington also welcomed Singapore's move into multilateral arrangements with other regional states as ASEAN was set up.

The foundational defence and diplomatic elements of the relationship remained strong, but became, in relative terms, less conspicuous from the early 1970s onwards. Forward defence ceased being the primary rationale for Wellington's engagement, particularly following its diplomatic recognition of the PRC in 1972.[114] However, there continued to be much value in strategic engagement, including through the Five Power Defence Arrangements (FPDA), which effectively replaced AMDA in November 1971 as a form of 'functional co-operation'. The PAP Government valued New Zealand's army presence in Singapore under these arrangements, which lasted until 1989 and provided a "trip-wire" force that linked back to powerful partners.[115] This continuing engagement complemented strong diplomatic links, both throughout the remainder of Jim Weir's term and through the posting of a succession of senior diplomats to the High Commissioner role.

By the 1970s, a comparatively-strong and distinctive relationship had developed between Singapore and New Zealand. Through the unusual origins evidenced in this study, External Affairs representatives accompanying the defence presence moulded close diplomatic links directly with Singaporean leaders. From its inception, the relationship reflected a progressive trait in Wellington's external engagement and an increasing focus on New Zealand interests. These particular origins have themselves contributed to the robustness of the relationship, which remains strategically important to both countries to this day.

---

[113] External Affairs, Annual Report, March 1965, p. 67.
[114] Smith (2005).
[115] Carter (2007).

Bibliography

ABHS and AAEG File Series [EA and NYP], Records of the Prime Minister's Department and the Department of External Affairs (Selected Items). Wellington: National Archives.

Caird, R. J. (1970). *New Zealand's Foreign Policy and Malaya/Malaysia, 1955–65.* MA: University of Canterbury.

Carter, P. (2007). *A Yin-Yang Affair: The Development of a New Zealand — Singapore Bilateral Relationship, 1950–67.* MA: Victoria University of Wellington.

Chee, C. H. (1974). *A Sensation of Independence: A Political Biography of David Marshall.* Singapore: Oxford University Press.

Colombo Plan Bureau. Annual Reports 1951–1967. Consultative Committee.

External Affairs. Annual Report, March 1965. Wellington.

External Affairs Review (1951–1968). Wellington: Government of New Zealand.

Foreign Relations of the United States, 1964–1968, Washington. Available at: https://history.state.gov/historicaldocuments/frus1964-68v26.

Hack, K. (2000). *Defence and Decolonisation in South-East Asia: Britain, Malaya and Singapore, 1941–67.* Richmond: Curzon.

McGibbon, I. (2022). *New Zealand's Foreign Service: A History.* Chicago: Massey University Press.

McGibbon I. (1999). *Unofficial Channels: Letters between Alister McIntosh and Foss Shanahan, George Laking and Frank Corner, 1946–1966.* Wellington: Victoria University Press.

McKinnon, M. (1993). *Independence and Foreign Policy: New Zealand in the World Since 1935.* Auckland: Auckland University Press.

MS Papers 6759, A.D. McIntosh Papers (Selected Items). Wellington: Alexander Turnbull Library.

Murfett, M. (1999). *Between Two Oceans: A Military History of Singapore from first Settlement to Final British Withdrawal.* Singapore: Oxford University Press.

Rabel, R. (2013). *New Zealand and the Vietnam War: Politics and Diplomacy.* Auckland: Auckland University Press.

Singh, L. P. (1963). *The Colombo Plan: Some Political Aspects.* Canberra: Australian National University.

Smith, A. (2005). *Southeast Asia and New Zealand: A History of Regional and Bilateral Relations.* Singapore: Institute of Southeast Asian Studies.

Trotter, A. (1990). *New Zealand and Japan, 1945–52: The Occupation and the Peace Treaty.* London: Athlone Press.

UNZ File Series, Official Records of the University of New Zealand (Select Items). Wellington: National Archives.

Watt, A. (1972). *Australian Diplomat: Memoirs of Sir Alan Watt.* Sydney: Angus and Robertson.

Wood, F. L. W. (1956). New Zealand and South East Asia. *Far Eastern Survey,* 25.

Wright, M. (2003). *Pacific War: New Zealand and Japan 1941–45.* Auckland: Reed Books.

Yew, L. K. (1998). *Singapore Story: Memoirs of Lee Kuan Yew.* Singapore: Times Editions and Singapore Press Holdings.

Chapter 3

Settling Historic Grievances:
Settlements with Māori Tribes

Hon. Christopher Finlayson KC

Introduction

The purpose of this chapter is to explain attempts by the New Zealand Government over the last 50 years to address longstanding grievances between the Māori (the indigenous people of New Zealand) and the Crown (the State). For a comprehensive analysis of Treaty settlements in New Zealand, see *He Kupu Taurangi* (Finlayson and Christmas, 2021) and *Yes, Minister: An Insider's Account of the John Key Years* (Finlayson, 2022, Ch. 9).

Historic Background

In 1840, the British Crown entered into a Treaty with the various tribes (or iwi) of New Zealand. This Treaty, signed on 6 February 1840, is known as the Treaty of Waitangi. It is New Zealand's most important constitutional document. Over the years, there has been spirited debate over the meaning of the Treaty, and whether the English version is different in material respects from the Māori version. It is beyond the scope of this chapter to explore those constitutional arguments. Broadly speaking, the Treaty (the English version) set out the following provisions:

- Sovereignty in and over New Zealand was ceded to the British Crown. The session of sovereignty is disputed by some Māori. It is beyond the scope of this chapter to consider those claims.
- The Crown agreed that it would recognise the Rangatiratanga (leadership) of the Māori chiefs and would ensure that the treasures (taonga) of the Māori were protected. Particular reference was made to lands, fisheries, and forestry.
- Thirdly, the Māori were to have all the rights and privileges of British citizens.

From the start, the Treaty was not honoured by the Crown. Breaches of the Treaty included the unlawful and brutal taking of land (*raupatu*), unfair taking or compulsory acquisition under the Public Works Act, and dishonest or irregular contracts which resulted in the Māori losing their land. As early as the mid-19th century, visitors to New Zealand were disgusted by the actions of the settlers. A very good illustration of this is the comments of Robert Cecil (a member of the great Cecil family of England which has been involved in English politics since the time of Elizabeth 1st). Cecil subsequently became the Third Marquess of Salisbury and served as Prime Minister in the late 19th and early 20th centuries under Queen Victoria and Edward VII. In his magisterial biography of the Marquess of Salisbury, Andrew Roberts recounts Cecil's visit to the colonies:

Cecil blamed what he called the Empire's prodigal sons — those local governors who indulged in semi-authorised military expeditions ... for unnecessarily violent and costly little wars. He wrote a series of philippics against Sir Thomas Browne, the Governor of New Zealand, whom he accused of precipitating the war against the Māoris and abrogating their "scrupulously reserved" land rights as prescribed in the 1840 Treaty of Waitangi. Browne's crushing of the Māoris, "the sovereign nation who voluntarily entered into an agreement to live under our flag under specified conditions", struck Cecil as "flagrantly unrighteous" and not really warfare so much as "man stalking". The New Zealand Government he dismissed as nothing "but a firm of Auckland attorneys", and settlers in general as "incorrigible, plausible scapegraces" whom Westminster should not continue to subsidise (Roberts, 1999, p. 43).

Mrs. Thatcher once observed that "the veneer of civilisation is very thin" (Thatcher, 1981). And, as Cecil noted, it was virtually non-existent in colonial New Zealand.

A few examples will illustrate what so repelled Cecil and other visitors to New Zealand in the mid-19th Century. First, the appalling actions of the settlers and the Crown in what is now the very wealthy dairy farming area of Taranaki, on the west coast of the North Island of New Zealand. In the 1860s, the settlers desired the rich land of the Māori for farming. During the land wars, the Māori were simply forced off their land. Several hundred Taranaki Māori sought protection in a little hamlet called Parihaka. In 1881, the English Army invaded Parihaka. The leaders were imprisoned without trial and exiled to the South Island. Respect for property rights was ignored and, more importantly, the rule of law and the protection afforded to individuals by the law were knowingly disregarded by all branches of government (see Parihaka Reconciliation Act 2019).

Another example of a breach of the Treaty can be seen in the history of the Whanganui River, which runs from the Central North Island to the Tasman Sea several 100 kilometres to the south of Taranaki. Local Māori had lived alongside the Whanganui River for hundreds of years. It was their source of sustenance, recreation, and livelihood. The river was so intrinsically part of their being that they had a saying, *Ko au te awa, ko te awa ko au* which means "I am the river and the river is me." The settlers arrived, destroyed the eel weirs of the Māori, introduced a paddle steamer to the river which caused damage to the banks of the river, and engaged in farming practices that degraded the quality of water in the river. The Crown developed what was known as the Tongariro Power Development, an enormous engineering project in the middle years of the 20th century, which took water from the Whanganui River and turned it north. This caused extensive environmental damage. The Whanganui River people were determined that these wrongs needed to be addressed. They petitioned Parliament, sued the Crown, and eventually obtained a settlement, as a result of which they have a substantial say over the care of the river (Te Awa Tupua Act 2017).

The law was often used as an instrument of oppression against the Māori. For example, the Waitomo Caves in central North Island are world famous for their glow worms. The caves were a treasure or *taonga* for the local Māori. In 1904, the government wanted to develop tourism in this country, so it simply took the caves under the Scenery Preservation Act (Doorne, 1999). The compensation provided to the local Māori was derisory.

It is beyond the scope of this chapter to recount the full litany of maltreatment that was perpetrated on people who, as Cecil had observed, voluntarily entered into a contract with the British Crown, an essential term of which was that their rights would be preserved. Over the years, however, there was an increasing recognition that what had happened to the Māori was wrong and unfair, and that these historical injustices needed to be addressed.

Treaty of Waitangi Act 1975

In 1975, Parliament enacted the Treaty of Waitangi Act (Treaty of Waitangi Act 1975). This established the Waitangi Tribunal, a body with inquisitorial powers like a commission of inquiry. Its task was to investigate contemporary breaches of the Treaty by the Crown. This was the first step in the modern reconciliation process.

In 1985, the jurisdiction of the Tribunal was extended so that it could inquire into grievances between the Crown and Māori dating back to 6 February 1840 (the date the Treaty was first signed at Waitangi) (Treaty of Waitangi Amendment Act 1985, s 3(1)). Thereafter, various Māori tribes and sub-tribes (iwi and hapū) commenced claims against the Crown in the Tribunal. By the end of the 1980s, the reports of the Tribunal were starting to be released. These provide a very comprehensive record of Crown actions and omissions over the years.

National, in the early 1990s, had to determine what to do with these reports. Were they to be nothing more than a historical record or were they to provide a principled justification for compensation? The Prime Minister at the time, Jim Bolger (1990–1997), was the son of Irish immigrants. He had grown up in Taranaki, not far from Parihaka. He decided that something needed to be done to address the wrongs of the past. So, he appointed one of his colleagues, Douglas Graham, as the first Minister for Waitangi Negotiations, and the government set aside $1 billion (in 1992 dollars), which could be used as financial redress. The quantum set aside was the subject of much debate (see Harris, 1996; Shand, 1998). The Māori regarded $1 billion as derisory but were nonetheless prepared to enter into settlement discussions with the Crown. The government designed a settlement framework which was to provide how negotiations were to proceed and set out settlement parameters.

Settlements with Iwi (Māori Tribes)

The first major settlement was with Waikato iwi, Tainui. It received US$170 million in compensation for lands that had been forcibly taken from it. Redress over the Waikato River and the West Coast harbours was to be negotiated later (Waikato-Tainui Raupatu Claims Settlement Act 2010). Then, in 1997, the Bolger Government settled with the South Island tribe, Ngāi Tahu, for US$170 million (Ngāi Tahu Claims Settlement Act 1998).

The financial component is only one part of the settlement package. The other components of the settlement include the following:

- A right of first refusal (RFR) mechanism whereby the settling tribe has the right of first refusal over all surplus Crown property for a period of 150 years from the date of the settlement. This is a very valuable form of commercial redress.
- The settling tribe can also be given an opportunity to purchase Crown land where schools, police stations, hospitals, and courts are situated. They can then lease those properties back to the Crown.
- Important cultural redress is also provided for in a settlement. This often means returning to the settling group lands of cultural significance such as burial sites (*urupā*) or sites of

villages (*pās*). Originally, the approach taken on the return of culturally-significant land was that the return involved 'small and discrete' parcels of land, but, in recent years, the amount of land transferred has greatly increased.

- Agreements often address very important cultural matters. For example, the names of landmarks may be changed from English to their traditional Māori names. Promises are made about revitalisation of the Māori language (*Te Reo*), and occasionally-difficult intellectual property issues are addressed. For example, in the 19th century, the feared Māori leader Te Rauparaha composed the famous *Ka Mate haka*. Even non-New Zealanders will recognise this *haka* or war dance as it is performed by, for example, the All Blacks (the national rugby team of New Zealand) before major international games. The *haka* is also extensively performed within New Zealand. The descendants of Te Rauparaha, who are members of the Ngāti Toa tribe, sought to have greater recognition of the *haka* for Ngāti Toa. This involved discussions between the Crown and Ngāti Toa representatives because the *haka* had effectively been appropriated by all sections of New Zealand and was regarded as common property. Much work has been done at the international level on the protection of traditional cultural expressions but the law had yet to develop to provide an adequate basis for protection of something like the *haka*. As part of its settlement with the Crown, Ngāti Toa obtained limited recognition of the *haka* (Haka Ka Mate Attribution Act 2014). The authorship by Te Rauparaha was recognised and certain limited moral rights were recognised. When the settlement package was announced, a local Wellington newspaper had as its headline, "All Black haka goes to Maoris".
- Importantly (and in some respects most importantly), any deed of settlement with the Crown sets out the facts of what happened and the Crown gives a formal apology. Both the account of historical facts and the apology are often contested. Māori and Crown historians will argue over what happened. The Crown does not simply apologise 'for the sake of it'.

For example, in the apology given at Parihaka, the Crown apologised for the first time for rape committed by soldiers (Parihaka Reconciliation Act 2019, schedule 1). Such an apology remains very sensitive even all these years later.

- In recent years, redress has been developed which recognises the significant interest that tribes have in natural resources in their area. As noted earlier, the members of the Whanganui tribes had lived alongside the Whanganui River for hundreds of years. It was part of them. They wanted a say in how it was to be looked after. Over the last 15 years, this has given rise to various types of co-governance or Treaty-based co-management. The concept of 'co-governance' has been the subject of some political debate in this country over the last few years, but there seems to be a general consensus that, insofar as natural resources are concerned, the Māori have a legitimate interest in, for example, the clean-up of a lake or river and can add value by being actively involved (for example, ss 14 and 34 Te Awa Tupua (Whanganui River Claims Settlement) Act 2017; Ngāti Manawa Claims Settlement Act 2012 s 104(1)).

Requirements for Settlements

Starting with the Bolger Administration, the procedure for negotiating and concluding settlements has been developed and refined. In particular, the following points are noted:

- The Crown needs to know that the settling group can speak for its members when negotiating with the Crown. It, therefore, needs to obtain a mandate from its people that is recognised by the Crown. This is often easier said than done because of overlapping interests and internal divisions.
- Once a Crown-recognised mandate is obtained, the Crown and the settling tribe will sign terms of negotiation which will govern how the negotiation is to be conducted and concluded.
- When the outlines of settlement are reached, the parties will sign a heads of agreement or agreement in principle.

- They then negotiate the deed of settlement, which sets out all the details of what is agreed between the Crown and the settling group. Once the deed of settlement is initialled, it goes to the members of the tribe for ratification. The Crown needs to be satisfied that the terms of what is proposed are broadly accepted by the settling group.
- When the deed is ready to be signed, there is a ceremony, sometimes in Parliament but more often at one of the key meeting places of the settling group, where the Minister for Treaty of Waitangi Negotiations will sign the deed on behalf of the Crown and apologise for what has happened and that "the future between the Crown and the iwi will be governed by the spirit of the Treaty of Waitangi and its principles." When I used to read out those apologies, more often than not, I had my fingers crossed because, fine rhetoric though it may have been, I was not responsible for the Crown's actions in the years ahead and I knew that the threat to the durability of Treaty settlements came not from the Māori signing the agreement but from the Crown. One example shows how the Crown is a threat to the durability of settlements. In the years before I became Minister for Treaty of Waitangi Negotiations, a tribe in the North Island, the Ngāti Apa, was negotiating with my predecessor. They indicated they would very much like to purchase some land which incorporated a former agricultural training establishment, Flock House, and an adjoining farm. The school and land were vested in a Crown entity. The then Minister received advice from the Crown entity that the land was strategic and could not be made available for settlement. The settlement proceeded, and some years later, the so-called strategic asset was put on the market. It is difficult to know whether the settling tribe were deliberately misled or whether it was a comedy of errors. Regardless, members of Ngāti Apa were outraged and felt they had been shabbily treated. I agreed with them. They were threatening to occupy the land (and I would have been in full support of this action). It was made very clear by Ministers to the Crown entity that this kind of behaviour was not to be toler-

ated and that they had better sort the matter out. Fortunately, the Ngāti Apa acquired the so-called strategic asset (which was, in fact, very rundown) and turned it into a highly-successful agri-business operation. This is a good illustration of what happens when the Crown, for all its fine words when a deed of settlement is signed, simply forgets its obligations or, worse still, does not tell the truth to its Treaty partner.

- The last stage in the settlement journey is legislative. A bill to give effect to a settlement is introduced to the House and is reviewed by a select committee. Then, the bill is signed into law (see Schedule 3 of the Treaty of Waitangi Act 1975).

Economic Consequences of Settlements

The amount spent on settlements is currently $2.2 billion (in today's dollars) (*Te Ōhanga Māori* — The Māori Economy 2018, p. 19). This has been a significant component of the Māori economy's growth in the last 20 years. The Māori economy was valued at US$68.7 billion in 2018 (*Te Ōhanga Māori* — The Māori Economy 2018, p. 20) and is projected to reach US$100 billion by 2030 (Fit for a Better World Update 2023, p. 26). To compare, the entire GDP of NZ was measured at US$400 billion in 2023 (Gross Domestic Product, 2023). The economic performance of the two largest *iwi* in New Zealand illustrates the influence that Treaty settlements can have on an *iwi*'s financial status. In the 1990s, Waikato-Tainui and Ngāi Tahu were the first two major *iwi* to settle. These two *iwi* settled for US$170 million each. However, they also had relativity clauses in their settlements to ensure that the value of their settlements was proportionate to the quantum of future settlements. These clauses have augmented the amount each *iwi* originally received on the settlement by US$293 million and US$315 million, respectively (Iwi Investment Report 2022, p. 11 and 29). These *iwi* are now the wealthiest in New Zealand, with their respective asset bases totalling US$1.98 billion and US$2.28 billion in 2022 (Iwi Investment Report 2022, p. 5). Waikato-Tainui and Ngāi Tahu have predominantly invested in property and primary industries, with some further investment in financial assets. This has resulted in them becoming significant stakeholders in their *rohe* (tribal territory). Another example is Ngāti Whātua Ōrākei, one of the tribes in Auckland. Its asset base is composed of 98% property, and it has the third-largest asset base of all *iwi*, valued at US$1.66 billion, clearly illustrating the correlation between property investment and *iwi* wealth (Iwi Investment Report 2022, p. 23). Overall, the combined assets of every *iwi* in NZ are estimated at US$11.7 billion in 2022, with the assets of 10 tribes making up 69% of this amount (Iwi Investment Report 2022, p. 5). However, while some tribes have become very wealthy post-settlement, all with asset bases exceeding or nearing a billion dollars, other tribes have not fared so well financially. A clear example of the impact when settlement with the Crown is not reached is seen with the Ngāpuhi, the largest tribe in New Zealand. This tribe currently has limited resources, with its asset base amounting to only US$86 million (Iwi Investment Report 2022, p. 13). This is a negligible sum when compared not only to the iwi previously outlined but also to the Ngāpuhi's population of approximately 151,000 people in 2022 (Iwi Investment Report 2022, p. 13). The Ngāpuhi's failure to reach a settlement with the Crown can be mainly attributed to its poor leadership over many years.

Of course, had the Crown not committed breaches of the Treaty, *iwi* would not be so financially reliant on the Crown for their economic prosperity. When assessing financial success, it always needs to be evaluated with respect to the position the Māori could have been in, with no Crown involvement, when they collectively-exercised authority or *rangatiratanga* over the country. Furthermore, this is only an overview of the financial impact of Treaty settlements, which is by no means the sole indicator of tribal well-being. If success, or lack thereof, was measured from a *Te Ao Māori* (the Māori worldview) perspective, rather than a European one, a very different outcome may be reached, as *Te Ao Māori* emphasises relationships, including with the environment, over the accumulation of assets.

The Future

Because of my concern that the Crown could either ignore Treaty settlements or forget its obligations, in my last term as a Minister, I established the Post-Settlement Commitments Unit. Its task was to ensure that the Crown honoured its obligations. The first step was to tabulate all the various commitments (which in my time as a Minister came to about 7,000, some of which were one-off but others imposing continuing obligations). Under my successor, this office was expanded and the Crown also appointed a Minister for Crown–Māori Relationships.

It is an open question as to whether this exercise in historical dispute resolution will be successful. It will be if the Crown honours settlements. The Māori can, without exception, be relied on to honour their obligations. The problem is always that the Crown forgets, or the needs of a particular generation (for example, a roading or some other development project) mean that land transferred to the Māori can be taken again under the Public Works Act. For that reason, it is by no means guaranteed that this interesting intergenerational dispute resolution project will be successful. If it fails, then we will all know why — because the Crown was responsible.

Perhaps there are those who, having read this, will say that the Crown has learnt from its mistakes. Experience would suggest that this is not the case. The rights of indigenous people in New Zealand are never guaranteed. So, in the early 2000s, when certain Māori groups applied for the customary title of the foreshore and seabed, the Court of Appeal found that the customary title had not been extinguished. The Crown then quickly moved to enact the Foreshore and Seabed Act, which had the effect of preventing 15% of the population (i.e. Māori) from going to court to prove their rights over the foreshore and seabed (Foreshore and Seabed Act 2004). All uninvestigated customary titles were extinguished. The government (of which I was a member) enacted the Marine and Coastal Act 2011, which restored all uninvestigated customary titles, provided a statutory test for establishing such titles, and gave the

Māori the right to go to the courts to prove their case (Marine and Coastal Area (Takutai Moana) Act 2011). It may seem incredible that, in the early years of this century, the Māori should have had fundamental rights of justice (i.e. access to courts) taken away from them, but that is what happened in this country. At the end of the day, the State will always act in accordance with what it perceives to be the needs or desires of the general population and this has often meant that the indigenous people of this country have suffered as a result.

Bibliography

Doorne, S. M. (1999). Visitor experience at the Waitomo Glowworm Cave. *Science for Conservation*, 95, 6. Available: https://www.doc.govt.nz/documents/science-andtechnical/sfc095.pdf. (Accessed 20 December 2023).

Finlayson, C. F. and Christmas, J. (2021). *He Kupu Taurangi.* Wellington: Huia Publishers.

Finlayson C. F. (2022). *Yes, Minister: An Insider's Account of the John Key Years.* Auckland: Allen & Unwin.

Fit for a Better World Update (2023). Ministry for Primary Industries. https://fitfora-betterworld.org.nz/assets/publications/2023-Fit-for-a-Better-World-Update-WEB.pdf. (Accessed 20 Dec 2023).

Foreshore and Seabed Act 2004. Available: https://www.legislation.govt.nz/act/public/2004/0093/latest/DLM319839.html. (Accessed 20 December 2023).

Gross Domestic Product (2023). Stats New Zealand. https://www.stats.govt.nz/indicators/gross-domestic-product-gdp/. (Accessed 20 December 2023).

Haka Ka Mate Attribution Act 2014. Available: https://www.legislation.govt.nz/act/public/2014/0018/latest/DLM5954403.html?search=sw_096be8ed80de95bc_ka+mate_25_se&p=1#DLM5954402. (Accessed 20 December 2023).

Harris N. (1996). Ko Ngaa Take Ture Māori. *Auckland Law Review*, 11, 205–208.

Iwi Investment Report 2022. TDB Advisory. https://www.tdb.co.nz/wp-content/uploads/2023/02/TDB-Advisory-Iwi-Investment-Report-2022.pdf. (Accessed 20 December 2023).

Marine and Coastal Area (Takutai Moana) Act 2011. Available: https://www.legislation.govt.nz/act/public/2011/0003/latest/DLM3213131.html. (Accessed 20 December 2023).

Ngāi Tahu Claims Settlement Act 1998. Available: https://www.legislation.govt.nz/act/public/1998/0097/latest/DLM429090.html. (Accessed 20 December 2023).

Ngāti Manawa Claims Settlement Act 2012. Available: https://www.legislation.govt.nz/act/public/2012/0027/latest/DLM3277089.html?search=sw_096be8ed81c10a72_forum_25_se&p=1&sr=1. (Accessed 20 December 2023).

Parihaka Reconciliation Act 2019. Available: https://www.legislation.govt.nz/act/public/2019/0060/latest/DLM7397104.html. (Accessed 20 December 2023).

Roberts A. (1999). *Salisbury: Victorian Titan.* London: Weidenfeld & Nicholson.

Shand P. (1998). Fixing settlement: An analysis of government policy for settling tiriti grievances. *Auckland Law Review*, 5, 739–767.

Te Awa Tupua (Whanganui River Claims Settlement) Act 2017. Available: https://www.legislation.govt.nz/act/public/2017/0007/latest/whole.html. (Accessed 20 December 2023).

Te Ōhanga Māori — The Māori Economy 2018. The Reserve Bank of New Zealand. Available: https://www.rbnz.govt.nz/-/media/project/sites/rbnz/files/research/teohanga-maori-report-2018.pdf. (Accessed 20 December 2023).

Thatcher, M. H. (1981). *Speech to Parliamentary Press Gallery Centenary Dinner* [speech], 10 July, London. Available: https://www.margaretthatcher.org/document/104682. (Accessed 20 December 2023).

Treaty of Waitangi Amendment Act 1985. Available: http://www.nzlii.org/nz/legis/hist_act/towaa19851985n148306/. (Accessed 20 December 2023).

Treaty of Waitangi Act 1975. Available: https://www.legislation.govt.nz/act/public/1975/0114/latest/whole.html. (Accessed 20 December 2023).

Waikato-Tainui Raupatu Claims (Waikato River) Settlement Act 2010. Available: https://www.legislation.govt.nz/act/public/2010/0024/latest/DLM1630002.html. (Accessed 20 December 2023).

Chapter 4

New Zealand - Singapore Relations: An Outlook*

Gabrielle Rush and William Tan

It is difficult to encapsulate the relations of two countries as close as ours that have broadened and deepened over almost 60 years. Some 8,500 km lie between us, yet Singapore and New Zealand share the same hopes for a world where smaller countries have their own voice and where they can prosper and thrive. With populations of similar size, our bilateral relations are grounded in complementarity that benefits both our peoples. We have supported each other in times of crisis and both work tirelessly to uphold the rules-based international order. Statistics and numbers cannot fully reflect the friendships that have formed between our leaders, officials, business people, and communities. Yet, the deep reserve of trust this has built will continue to serve us in years to come.

New Zealand and Singapore are trusted partners. New Zealand was among the first countries to officially recognise Singapore when the latter became independent in 1965. New Zealand troops were the last to leave in the nascent years of Singapore's nationhood, providing much-needed stability for Singapore's external security. New Zealand also readily agreed to provide training areas for the armed forces of Singapore in the 1970s. Defence ties between the

---

*Joint article by the New Zealand and Singapore High Commissioners.

two countries remain strong to this day. The Singapore Armed Forces continue to train with their New Zealand counterparts in Waiouru under the Exercise Thunder Warrior initiative since 1997. New Zealand and Singapore also cooperate closely on other defence platforms such as the Five Power Defence Arrangements and ASEAN Defence Ministers' Meeting-Plus.

Our bilateral economic relations are robust. Singapore is New Zealand's fourth-largest trading partner. New Zealand was the first country to sign a bilateral Free Trade Agreement with Singapore, which came into effect in 2001. We jointly laid the foundation for what became the Comprehensive and Progressive Agreement for Trans-Pacific Partnership (CPTPP). Our countries are also pathfinders with Chile in the Digital Economic Partnership Agreement (DEPA). Together, there are six trade agreements currently in force between New Zealand and Singapore.

Recently, the deep friendship between our countries was most evident during the COVID-19 pandemic. Both our countries recognised early on the critical importance of global supply chains, especially for essential goods and services as well as the essential movement of people. We worked hard together on supply chain resilience and saw our efforts serve as catalysts for similar initiatives on the regional and international fronts. We helped each other repatriate our nationals, and Singapore Airlines continued to fly between our two countries throughout this period. We cooperated on the airfreight of much-needed food supplies from New Zealand to Singapore, while key medical supplies were sent from Singapore to New Zealand. Since then, we have set up a joint Supply Chain Working Group to further strengthen security and resilience in this area.

As small states, New Zealand and Singapore have an abiding interest in upholding a rules-based international order, multilateralism, free trade, supply chain connectivity, and the rule of law. We cooperate closely at various multilateral fora, including the UN and WTO. New Zealand and Singapore are also keen to do more together in ASEAN and the Pacific. Our partnership has evolved and deepened over time in support of these shared interests. The signing of the Enhanced Partnership between New Zealand and

Singapore in 2019 underpins our relations and focuses cooperation in the areas of (i) trade and economics, (ii) security and defence, (iii) science and innovation, and (iv) people-to-people links. The additions of the climate change and green economy pillar in 2022, and supply chains and connectivity pillar in 2024, further broadened the Enhanced Partnership. They reflect our shared concern about climate change and supply chain resilience. There is great potential for green economy and connectivity cooperation under these pillars in the energy, transport, maritime and aviation sectors.

Links between our peoples are strong and continue to flourish. New Zealand is a popular travel destination for Singaporeans. Singapore is a major air transit hub for New Zealanders to other parts of the world and is a favoured destination in its own right. Young Singaporeans study in New Zealand universities, as do New Zealand students in Singapore universities. In 2019, we signed an Arrangement on Science, Technology, and Innovation to support research collaboration in areas of mutual interest, such as Data Science and Future Foods, and the exchange of Science and Technology experts. We are also engaging in critical and emerging technologies. The Working Holiday Scheme was upgraded in 2022 to facilitate a freer flow of Singaporeans and New Zealanders to each other's country. Under our cultural cooperation that same year, New Zealand installed a Māori *kūwaha* sculpture at Singapore's iconic Gardens by the Bay.

New Zealand and Singapore have been trusted, steadfast, and reliable partners for each other through the years. Yet, we are not complacent. We continue to look for new ways to add value to the relationship, exploring avenues for enhanced cooperation to keep our relationship fresh and forward-looking. There will be new, exciting opportunities for our two countries to tap into as Southeast Asia grows with promise and we continue working together in the Pacific. The year 2025 will be a significant milestone as we look to celebrate 60 years of close relations between New Zealand and Singapore.

II

FOREIGN POLICY IN A CHANGING ENVIRONMENT

Chapter 5

Singapore's Foreign Policy Challenges

Tommy Koh

Introduction

New Zealand and Singapore are small countries. In the ancient world, small countries had no agency. They had to follow the dictates of the big countries. Some small countries were swallowed up by big countries. Since 1945 and the founding of the UN, the world has been kinder to small countries. Today, small countries like New Zealand and Singapore have agency and can decide on their foreign policies.

The Early Years

Singapore did not seek independence. It was thrust upon her when she was expelled from Malaysia in 1965. The first foreign policy objective was to gain the recognition of the world. In 1968, I was sent to the UN, at the tender age of 30, to achieve this objective. Our second objective was to bring peace to the region through ASEAN. Our third objective was to fill the vacuum left by the British withdrawal from its bases in Singapore. The Five Power Defence Arrangement, involving Singapore, Malaysia, the UK, Australia, and New Zealand, helped psychologically. The final objective was to establish diplomatic relations with as many countries as possible and learn how the international political system worked.

Alignment versus Non-Alignment

During the Cold War, the world was divided into two rival blocs, one led by the US and the other led by the Soviet Union. In the contemporary world, the world is again divided into two rival blocs, one led by the US and the other led by China.

New Zealand has decided to align itself with the US. Singapore has chosen a policy of non-alignment. Singapore is on excellent terms with both the US and China. Singapore's policy is to be close to all the major powers but not to be aligned with any of them.

Relations with the Two Superpowers

Singapore has very substantive relations with both the United States and China. The US is our largest investor. There are over 3,000 US companies in Singapore. We have a free trade agreement with the US and Singapore is the largest market for US exports in ASEAN. The US is the main provider of Singapore's defence needs, including advanced fighter aircraft. Some of our aircraft and pilots are based in the US. Singapore gives the US Air Force and Navy access to our facilities.

China is our largest trading partner. Singapore is China's largest foreign investor. China is the only country in which there are three government-led iconic projects, in Suzhou, Tianjin, and Chongqing. There is a high-level bilateral council, co-chaired by Deputy Prime Ministers. Almost every member of the Singapore cabinet co-chairs a bilateral council with a province of China. For the past 17 years, I have co-chaired the China–Singapore Forum which brings together opinion-makers from both sides.

The relationship between the US and China has become increasingly acrimonious and confrontational. For the time being, neither superpower has demanded that Singapore should end its policy of neutrality. However, an evil day may come when one or both superpowers will demand that we choose sides. If Singapore had to choose between the US and China, who would it choose? I don't know the answer, and I am not prepared to make a guess.

ASEAN Unity and Neutrality

One advantage that Singapore enjoys over New Zealand is that we belong to an important regional organisation called the Association of Southeast Asian Nations or ASEAN. It was founded in 1967 with five founding members, Indonesia, Malaysia, the Philippines, Thailand, and Singapore. Today, ASEAN consists of 10 countries of Southeast Asia. This will increase to 11 when Timor-Leste joins.

ASEAN has kept the peace in Southeast Asia for the past 50 years. ASEAN has integrated the 10 economies into a single economy. The experts predict that by 2030, the ASEAN economy could be the fourth-largest economy in the world.

ASEAN has also succeeded in becoming the convener and neutral chairman of the region's forums, such as ASEAN + 3, ASEAN Regional Forum, East Asia Summit, and the ASEAN Defence Ministers +. Except for ASEAN + 3, New Zealand is a member of all the other forums.

ASEAN has been able to play the role of convener and chairman because it is neutral and acceptable to the two superpowers and the other major powers. ASEAN has done a good job of promoting peace and amity in the region.

Is there a danger that ASEAN will be pulled apart by the United States and China? After all, Cambodia has become a Chinese ally and the Philippines is an American ally. The good news is that, when the 10 leaders of ASEAN meet by themselves, there is consensus among them — that ASEAN as an organisation must remain united and neutral. At the recent ASEAN Summit, in Indonesia, the chairman, President Joko Widodo, said that ASEAN is not an ally of any great power.

Free Trade versus Protectionism

Small, open economies, like New Zealand and Singapore, thrive and prosper when the world supports free trade. When Donald Trump became the President of the United States, he opposed free trade and championed protectionism. His first act in office was to withdraw from the Trans-Pacific Partnership (TPP), a mega free trade agreement negotiated by the Obama Administration and 10 other countries, including New Zealand and Singapore. Incidentally, the TPP began life as an agreement among four countries, New Zealand, Chile, Brunei, and Singapore.

Public opinion in the United States has turned against free trade and free trade agreements. For this reason, President Biden is unable to rejoin the TPP. At the WTO, the Biden Administration is continuing to block the appointment of appellate judges. This has, effectively, paralysed the compulsory dispute settlement system under the WTO. I feel strongly about the misguided action of the US for the following reasons.

I have served twice as the chairman of dispute panels at the WTO. In the first case, New Zealand and the United States had complained that Canada had illegally subsidised its milk and dairy industry. The three countries had requested me to chair the panel. The panel found in favour of New Zealand and the United States. After failing in its appeal, Canada complied with the panel's finding.

In the second case, Australia and New Zealand complained that the US domestic law on 'safeguards' was inconsistent with the WTO law. The US had invoked its law to protect its domestic industry against the imports of frozen lamb meat from Australia and New Zealand. The panel found in favour of Australia and New Zealand. After failing in its appeal, the US complied and changed its law.

The US narrative that the WTO's dispute settlement system is unfair is not true. The truth is that the system is fair and the US has won more cases than it has lost. It is very disappointing for a country which purports to believe in the rule of law and the peaceful settlement of disputes to block the working of the system.

Apart from the United States, the support for free trade in the rest of the world has also weakened. Support for industrial policy and protectionism has strengthened. This poses a threat to the prosperity of New Zealand and Singapore. We must rise to the challenge and mobilise other like-minded countries to support free trade and oppose protectionism. We must support the WTO and oppose any attempt to undermine it. We will continue to conclude free trade agreements with other countries and regions. We will protect the CPTPP (the reincarnation of TPP) and the Regional Comprehensive Economic Partnership (RCEP) and ensure their success.

Multilateralism versus Unilateralism

New Zealand and Singapore believe in international cooperation, both at the regional and global levels. New Zealand and Singapore believe in multilateralism and the system of multilateral institutions, such as the UN, WTO, IMO, ICAO, WMO, and WHO.

Countries that oppose free trade and champion protectionism prefer unilateralism or bilateralism. They believe that they are strong enough to act alone. They prefer bilateral cooperation because they can use their superior power to coerce their weaker partner. They don't like multilateralism and multilateral institutions because their power is diluted in a larger grouping and they are unable to dominate such institutions.

When we deal with problems, such as climate change or pandemics, there is no substitute for international cooperation and multilateralism. New Zealand and Singapore must therefore work together, and with other like-minded countries to champion international cooperation and multilateralism. We must not be afraid to oppose the enemies of multilateralism, no matter how powerful they may be.

Rule of Law versus the Law of the Jungle

New Zealand and Singapore would not survive if the world were governed by the law of the jungle. We thrive best when the world is governed by the Rule of Law and by the peaceful settlement of disputes.

Since 1945, the world has been strengthening the rule of law and the peaceful settlement of disputes. The progress had been uneven. It is often two steps forward and one step backward. Nevertheless, the trajectory has been in the right direction.

In recent years, there has been a tendency by some great powers to take the law into their own hands. The most egregious case is Russia's invasion of Ukraine.

Russia's invasion is unprovoked and unjustified. It is a violation of the UN Charter, international law, and international humanitarian law. We must condemn Russia's action and support Ukraine, which is fighting for its sovereignty, independence, and territorial integrity.

It is important for small countries to act with courage and consistency in defending the UN Charter and international law. I was at the UN from 1974 to 1984. I condemned Vietnam when it invaded Cambodia in 1978. I condemned the Soviet Union when it invaded Afghanistan in 1979. I also condemned the United States when it invaded Grenada in 1983. If I had failed to condemn the US invasion of Grenada, then Singapore could have been accused of double standards. Fortunately, we did so. In view of this, the Russians cannot complain that we are guilty of double standards.

Conclusion

Small countries like New Zealand and Singapore must try to be relevant and useful to the world. This applies to both government and individuals. I served as the President of the Third UN Conference on the Law of the Sea and Chairman of the 1992 Earth Summit. I had also served as the UN Secretary-General's Special Envoy to make peace between Russia, on the one hand, and Estonia, Latvia, and Lithuania, on the other. Another Singaporean, Rena Lee, chaired the UN Conference on Biological Diversity Beyond the Limits of National Jurisdiction. The conference was successfully concluded with a new international agreement on the high seas. Another Singaporean, Darren Tang, is the Director-General of the World Intellectual Property Organization.

Chapter 6

New Zealand's Foreign Policy in a Changing Strategic Environment

Nicholas Khoo

Introduction

When the history of New Zealand's foreign policy in the post-Cold War era is written, analysts will highlight the years from 2017–2023 as a watershed. And, they will likely point to Defence Minister Andrew Little's remark that "in 2023, we do not live in a benign environment" as evidence of the *zeitgeist* (Little, 2023). Little's statement is important because of the speech's larger message — that New Zealand is at a historic turning point in its foreign and security policy. Indeed, the speech itself is one of the five government documents buttressing that message. The documents were released over the July–August 2023 period, and cover national security, foreign policy, defence, and intelligence (DPMC, 2023; NZMOD, 2023a, 2023b; NZMFAT, 2023; NZSIS, 2023). Collectively, they catalogue the reality that Wellington faces the most complex foreign policy environment since the breakdown of the US–New Zealand leg of the ANZUS alliance from 1985–1987. Indeed, the current era is at least as important as previous watershed eras, including the weakening of New Zealand's imperial-era economic ties following the United Kingdom's entry into the European Economic Community in 1973, the formation of the ANZUS alliance from 1951–1952, and the tensions during 1985–1987. Following a discussion of the role of interests and values in New Zealand's foreign policy, this chapter examines what are arguably the critical foreign policy challenges facing Wellington in this new era. These include a discussion of nuclear weapons; the environment; and Wellington's management of relations with China, in the context of Beijing's increasingly-fractious relationship with New Zealand's sole treaty ally, Australia, and its close partner, the US.

New Zealand's Foreign Policy — Interests and Values

While allowing for inevitable differences in emphasis and interpretation, the Labour and National Parties, the main political parties in New Zealand, agree substantially on the definition of the country's foreign policy interests and values, in their capacity as essential components in an 'independent foreign policy'. Given the significant changes in the regional and global environment that occurred during Jacinda Ardern's tenure as Prime Minister from 2017–2023, her administration's foreign policy represents the ideal place to begin our discussion.[1] We then seek to capture the elements of continuity and change in foreign policy under Ardern's successors, Christopher Hipkins (January–November 2023) and Christopher Luxon (since November 2023).

In a keynote speech at the July 2021 conference of the New Zealand Institute of International Affairs (NZIIA) in Wellington, Ardern highlighted the importance of five fundamental principles as a concise statement of New Zealand's foreign policy interests. The first relates to the privileging of action through multilateral international institutions, as part of a deep respect for rules that forms the basis of a "rules-based international order" (Ardern, 2021a). Ardern

---

[1]The full list of New Zealand's Post-Cold War era Prime Ministers from the National Party includes Christopher Luxon (2023–present), Bill English (2016–2017), John Key (2008–2016), Jennifer Shipley (1997–1999), and Jim Bolger (1990–1997). From the Labour Party, we have Jacinda Ardern (2017–2023), Christopher Hipkins (2023), and Helen Clark (1999–2008).

highlighted the imperative for states to behave in ways that reflect "consistency with international law, including the United Nations Convention on the Law of the Sea, freedom of navigation and over-flight" (Ardern, 2021a). The second principle is openness. This refers to the importance "that the region is open for trade, invest-ment, and the movement of people to support prosperity and open supply chains" (Ardern, 2021a). Next, there is the principle of inclu-sivity. This refers to the idea that "all countries in the region can participate" (Ardern, 2021a). Also important is upholding of sover-eignty. This explains New Zealand's strong criticism of Russia's annexation of Crimea in 2014 and the subsequent war in Ukraine since 2022. Finally, there is transparency. This is the idea that "states are honest about their foreign policy objectives and initia-tives beyond their borders" (Ardern, 2021a). The core point to note in this discussion is that while these principles may not always align completely with state practice, when they are upheld, they effec-tively uphold the post-1945 US-constructed international order. In this respect, New Zealand is very much a state supporting the international status quo.

These foreign policy principles are underpinned by an empha-sis on values that New Zealand advocates. The use of the vocab-ulary of values is a common rhetorical device for foreign policy makers across the spectrum of political regimes. And, New Zealand is no exception. Thus, Ardern noted in her 2021 NZIIA speech that "while we welcome the concept of an Indo-Pacific region, we do so based on the principles that have served New Zealand well and are consistent with our values" (Ardern, 2021a). These values anchor the speech but remain undefined there. To get a clearer sense of these values, we need to investigate her 7 July 2022 speech at the Lowy Institute in Sydney. In it, Ardern forthrightly stated that "the honest reality is that the world is bloody messy" and highlighted the role of "values" as an antidote in New Zealand's foreign policy (Ardern, 2022). In this view, val-ues stem from "a conviction that we have a moral responsibility to do our part to maintain the rules-based order" (Ardern, 2022). Ardern noted that when multilateral institutions fail, New Zealand looks to cooperate with like-minded states who share the "basic values of human rights, gender equality, state sovereignty, climate action," where it "falls on each of us to defend and uphold" (Ardern, 2022). Of course, to what degree values translate into actual practice is an empirical question that needs to be investigated rather than assumed. This is particularly the case since it is not unusual for a divergence to exist between values and interests in foreign policy practice.

In January 2023, Ardern stepped down to allow her successor Christopher Hipkins time to prepare for the October General Election. Not surprisingly, Hipkins' foreign policy also reflected a recognition of the role of interests and values. An example will serve to illustrate the point. New Zealand shares deep and expanding economic interests with China, its top trading partner since 2017, which are juxtaposed by serious interest- and values-based differences over aspects of Beijing's domestic and foreign policies. This is underlined by an examination of Hipkins' week-long visit to China in late June. The economic imperative underpinning this visit is reflected in the joint statement issued by Hipkins and Chinese Premier Li Qiang, which celebrated the 2022 upgrade in the China–New Zealand Free Agreement signed in 2008 (Beehive.govt.nz, 2023a). Shortly after his China trip, in a speech to the NZIIA on 7 July, Hipkins began the section on China by noting that he had "just arrived back from China and a very successful trade mission" (Hipkins, 2023a). He immediately pivoted to his next sentence, noting that "China is our most complex relationship" (Hipkins, 2023a). Why complex? This is principally because of the above-mentioned interest- and values-based differences between Beijing and Wellington (Khoo, 2022a, 2022b, 2023).

Accordingly, to achieve a balance in Wellington's foreign policy, the Hipkins administration paired improvements in its relationship with Beijing with increased engagement with Canberra and Washington. In effect, the administration doubled down on relations with Australia and the US at a time when China was experiencing its worst period of tensions with both these states since the watershed year of 1972.[2] In full knowledge that China objects to AUKUS, in March 2023, Defence Minister Andrew Little announced that New Zealand was looking at exploring a partnership role in the non-nuclear Pillar II component of AUKUS, the technology-sharing agreement involving Australia, the United Kingdom, and the US (Manch, 2021). Formalized in September 2021, AUKUS is princi-pally an Australian response to a Chinese economic and diplomatic sanctions policy that began in 2020 and continues to this day. Declassified New Zealand government documents written in March 2023 emphasise that Wellington "understands the strategic ration-ale for AUKUS" (NZMOD, 2023c). Furthermore, Hipkins welcomed the Biden administration's increased engagement in the Pacific Islands region, including the US's establishment of diplomatic rela-tions with the New Zealand dependencies of Cook Islands and Niue in September 2023 (Lewis, 2023). He also drew a favourable distinction between New Zealand's view of the May 2023 US–Papua New Guinea security agreement, which it endorsed as "a very transparent arrangement," and its view of the China–Solomon Islands agreement of 2022, which it saw as "different" (Ensor, 2023).

The November 2023 General Election saw the National Party emerge as the largest party in Parliament. The National Party's election on the basis of a plurality rather than an absolute majority of the votes cast required it to enter into a coalition with the David Seymour-led ACT party and the Winston Peters-led New Zealand First party. The emphasis on a strong economic interest-based relationship with China and a deepening of New Zealand's interest- and values-based relationship with Australia and the US will con-tinue. Prime Minister Luxon's first international trip was a visit to Sydney in late December. This came after Foreign Minister Winston Peters had set out a clear vision in his first foreign policy-related speech, which was the keynote address at the US Business

---

[2] China established diplomatic relations with Australia and New Zealand in December 1972. Sino-American rapprochement occurred in February 1972.

Summit in Auckland on 30 November. To highlight the importance of the message, Luxon was in attendance. The symbolism of the event was reinforced by the content of the speech. Peters emphasised that New Zealand "seek(s) to strengthen engagement with the US on strategic and security challenges, centred on our common interest in a stable, peaceful and prosperous Indo-Pacific," noting that "there are few relationships that matter more to New Zealand than our relationship with the United States" (Peters, 2023). At the same time, Peters underlined that there was scope to "unlock the potential in our economic relationship" (Peters, 2023). While it is inevitable that there will be a public reaching out to China, this has not yet occurred. In the context of contemporary regional developments, this pattern of diplomatic activity is unlikely to have been unplanned. Having discussed the broad role of values and interests in New Zealand's foreign policy, we move to a discussion of some of the central themes in New Zealand's foreign policy. These include policy toward nuclear weapons and the environment, as well as a more detailed discussion of the politics of New Zealand's relations with China, in the context of its close relationship with Australia and the US.

New Zealand's Foreign Policy Challenges: Nuclear Weapons and The Environment

As New Zealand navigates international politics in the third decade of the 21st century, it encounters a very different international context from that which existed in the second half of the 1980s, which is when Wellington defined its interests and values more sharply with respect to the policy issues discussed in this section — nuclear weapons and the environment — and set the baseline for the understanding of Wellington's current perspective.

In July 1984, the Labour Party secured a victory in the general election, running on a platform that included refusing entry to nuclear-powered or nuclear-armed vessels in New Zealand's waters. The inevitable test followed. In January 1985, the US government formally requested permission for the USS Buchanan to visit New Zealand. The USS Buchanan possessed the capability of launching nuclear depth bomb anti-submarine missiles with its MK-11 missile launcher. Washington followed its standard policy of declining to confirm or deny the presence of nuclear weapons technology on the vessel. Extensive efforts to resolve the issue proved unsuccessful. In August 1986, the United States suspended its ANZUS security obligations to New Zealand, with Secretary of State George Shultz stating that "we remain friends, but we are no longer allies" (Gwertzman, 1986). The rift widened as New Zealand played a central role in the adoption of the Treaty of Rarotonga, which established a South Pacific Nuclear Free Zone, entering into force on 11 December 1986. The New Zealand Nuclear Free Zone, Disarmament, and Arms Control Act of 8 June 1987 followed. This formally prohibited nuclear-armed and nuclear-propelled vessels from visiting New Zealand. The US responded by codifying the Broomfield Act of 1987, which formally changed New Zealand's status to that of a non-ally on 20 October 1987. Ultimately, the implementation of this non-nuclear policy shift effectively prevented practical alliance cooperation under the trilateral ANZUS alliance.

It is against this background that we can understand Ardern's statement in her 2021 Lowy Institute speech that "our values dictated that we had to stand up and speak out against the decades of nuclear testing in the Pacific. Opposing nuclear weapons is now a central tenet of New Zealand's foreign policy" (Ardern, 2022). The flip side of the anti-nuclear stance is that the eroding effectiveness and declining support for nuclear disarmament and arms control among the major powers is seen as a highly-negative development by New Zealand. As Minister for Disarmament Philip Twyford noted in November 2022, "the nuclear weapon states are doubling down on deterrence", and "this is not an argument that New Zealand can subscribe to" (Twyford, 2022). Twyford further observed that "more nuclear weapons … will not make us safer" (Twyford, 2022).

That said, it bears noting that while nuclear weapons are often interpreted as a values-laden issue in New Zealand's foreign policy, there is more to the issue than meets the eye. Wellington's nuclear stance can be equally well understood with reference to

New Zealand's security interests and nationalism. These are a characteristic of all states. Which state, if it does not face a nuclear-armed adversary and has a choice in the matter, would welcome nuclear weapons in its region? The successful implementation of the South Pacific Nuclear Free Zone Treaty has been of objective security benefit to New Zealand. In addition to reducing the likelihood of the use of nuclear weapons in the region, it allows Wellington to credibly project itself to its neighbours as a responsible partner in regional security. This is buttressed by the nationalist aspect of this issue. An illustrative statement of this point can be seen on the website of the New Zealand Ministry of Foreign Affairs and Trade. The website notes that "the fight against nuclear weapons provides one of the most sustained examples of the independence with which New Zealand has crafted much of its foreign policy over the past 75 years" (MFAT, 2024). This is as clear a statement of nationalism as any. To be sure, there is a trade-off with such as stance. Wellington has explicitly ruled out participation in Pillar I of the AUKUS security partnership because it involved the sharing of nuclear propulsion technology. Notably, this still presents the newly-elected Luxon administration with a significant decision on its involvement in the non-nuclear Pillar II component.

Closely related to nuclear weapons is the environment, reflected in the climate change issue. While the environment is often seen as a 21st century issue, it has been very much central to New Zealand's foreign policy since the early days of the Cold War. Environmental concerns formed a substantial part of New Zealand's role as a key player in the region's opposition to nuclear testing in the South Pacific. And, the past is prologue. Concern about global warming in the South Pacific is of national interest to New Zealand. The 2021 New Zealand Ministry of Defence Assessment identified climate change and strategic competition as the two principal strategic challenges for the coming decades (MOD, 2021). Indeed, Ardern foreshadowed the physical threat to New Zealand presented by climate change in her first speech to the United Nations in 2018. In it, she noted the regional dimension of the threat, commenting that "of all of the challenges we debate and discuss, rising sea levels present the single biggest threat to our region" (Ardern, 2018a). And, when the effects of climate change in the South Pacific are paired with multilateralism, regional security is clearly at stake. Thus, Ardern stated that "any disintegration of multilateralism — any undermining of climate related targets and agreements — aren't interesting footnotes in geopolitical history. They are catastrophic" (Ardern, 2018a).

New Zealand's Foreign Policy Challenges: Navigating China's Rise and Relations with Australia and the US

If New Zealand's relationship with its traditional allies and partners is marked by deep historical, political, and strategic ties, New Zealand's relationship with China stands out in its instrumental economic focus. As highlighted previously, China has been New Zealand's top trade partner since 2017 (Stats NZ, 2019). In many respects, this outcome represents the successful fulfilment of Wellington's vision for the relationship. At the time of signing the 2008 New Zealand–China Free Trade Agreement, Prime Minister Helen Clark expressed the view that "it's a strategic agreement — it is acknowledging on our part that China will be, in my lifetime, the world's biggest economy" (Young, 2017, p. 523). Viewed in economic terms, this has been a spectacularly-successful relationship. In her 2018 NZIIA speech, Ardern correctly noted that the China–New Zealand Free Trade Agreement has been "a runaway success for both countries" and was "enormously beneficial for New Zealand" (Ardern, 2018b).

That said, trade always occurs in a strategic political context. Notwithstanding expanding economic ties, by May 2021, in Ardern's speech to the China Business Summit, there was an imperative to underline the point that political differences were real and growing. Ardern noted that "it will not have escaped the attention of anyone here that as China's role in the world grows and changes, the differences between our systems — and the interests and values that shape those systems — are becoming harder to reconcile"

(Ardern, 2021b). At the July 2021 NZIIA conference, Ardern presented a nuanced view of China, which reflected the perceived increase in Beijing's challenges to aspects of the existing international order and a consolidation of authoritarian practices domestically. Ardern referred to China as "an engine of global growth and one of our most significant, but also one of our increasingly complex relationships" (Ardern, 2021a). Significantly, this is the first instance of Ardern describing the bilateral relationship as "complex" (Ardern, 2021a). Her 2020 China Business Summit speech did not use such a characterisation (Ardern, 2020). Moreover, Ardern's description of Australia and the US in the July 2021 NZIIA speech contrasted markedly with that of China. Canberra was described as "New Zealand's indispensable partner and ally", and for the first time, the speech explicitly adopted the US's framing of the region as "the Indo-Pacific" (Ardern, 2021a).

An explanation for why this is the case involves reference to China and New Zealand's diverging values and interests. We discuss the values component first. To state the obvious, New Zealand's values are profoundly different from those represented by the Communist Party of China's governance model. What Beijing views as a threat to its sovereignty and the Marxist–Leninist political model, Wellington sees as human rights violations and the use of coercion to thwart alternative political voices. The issues of Hong Kong, Taiwan, Tibet, and Xinjiang have been regularly raised by the New Zealand government's representatives in their meetings with their Chinese counterparts. As Jacinda Ardern noted in her 3 May 2021 address to the China Business Council, "we need to acknowledge that there are some things on which China and New Zealand do not, cannot, and will not agree. This need not derail our relationship, it is simply a reality" (Ardern, 2021b). And, New Zealand has repeatedly handled this issue by specifying clearly that fundamental political differences need not define the relationship. But, that formula has increasingly come under strain under the more authoritarian domestic politics and activist foreign policy of the post-2012 Xi Jinping leadership.

This brings us to diverging interests which have intensified over China's more activist foreign policy. Space limitations require that we note Beijing's role in the contentious South China Sea and East China disputes, but focus on Chinese policy in the South Pacific region. This is the region in which New Zealand is physically located and whose stability no government in Wellington can be indifferent to. The Pacific region was identified in both Ardern's 2018 and 2021 NZIIA speeches as New Zealand's core geographical area of interest. In 2018, Ardern explicitly identified New Zealand as a "member of the Pacific community" (Ardern, 2018), while in 2021, the Pacific was identified as "our home" (Ardern, 2021a). She noted in her 2021 NZIIAA speech that "the Pacific itself is an increasingly contested region" (2021a). This message was underlined in the 2021 New Zealand Ministry of Defence Assessment. The report highlighted that "New Zealand faces significant and likely increasing challenges to its interests in this region, and particularly in the Pacific" (MOD, 2021, p. 7). It went further in identifying that "New Zealand also has a much greater responsibility to act in this region than elsewhere" (MOD, 2021, p. 7).

The 2021 Defence Assessment was deeply prescient. News emerged in late March 2022 that China had signed a security agreement with the Solomon Islands. This was, to a large degree, a response by China to the formation of AUKUS in September 2021 (Khoo, 2022a). Nevertheless, this development elicited a forceful response from Ardern. Taking time out from a visit to Singapore, she pointedly observed that the agreement was "gravely concerning" and highlighted "the ongoing issues with the Solomon Islands and their engagement with China in a way that may add to the militarisation of the Pacific" (Manch, 2022). To underline Wellington's concern, on 31 May, a very strong joint statement was released after Ardern's meeting in the White House with US President Biden. The statement articulated an unequivocal shared concern about the China–Solomon Islands agreement. The gravity of the statement merits its repetition here. It was pointedly noted that both sides were "concerned with growing strategic competition in the

Pacific region", and stated that "in particular, the United States and New Zealand share a concern that the establishment of a persistent military presence in the Pacific by a state that does not share our values or security interests would fundamentally alter the strategic balance of the region and pose national security concerns to both our countries" (Office of the President, 2022). Ardern subsequently underlined the issue in her July 2022 Lowy speech in Sydney, where it was noted that "priorities should be set by the Pacific. They should be free from coercion. Investment should be of high quality. And issues that affect the security of all of us, or may be seen as the militarisation of the region should come through the PIF as set out in the Biketawa and Boe Declarations, as such a change would rightly effect and concern many" (Ardern, 2022).

The Hipkins administration reiterated this basic message and went further in its candour, specifically on the Chinese policy toward the Pacific Islands region and in respect to the Chinese foreign policy more generally. Thus, on 3 May 2023, New Zealand Foreign Minister Nanaia Mahuta observed that "the Pacific is a primary consideration for New Zealand as we think about our place in the world and what really matters to our sense of well-being … we cannot reference the Indo-Pacific geo-strategic challenges and the Pacific ends up being a footnote" (Mahuta, 2023). More was to come. After Hipkins' 28 June 2023 meeting with Chinese Premier Li Qiang, the New Zealand side released a *separate* summary statement where areas of difference in the discussions with Li were noted (Beehive.govt.nz, 2023a). In particular, there was an insistence that "engagement in the Pacific takes place in a manner which advances Pacific priorities and supports regional organisations — in particular the Pacific Islands Forum" (Beehive.govt.nz, 2023a). Indeed, at the 7 June 2023 NZIIA conference in Auckland, Hipkins went further than Ardern by stating that "China is our most complex relationship" (Hipkins, 2023a) rather than "one of our increasingly complex relationships" as his predecessor had done in 2021 (Ardern, 2021a). After opening his speech with a comment on his successful June trip to China, Hipkins devoted majority of his speech to laying out differences between the two sides, including a sentence acknowledging that Foreign Minister Mahuta had a "robust conversation" with her counterpart Qin Gang during a meeting in China in March to prepare for Hipkins' China visit (Hipkins, 2023a). At his subsequent 12 July speech in Brussels at the NATO summit session for Indo-Pacific partners, Hipkins stated forthrightly that "China's increasing assertiveness is resulting in geopolitical change and competition" (Hipkins, 2023b). Moreover, the second section of Hipkins' 17 July speech at the China Business Council was titled "A Complex Relationship" (Hipkins, 2023c). Interestingly, there was a clear statement in the section that "China's rise and how it exerts that influence is also a major driver of the increasing strategic competition, particularly in our wider home region, the Indo-Pacific" (Hipkins, 2023c). Indeed, what is notable about the summary section of Hipkins' speech is the emphasis on differences rather than similarities between the two countries (Hipkins, 2023c).

Any analysis of New Zealand's China policy has to involve a discussion of New Zealand's relationship with Australia, and AUKUS specifically. Following the 13 March 2023 AUKUS Leaders' Summit in San Diego, AUKUS now constitutes an increasingly central component of the international order in the Indo-Pacific. Given Canberra's investment in AUKUS, and the fact that Australia is New Zealand's only formal alliance partner, Wellington's position on AUKUS has emerged as a focus of attention and an important barometer of the relationship. Commenting immediately after the event, New Zealand academic David Capie noted that "no one expects Wellington to see the world in exactly the same way to Canberra, but there will definitely be some on this side of the Tasman wondering whether we're at risk of disappearing off a radar of relevancy" (Sachdeva, 2023). Such hard-headed calculations explain why in late March 2023, Defence Minister Andrew Little announced that New Zealand is exploring participation in the non-nuclear Pillar II part of the AUKUS technology agreement that does not involve nuclear propulsion technology (Guardian, 2023). This stance was affirmed by Prime Minister Luxon on his first international trip. Speaking during a visit to Sydney, Luxon reiterated that New Zealand was interested in "exploring" membership in Pillar II, describing it as a "very important element in ensuring we've got stability and peace" (Albanese, 2023). He then asserted that Wellington would do its "share of the heavy lifting in the alliance" and "want(s) to see more interoperability, frankly, between our respective defence forces" (Albanese, 2023). As the Luxon administration seeks to operationalise its role in AUKUS, Canberra and Wellington's perspectives on international developments are increasingly converging. At the inaugural Australia–New Zealand Foreign and Defence Ministerial Consultations in Melbourne on 1 February 2024, attention was focused on four specific issues: the general Australia–New Zealand alliance; coordination on global strategic issues; the Indo-Pacific region; and partnership in the Pacific. Significantly, the AUKUS partnership was discussed as "a positive contribution toward maintaining peace, security and prosperity in the Indo-Pacific" (Collins and Peters, 2024). The Chinese embassy in Wellington offered a less positive interpretation, stating that "China has serious concerns over AUKUS" (Embassy of the PRC, 2024). The statement also posited that "AUKUS is a stark manifestation of [a] Cold War mentality" which "will undermine peace and stability, sow division and confrontation in the region, and thus runs against the common interests of regional countries pursuing peace, stability, and common security" (Embassy of the PRC, 2024).

Conclusion

By any standard, the post-Cold War era from 1991–2008 represented a prosperous and stable era during which New Zealand profited immensely. Great power relations were on an even keel; the more positive aspects of globalisation had a clear edge over the negative; and security threats were manageable. This geopolitical dispensation changed dramatically from 2009 to 2023. Looking to the future, the trajectory of the issues in New Zealand's foreign policy as discussed in this chapter is at best mixed. The nuclear proliferation regime is at a crisis point, even as there has been progress on environmental issues, reflected in the commitments made at the COP 28 meeting in Dubai in late 2023. Moreover, to state the obvious, while Wellington clearly has agency in its foreign policy, particularly in its relationship with Australia, there are distinct limits on New Zealand's capacity to influence the trajectory of its relations with China and the United States. Furthermore, other issues that have not been discussed in this chapter, including the ongoing Russian invasion of Ukraine since early 2022 and the escalation of the Hamas–Israel conflict, have further undermined global stability. The reality has finally struck home that a far less progressive and more conflictual era has dawned for New Zealand's foreign policy.[3]

Bibliography

Albanese, A. (2023, December 20). Press Conference — Sydney. Available at: https://www.pm.gov.au/media/press-conference-sydney-10. (Accessed 3 January 2024).

Ardern, J. (2018a). Full text: PM's speech to the United Nations. *Newsroom,* September 27. https://www.newsroom.co.nz/full-text-pms-speech-to-the-united-nations. (Accessed 3 January 2024).

Ardern, J. (2018b). Speech to New Zealand Institute of International Affairs. Available at: https://www.beehive.govt.nz/speech/speech-new-zealand-institute-international-affairs-2. (Accessed 3 January 2024).

Ardern, J. (2020). Speech Notes Prepared for the China Business Summit. Available at: https://www.nzcta.co.nz/chinanow-profile/2075/rt-hon-jacinda-ardern-speech-notes-prepared-for-the-china-business-summit/.

Ardern, J. (2021a). Prime Minister's Speech to NZIIA Annual Conference. Available at: https://www.beehive.govt.nz/release/prime-ministers-speech-nziia-annual-conference. (Accessed 3 January 2024).

---

[3] Thus, the Ministry of Foreign Affairs and Trade's 2023 report notes the following: "As New Zealand's strategic context becomes more complex and the foundations on which it has relied for several decades are challenged, New Zealand's foreign policy will be presented with difficult decisions with increasing frequency." The report continues with the observation that "with this in mind, there would be considerable value in having a more deliberate national conversation on New Zealand's foreign policy to help raise awareness of the priorities, risks, challenges and opportunities. It could also lead to a greater understanding of the difficult options and choices that New Zealand will need to navigate in pursuit of a safer, more prosperous and more sustainable world." MFAT, *Navigating a Shifting World*, 35.

Ardern, J. (2021b). Speech to China Business Summit. https://www.beehive.govt.nz/speech/speech-china-business-summit. (Accessed 3 January 2024).

Ardern, J. (2022). A Pacific Springboard to Engage the World: New Zealand's Independent Foreign Policy. Available at: https://www.beehive.govt.nz/speech/pacific-springboard-engage-world-new-zealand%E2%80%99s-independent-foreign-policy. (Accessed 3 January 2024).

Beehive.govt.nz. (2023a). Prime Minister and Premier Reaffirm Strong Economic Relationship. Available at: https://www.beehive.govt.nz/release/prime-minister-and-premier-reaffirm-strong-economic-relationship. (Accessed 3 January 2024).

Beehive.govt.nz. (2023b). Joint Statement between New Zealand and the People's Republic of China on the Strategic Partnership. Available at: https://www.beehive.govt.nz/sites/default/files/2023-06/PM%20China%20Visit%20June%202023%20Joint%20Statement%20-%20Final.pdf. (Accessed 3 January 2024).

Collins, J. and Peters, W. Joint statement on Australia New Zealand Ministerial Consultations 2024 (2024). Available at: https://www.beehive.govt.nz/release/joint-statement-australia-new-zealand-ministerial-consultations-anzmin-2024. (Accessed 9 February 2024).

Department of Prime Minister and Cabinet. (2023). Secure Together: New Zealand's National Security Strategy 2023–2028. Available at: https://www.dpmc.govt.nz/sites/default/files/2023-11/national-security-strategy-aug2023.pdf. (Accessed 3 January 2024).

Embassy of the Peoples' Republic of China in New Zealand (2024). Remarks of the Spokesperson of the Peoples' Republic of China in New Zealand on the Joint Statement on ANZMIN 2024. http://nz.china-embassy.gov.cn/eng/zyxw/202402/t20240202_11238593.htm. (Accessed 9 February 2024).

Ensor, J. (2023). Prime Minister Chris Hipkins calls United States-Papua New Guinea security deal 'different' to China's pact with Solomon Islands. *Newshub*, May 22. Available at: https://www.newshub.co.nz/home/politics/2023/05/prime-minister-chris-hipkins-calls-united-states-papua-new-guinea-security-deal-different-to-china-s-pact-with-solomon-islands.html. (Accessed 3 January 2024).

Guardian. (2023). New Zealand May Join AUKUS Pact's Non-nuclear Component, March 28. Available at: https://www.theguardian.com/world/2023/mar/28/new-zealand-may-join-aukus-pacts-non-nuclear-component. (Accessed 3 January 2024).

Gwertzman, B. (1986). Schultz ends US vow to defend New Zealand. *New York Times,* June 28. Available at: https://www.nytimes.com/1986/06/28/world/shultz-ends-us-vow-to-defend-new-zealand.html. (Accessed 3 January 2024).

Hipkins, C. (2023a, July 7). Prime Minister's Foreign Policy Speech to NZIIA. Available at: https://www.beehive.govt.nz/speech/prime-ministers-foreign-policy-speech-nziia. (Accessed 3 January 2024).

Hipkins, C. (2023b, July 12). Speech to NATO Summit Session for Indo-Pacific Partners. Available at: https://www.beehive.govt.nz/speech/speech-nato-summit-session-indo-pacific-partners. (Accessed 3 January 2024).

Hipkins, C. (2023c, July 17). Prime Minister's Speech to the China Business Summit. Available at: https://www.beehive.govt.nz/speech/prime-minister%E2%80%99s-speech-china-business-summit. (Accessed 3 January 2024).

Khoo, N. (2022a). New Zealand must lead the response to China's agreement with the Solomon Islands. *Dominion Post*, May 3. https://www.stuff.co.nz/opinion/128489174/new-zealand-must-lead-the-response-to-chinas-agreement-with-the-solomon-islands. (Accessed 3 January 2024).

Khoo, N. (2022b). Can the Anzac alliance meet increasing geopolitical challenges? *Dominion Post*, August 10. Available at: https://www.stuff.co.nz/opinion/129520670/can-the-anzac-alliance-meet-increasing-geopolitical-challenges. (Accessed 3 January 2024).

Khoo, N. (2023). New Zealand foreign policy turns a corner in Beijing. *Newsroom*, 1 July 2023. Available at: https://newsroom.co.nz/2023/06/30/new-zealand-foreign-policy-turns-a-corner-in-beijing/. (Accessed 3 January 2024).

Lewis, L. (2023). New Zealand 'welcomes' US diplomatic relations with Cook Islands and Niue. *New Zealand Herald*, September 23. Available at: https://www.nzherald.co.nz/talanoa/new-zealand-welcomes-us-diplomatic-relations-with-cook-islands-and-niue/CLCJMKETPVCKFOSCPVQJ7OTPKI/. (Accessed 3 January 2024).

Little, A. (2023). Speech to Announce Roadmap for Future of Defence and National Security. Available at: https://www.beehive.govt.nz/release/speech-roadmap-for-future-of-defence-and-national-security-released. (Accessed 3 January 2024).

Mahuta, N. (2023). Why the Pacific Way Matters for Regional Security. https://www.beehive.govt.nz/spee Manch, T. (2021). 'US and UK must Stop': Chinese diplomat warns New Zealand audience of Australia's nuclear ambitions, *Stuff*, November 2. Available at: https://www.stuff.co.nz/national/politics/126854210/us-and-uk-must-stop-chinese-diplomat-warns-new-zealand-audience-of-australias-nuclear-ambitions. (Accessed 3 January 2024).

Manch, T. (2021). 'US and UK must Stop': Chinese diplomat warns New Zealand audience of Australia's nuclear ambitions. *Stuff*, November 2. Available at: https://www.stuff.co.nz/national/politics/126854210/us-and-uk-must-stop-chinese-diplomat-warns-new-zealand-audience-of-australias-nuclear-ambitions. (Accessed 3 January 2024).

Manch, T. (2022). Solomon Islands PM rebukes NZ, Australia over China security deal dismay'. *Stuff,* March 29. Available at: https://www.stuff.co.nz/national/politics/128202394/solomon-islands-pm-rebukes-nz-australia-over-china-security-deal-dismay?rm=a. (Accessed 3 January 2024).

New Zealand Military Preference Suspension Act — 100th Congress (1987, October 20). Available at: https://www.congress.gov/bill/100th-congress/house-bill/85?s=1&r=16. (Accessed 3 January 2024).

New Zealand Ministry of Defence. (2023, March 7). AUKUS: Updating New Zealand's Approach. Available at: https://www.defence.govt.nz/assets/publication/file/Redacted-Aukus-Updating-New-Zealands-Response-v3.pdf. (Accessed 3 January 2024).

New Zealand Ministry of Defence. (2021, December). A Rough Sea Can Still Be Navigated: Defence Assessment 2021. Available at: https://www.defence.govt.nz/assets/publication/file/Defence-Assessment-2021.pdf. (Accessed 3 January 2024).

New Zealand Ministry of Defence. (2023a). Defence Policy and Strategy Statement 2023. Available at: https://www.beehive.govt.nz/sites/default/files/2023-08/Defence%20Policy%20Strategy%20Statement%202023.PDF. (Accessed 3 January 2024).

New Zealand Ministry of Defence. (2023b). Future Force Design Principles 2023. (Available at: https://www.beehive.govt.nz/sites/default/files/2023-08/Future%20Force%20Design%20Principles%202023.PDF. (Accessed 3 January 2024).

New Zealand Ministry of Foreign Affairs & Trade. (2023). Navigating a Shifting World. Available at: https://www.mfat.govt.nz/assets/About-us-Corporate/MFAT-strategies-and-frameworks/MFATs-2023-Strategic-Foreign-Policy-Assessment-Navigating-a-shifting-world-June-2023.pdf. (Accessed 3 January 2024).

New Zealand Ministry of Foreign Affairs & Trade (2024). Taking a Nuclear-Free Policy to the World. Available at: https://www.mfat.govt.nz/br/about-us/mfat75/taking-a-nuclear-free-policy-to-the-world/. (Accessed 3 January 2024).

New Zealand Security Intelligence Service. (2023). New Zealand's Security Threat Environment 2023. Available at: https://www.nzsis.govt.nz/assets/NZSIS-Documents/New-Zealands-Security-Threat-Environment-2023.pdf. (Accessed 3 January 2024).

Office of the President. (2022, May 31). United States — Aotearoa New Zealand Joint Statement. Available at: https://www.whitehouse.gov/briefing-room/statements-releases/2022/05/31/united-states-aotearoa-new-zealand-joint-statement/. (Accessed 3 January 2024).

Peters, W. (November 30, 2023). Keynote Address to the United States Business Summit, Auckland. Available at: https://www.beehive.govt.nz/speech/keynote-address-united-states-business-summit-auckland. (Accessed 3 January 2024).

Sachdeva, S. (2023). AUKUS alliance 'won't shut out NZ' — US official. *Newsroom*, March 14. Available at: https://www.newsroom.co.nz/aukus-alliance-wont-shut-out-nz-us-official. (Accessed 3 January 2024).

Statistics New Zealand. (2020, March 3). China Top Trade Partner for 2019. Available at: https://www.stats.govt.nz/news/china-top-trade-partner-for-2019. (Accessed 3 January 2024).

Twyford, P. (2022, November 1). Nuclear Weapons — Where Are We at? The Treaty on the Prohibition of Nuclear Weapons and the Nuclear Non-Proliferation Treaty. Available at: https://www.beehive.govt.nz/speech/nuclear-weapons-%E2%80%93-where-are-we-treaty-prohibition-nuclear-weapons-and-nuclear-non. (Accessed 3 January 2024).

US Embassy to Papua New Guinea, Solomon Islands, and Vanuatu. (2023, May 22). Secretary Antony J. Blinken Meeting with New Zealand Prime Minister Chris Hipkins. Available at: https://pg.usembassy.gov/secretary-antony-j-blinken-and-new-zealand-prime-minister-chris-hipkins/. (Accessed 3 January 2024).

Young, J. (2017). Seeking ontological security through the rise of China: New Zealand as a small trading nation. *Pacific Review*, 30(4), 513–530. DOI: 10.1080/09512748.2016.1264457.

Chapter 7

ASEAN and Regional Security: One Singaporean's Perspective

Lawrence Anderson

Introduction

ASEAN is one of the major pillars of Singapore's foreign policy. New Zealand was the second country to become a Dialogue Partner in 1975 and has been an able participant in ASEAN's main regional security platforms and activities spanning the three ASEAN Community pillars.

The last several years, however, have been difficult. Geopolitical tensions arising from the war between Israel and Hamas, Russia's invasion of Ukraine, and Sino-US strategic rivalry, coupled with ASEAN's inability to resolve its own trouble spots like Myanmar, have led some of its friends to question what ASEAN has achieved recently to resolve its internal difficulties or deal with regional problems.

These doubts have made it opportune to clear up certain misperceptions of what ASEAN is and is not and to reflect on some of ASEAN's major achievements. In the process, it would be pertinent to look at how the organisation deals with Sino-US strategic competition and, finally, reflect on what ASEAN can do moving forward to address regional challenges.

What ASEAN Is and Is Not

First, ASEAN's greatest achievement is internal, i.e. it has brought peace and stability to Southeast Asia by managing relations among its members. To put it bluntly, it has prevented war between its members. This is no small achievement given the chaos in Southeast Asia when ASEAN was formed in 1967. Over time, ASEAN countries have been singularly successful by pledging to settle their differences peacefully and working together for the good of all member states.

Second, an oft-quoted phrase is ASEAN Centrality, but what exactly does it mean? In 2019, ASEAN issued its "Outlook on the Indo-Pacific" that explicitly rejected zero-sum regional competition and regional dominance by any single power. Instead, it positioned ASEAN at the heart of the area's dynamics.

This is the basis underpinning ASEAN Centrality. ASEAN provides the main regional security platforms — the ASEAN Regional Forum (ARF), ASEAN Defence Ministers' Meeting-Plus (ADMM+), and the East Asia Summit (EAS) — to overcome challenges and engage with all the major external powers.

It means that ASEAN is not a defence alliance the way NATO is. ASEAN's purpose is to build confidence and trust among member states and external partners, to tackle common security challenges together.

Third, ASEAN's effectiveness should not be judged by its ability to address the ongoing troubles in Myanmar. No international grouping is free of internal problems, and just as ASEAN engages the major powers on a wide range of traditional and non-traditional security issues, so it must do so with those who have a stake in Myanmar, including Russia, China, and India. It is noteworthy that ASEAN has decided to form a 'troika mechanism' in 2024, which would comprise the immediate past, current, and incoming chairs — Indonesia, Laos, and Malaysia — to help find a way forward.

All the major powers continue to attend the major ASEAN Ministerial and Leaders Meetings, a testimony that ASEAN, collectively, has agency. It is a grouping of over 600 million people, most of whom are educated, skilled, and below 35 years of age. ASEAN is one of the wealthiest and fastest-growing regions with a gross domestic product of US$3.63 trillion in 2022. Barring a major regional catastrophe, ASEAN is on course to be the world's fourth-largest economy by 2030.

Being part of ASEAN has given Singapore a greater voice and influence than if it were on its own. In turn, the island state has contributed its fair share to the organisation. Singapore played a major part in transforming ASEAN's approach to regional exclusiveness to embrace inclusiveness. It also played a major role in the establishment of key ASEAN platforms like the ARF, EAS, ADMM+, and Asia–Europe Meeting (ASEM), as well as opening the Treaty of Amity and Cooperation in Southeast Asia to allow for accession by regional organisations and states outside Southeast Asia. These platforms have enabled ASEAN, its Dialogue Partners, and others to forge excellent relations in multilateral settings.

US–China Strategic Competition

ASEAN's major challenge is to navigate the shoals of US–China rivalry, in particular the strategic mistrust and negative perceptions that each has of the other. China views Southeast Asia as its 'backyard'. Beijing has embedded a military presence in the South China Sea and surrounding waters while relying on development and financial incentives through its Belt-and-Road and three 'Global' Initiatives to win friends and gain access to significant infrastructure like ports, airports, road connections, and raw materials in the Indo-Pacific and beyond.

China's economic heft is a great attraction. It is the number one trading partner of the ASEAN countries, but its economic deals often come at a cost. Huge loans have placed unsustainable debt on several recipients that Beijing can use against them.

For its part, Washington remains a vitally important security and economic partner to most countries in East Asia. In Southeast Asia alone, US investments are larger than those of China, Japan, and South Korea combined.

Moreover, China's 'wolf-warrior' diplomacy and incursions in the East and South China Seas and the Himalayas have led many countries to pivot towards the US.

Leveraging this substantial influence, the US has tried hard to lobby its friends and partners to support its ban on Chinese technologies. But, its attempts to get ASEAN countries to 'decouple' from China without offering market access and other incentives in its Indo-Pacific Economic Framework are not likely to persuade many to sign on.

Also, several Asian states are distinctly uncomfortable when Washington and its western allies couch the war in Ukraine and the rivalry with China as a struggle between democracies and autocracies. Democracy and human rights are important. But, the perception of many countries is that the overwhelming reliance on universal application and the imposition of values are not fully accepted even in developed economies. The fact is that Southeast Asia is home to many different political systems and its states work across ideological lines to advance their interests.

The Way Forward

Like most countries, ASEAN members do not want to be caught in the middle of a quarrel between the US and China — they do not want to choose sides. Each ASEAN member state has its own preferences and grievances towards the US and China, with considerable economic and/or security linkages. So far, most ASEAN members have managed to deal with China and the US simultaneously, which has been essential to their success.

This is why ASEAN has chosen a two-pronged approach to foreign policy:

- *First, Strategic neutrality is the preferred position of most ASEAN states.* It means positions taken are based on how they benefit each member and not because they benefit one great power at the expense of the other. Most ASEAN countries want good relations with both the US and China, and have actively worked towards this goal both individually and within ASEAN.

- *Second*, most ASEAN member states have chosen to ride on US naval and air power as insurance to ensure equilibrium is maintained in the Indo-Pacific.

ASEAN and its regional security platforms have their flaws, but ASEAN must strive harder to make better use of them. They provide the cover for quarrelling countries to meet in private to try to narrow their differences. Private meetings enable leaders and senior officials to put forward candid, alternative assessments of what leaders of the two superpowers might be receiving from their advisers.

For such institutions to work effectively, leaders and senior officials must be committed to searching for ways to avoid serious conflict and practicing preventive diplomacy. They must resist the urge to use such platforms to score public points through the staging of walkouts and disclosing details of sensitive discussions to the press and on social media.

ASEAN can also offer economic 'space' by being a relevant testbed for the major powers to build stronger economic linkages with individual ASEAN countries and with the organisation as a whole. ASEAN's value then is to be a neutral, reliable 'bridge' for the two hegemons to co-exist at the very least, and to build towards cooperation, instead of focusing only on strategic competition.

There is value for like-minded small and medium-sized states to come together and exercise agency to persuade the two major powers to build trust and reach an understanding on their respective red lines. The time is right because almost all states, whether US allies or China dependents, do not want to permanently align all their interests with one great power to confront the other.

There are concrete areas to work together for mutual benefit. Food security, the green and digital economies, regional supply chains, managing future pandemics, maritime cooperation, and cybersecurity are key areas that ASEAN wants to develop further.

They constitute productive sectors for business collaboration between companies from ASEAN and its like-minded partners, including New Zealand.

Conclusion

Great power competition is not new to the Indo-Pacific, certainly not to Southeast Asia. Throughout history, this part of the world has been a hotbed of power struggles among the great powers of the day. ASEAN alone cannot determine the fate of the region. It needs to work closely with its like-minded partners to help ensure continued peace, stability, and prosperity. Traditional and non-traditional security problems will be present for years to come. But, a strong, unified, and cohesive ASEAN would be better placed to meet these challenges, thereby lending true substance to the claim of ASEAN Centrality.

Chapter 8

Aotearoa New Zealand and the Pacific Challenges and Opportunities

Michael Powles

Climate Change

There are few communities on earth which stand to suffer as much from the harmful effects of climate change as the Island communities of the South and Central Pacific. Already, in the small island country of Tuvalu, for example, the evidence of rising sea levels is clear. And, in despair, legal steps are being taken to try to ensure that even if the islands, which at present comprise the state of Tuvalu, should be submerged by rising sea levels, the country itself will retain its legal identity.

The Tuvalu people face the loss of their culture and way of life. As climate change refugees, they will first need to secure homes elsewhere. So far, the Australian and New Zealand governments have indicated they could admit them into their countries. But, the Australian offer is strictly conditional on Tuvalu surrendering significant aspects of its sovereignty to Australia, and the New Zealand offer is still vague and imprecise.

The *Boe Declaration on Regional Security*, adopted by the Pacific Islands Forum in 2018, sends a clear message to the world about the plight of Tuvalu and similarly-threatened states. The Declaration cites climate change as the "single greatest threat to

the livelihoods, security and wellbeing of the peoples of the Pacific."
It is a blunt, emphatic, and united response by the member countries of the Pacific Islands Forum to the insensitive calls from major
global powers to Pacific Island states that, instead of focusing their
attention on the immediate and cataclysmic climate change threat
to their homes and countries, Pacific peoples should give higher
priority to the current global strategic competition.

Dame Meg Taylor, a former distinguished Papua New Guinea
diplomat and later Secretary-General of the Pacific Islands Forum,
is deeply critical of the policy pressure being put by overseas powers on Pacific Island states. She comments, "The emphasis should
be on prioritising the region's needs, particularly in addressing the
climate change impacts and economic development. Clearly
engaged in a competition for influence, both [the United States and
China] continue to prioritise geopolitical dominance and economic
interests over the paramount challenge of climate change. This
glaring misalignment between the global powers' narratives and
the Pacific's imperatives underscore the challenge of aligning the
region's narrative with those that revolve around geopolitical rivalry"
('Pacific-led Regionalism Undermined', posted September 2003).

Similar comments have been made by other Pacific leaders,
who clearly agree with Dame Meg's call to move the focus of attention from global geostrategic priorities to the Forum's emphasis on
the security threat posed by climate change.

The small island country of Tuvalu, with a population of just
11,200 people, has been particularly anxious about its plight with
increasing sea levels and the risk they pose to the country's continued existence.

With that in mind, Tuvalu has recently negotiated the text of a
treaty with Australia, called the Australia–Tuvalu Falepili Union,
which provides a "special human mobility pathway for citizens of
Tuvalu to access Australia to live, study and work" and to access
social services. In return, Tuvalu "shall mutually agree with Australia
on any partnership, arrangement or engagement with any other state
or entity on security and defence-related matters." These "matters"
are described as including defence, policing, border protection,

cyber security, and critical infrastructure, including ports, telecommunications, and energy infrastructure.

The Treaty has come under scathing criticism from Professor Steven Ratuva of New Zealand's Canterbury University. Ratuva is a frequent and widely-read commentator on Pacific affairs and he summarises the new Treaty as follows: "The crux of the agreement is that the people of Tuvalu can live in Australia, but in return, Tuvalu is essentially ceding part of its sovereignty to Australia. ... What this could mean is that Tuvalu as a sovereign state cannot, on its own, make decisions on its security interests across a whole range of areas including engagement with other countries ...".[1]

Ratuva comments that this could mean "unrestricted Australian access to, and control over, Tuvalu's sovereignty, including its 200-mile exclusive economic zone, under the rubric of 'border protection'." Ratuva describes this treaty as an applied version of a similar idea by former Australian prime minister Kevin Rudd, who suggested in 2019 that, as a strategy to adapt to climate change in the Pacific, Australia should offer citizenship to the people of Tuvalu, Kiribati, and Nauru — and in exchange, Australia would control their seas, exclusive economic zones, and fisheries. This 2019 proposal was described by Tuvalu's then prime minister, Enele Sopoanga, as "imperial thinking" and he said Tuvalu was not prepared "to be subjugated under some sort of colonial mentor; those days are over."

Of course, the Australia/Tuvalu treaty is not directly relevant to Aotearoa New Zealand's own relations with Tuvalu. But, New Zealand should closely follow developments regarding Australia's proposals if it does not wish to be similarly accused of "predatory imperial behaviour," the language used by Professor Ratuva to describe Australia following the latter's latest proposal to Tuvalu. Such a criticism of New Zealand would be more harmful to Aotearoa New Zealand's influence in the Pacific than similar criticisms of

---

[1] Ratuva, S. Good Faith lacking in Australia-Tuvalu Agreement, November 19, 2023. https://e-tangata.co.nz/comment-and-analysis/good-faith-lacking-in-australia-tuvalu-agreement/. (Accessed December 12, 2023).

Australia are to that country's influence; Australia is influential in the region not least because of its dominant economic and political strength which will barely be affected by such criticism, while Aotearoa New Zealand is heavily dependent for influence on its reputation among Pacific Island countries. That reputation would inevitably be harmed significantly if it were similarly criticised.

Regional Relationships

In seeking solutions for many of the issues affecting the Pacific Islands Forum and its member states, the first challenge is the difficulty in achieving, or maintaining, the unity of Pacific Island states. This is not a problem at all unique to the Pacific, as a glance at the challenges faced by multilateral and regional groupings elsewhere in the world proves. But, regional unity is often difficult to maintain.

Dame Meg Taylor recently wrote an article, 'Pacific-led Regionalism Undermined', in September 2023, stating that "It is crucial to recognise the Pacific's historical strength in regionalism. Amid the wrangling of superpowers for dominance, the Pacific's historic successes — from the movement for a Nuclear Free Pacific to collective protests against drift net fishing, we have shown unwavering commitment to safeguarding our home and our capacity to navigate complexity while preserving sovereignty. The Pacific's power lies in its ability to remain friends to all, fending off attempts to belittle us again. By remaining steadfast in its commitment to averting the climate crisis, the Pacific can assert its influence and contribute meaningfully to global challenges."

"As the Pacific nations strengthen their unity, seize opportunities, and face challenges with resolve, the essence of the Blue Pacific will guide them toward a future of self-determination, environmental resilience, and continued conversations begun by their ancestors."

Nevertheless, the vast and empty ocean spaces physically separating the member states of the Pacific Islands Forum inevitably make effective communication and understanding difficult. Cultural and language differences, in addition to different historical backgrounds between Polynesians, Melanesians, and Micronesians, all serve to compound the situation. Recently, these complications made aspects of Forum cooperation and unity quite fragile, but now, at least, steps are being taken to improve the situation.

Aotearoa New Zealand could itself do more in support of regional unity and improved relationships. New Zealanders' attitudes toward their Pacific neighbours have long included a significant element of condescension. Some years ago, with the backing of the Pacific Cooperation Foundation, I campaigned quite hard against the New Zealand tendency to describe our regional neighbours as being a part of 'our backyard'. The campaign seemed to be successful — but only for a time. Now, the term "backyard" has crept back into common use.

A related New Zealand attitude seems to expect Pacific Islanders' gratitude for the aid Aotearoa gives. Certainly, the Pacific is one of the most aid-dependent regions in the world. But, instead of pushing our own ideas, we could best help by encouraging and supporting Pacific Island initiatives designed to promote economic development. New Zealand will never be able to compete in the volume of its aid with the region's major donors. But, if we can treat our neighbours more as allies and partners rather than as mere recipients of aid, our relationships within the Forum, and thereby also New Zealand's wider influence, will grow significantly.

Further afield, Aotearoa New Zealand could also focus more strongly on our relations with the countries of Southeast Asia and their regional organisation, the Association of Southeast Asian Nations. Again, we will never be major players in this larger environment, but we can certainly improve our standing — and benefit significantly from that.

Geoff Miller is a former Australian diplomat and government official. He headed Australia's Office of National Intelligence and served as ambassador to Japan, Indonesia, and Korea, and (most important of all) as high commissioner to New Zealand. He is much respected on both sides of the Tasman Ocean and much of his thought on how Australia should behave in Southeast Asia can be applied to New Zealand, too.

On the South Pacific, Miller does not mince words: "We need to put the work in. … Our attitude to climate change is one very good example, with one Pacific commentator saying that our position led to Pacific nations viewing us with feelings of 'revulsion'".[2]

The late Terence O'Brien, one of Aotearoa New Zealand's ablest and most thoughtful diplomats, argued frequently that New Zealand should put more effort into its relations with the countries of both the South Pacific and Southeast Asia. He had several reasons for this, but the one which impressed me most, having spent over a decade in Asia myself, was that the countries of Asia had had decades, generations even, of experience in dealing both with each other and, sometimes collectively and sometimes alone, with China. We seem to forget how much we could learn from them. The same applies to the importance of listening to Pacific Island countries. These countries often have perspectives of their own on regional and strategic issues, perspectives which can significantly improve Aotearoa New Zealand's understanding of these issues.

Strategic Competition and Its Impact

Deepening and intensifying competition in recent years between China and the US (and its allies) has inevitably had a significant impact on Pacific Island states. While the competition between the United States and China to gain favour and influence from generous aid contributions has brought significant material benefit to many Pacific Island countries, such aid has sometimes had deficiencies and disadvantages, including occasional corruption. Concerns on several fronts are increasing. And, as Dr. Tess Newton Cain of Australia's Griffiths University predicted earlier this year, there is an increasing convergence of 'climate change' and 'security' narratives in the region.

---

[2] [Australian] Ministers in a new government should do — climate change, China-US relations and our region (Pearls and Irritations, *Public Policy Journal*, 12 May 2022).

Unfortunately, as Dame Meg Taylor has stated, the US and its allies, motivated by a geostrategic calculation that China poses a credible threat to their supremacy, have adopted aggressive and conspicuous measures to safeguard their positions.

Bringing a similar New Zealand perspective to the strategic competition discussion, Dr. Anna Powles, of Massey University, New Zealand, has written, "Strategic competition between the US, its regional allies and partners, and the PRC has intensified in the Pacific Islands region, reflecting the broader security trends and dynamics across the Indo-Pacific ... This intensification of strategic competition has raised concerns about the impact of the geopolitical ambitions of external actors on the Pacific security agenda and architecture, as well as the ways in which geopolitics intersects with national interests. The Pacific Islands Forum's *Boe Declaration on Regional Security* (2018), for example, acknowledges the increasingly crowded and contested geopolitical context ..."

"As competition intensifies in the Pacific, New Zealand will likely have to make a series of defining strategic choices which challenge its relationships with its Pacific partners and its security alignment with traditional partners, notably Australia and the United States".[3]

While most New Zealanders accept Aotearoa New Zealand's close relationship with Australia and the United States, their opposition to any militarisation, particularly nuclear militarisation, of their country remains strong. The history on that score is clear. Anti-nuclear sentiments were fed by France's long period of nuclear testing in the Pacific (in breach of an injunction by the International Court of Justice in 1973 ordering it to stop) and then elevated in the 1980s by the sinking of the Greenpeace protest vessel *Rainbow Warrior* in Auckland Harbour by French government agents.

Anti-nuclear opinion in New Zealand then escalated further in an argument between the United States and New Zealand in the 1980s over access by US nuclear-armed or -powered warships to New Zealand's ports. New Zealand's Prime Minister at the time,

---

[3] How Aotearoa New Zealand is Responding to Strategic Competition in the Pacific Islands Region Georgetown *Journal of Asian Affairs*, Vol. 9, 2023, 33.

David Lange, vigorously opposed such visits while the US Secretary of State, George Schultz, remained firm that the ANZUS security treaty relationship between the two powers required New Zealand to accept such visits. Moreover, the United States "would neither confirm nor deny" the presence of nuclear weapons.

Neither side would give way and eventually the United States advised that, in light of New Zealand's position, it would no longer consider itself committed to the defence of New Zealand under the ANZUS alliance.

For its part, New Zealand enshrined its new anti-nuclear policy in legislation with Parliament enacting the *1987 New Zealand Nuclear Free Zone, Disarmament and Arms Control Act.* The strength of anti-nuclear opinion in New Zealand remained strong. Many had expected that when New Zealand's centre-right National Party next won a general election, it would use its parliamentary majority to repeal the anti-nuclear legislation. But popular support for the Labour government's anti-nuclear policies was such that the National Party decided not to try to change the legislation when it could have done so.

New Zealand has also pursued its anti-nuclear policy internationally. First, during France's nuclear testing on the island of Mururoa in French Polynesia, the then New Zealand government signalled the strength of its opposition by dispatching two warships in turn to the testing area in French Polynesia, each carrying Greenpeace and other protesters. New Zealand also strongly supported the South Pacific Nuclear Free Zone Treaty ('SPNFZ' — also called the Treaty of Rarotonga) which was concluded in 1985. It bans the use, testing, and possession of nuclear weapons within a designated Nuclear Free Zone in the South Pacific.

More recently, the United Nations General Assembly has adopted the text of a new comprehensive nuclear treaty: *Treaty on the Prohibition of Nuclear Weapons.* As of 6 July 2022, the Treaty had been signed by 86 states, and 66 states had become full parties to the Treaty. Of the countries in our Pacific neighbourhood, Fiji, Kiribati, Niue, Palau, Vanuatu, Cook Islands, Nauru, New Zealand, Samoa, and Tuvalu had all become parties to the Treaty. Of the remaining states in the Pacific neighbourhood, Australia, the Federated States of Micronesia, and Marshall Islands voted against the adoption of the Treaty by the UN General Assembly.

Dame Meg Taylor reminds us that the US and its allies, motivated by a geostrategic calculation that China poses a credible threat to their supremacy, have adopted aggressive and conspicuous measures to safeguard their positions. A significant development has been the AUKUS partnership (of Australia, the United Kingdom, and the United States) which is at the centre of Western-led predominance in the Indo-Pacific, including, of course, the Pacific Islands region.

This new defence partnership was announced unexpectedly and caused unease across a region that has prided itself on working toward a demilitarised, peaceful Pacific and a world free of nuclear weapons. The AUKUS partners will produce nuclear-propelled long-range submarines, several of which are to be bought by Australia. The project may yet be in some doubt, however: A startling US congressional report (from the respected US Congressional Budget Office) suggests that the fleet of submarines will not achieve the stated objectives of the programme. It would degrade, not enhance, deterrence against China. And, according to the congressional report, it would undermine rather than sustain the global non-proliferation regime. And, all this for a projected cost of AU$368.

The AUKUS project underlines the glaring misalignment between the global powers' narratives and what the Pacific states see as their immediate imperatives.

Aotearoa New Zealand, of course, owes loyalty to its Pacific Island partners, on the one hand, and to its longstanding friend the United States, and ally Australia, on the other. It is suggested that New Zealand will have to make a series of defining strategic choices as competition intensifies in the Pacific. A decision to abandon the Pacific Islands' clear and emphatic position in favour of supporting instead the AUKUS military group would be highly contentious.

Former Prime Minister Jacinda Ardern, in emphasising the importance of the Pacific in New Zealand's foreign policy, said, "The Pacific is who we are as well as where we are. It is both our identity and our place in the world."

Many New Zealand politicians have taken the same or similar positions, although it is possible the new centre-right coalition which took office in December 2023 will not give as high a priority to the country's interests in the Pacific Islands region as its predecessor did. Nevertheless, the strength of New Zealanders' commitment to the country's longstanding anti-nuclear stance should not be underestimated. Moreover, many of the country's politicians and commentators have connected New Zealand's nuclear-free status with its independent foreign policy. Moves to change that status would be enormously controversial.

Following the unresolved dispute in the early 1980s between the United States and the then New Zealand government led by Prime Minister David Lange over the access of US warships to New Zealand waters, the US had argued that admitting US warships unconditionally to New Zealand waters was essential under the ANZUS Treaty while New Zealand would not do so without an assurance from the United States that the ship was neither nuclear-armed nor nuclear-powered. As mentioned, New Zealand's policy was then enshrined in domestic legislation, namely, the 1987 *New Zealand Nuclear Free Zone, Disarmament and Arms Control Act.* Public support for the nuclear-free policy has been such that even right-wing New Zealand governments since 1987 have declined to seek any change to the legislation.

It is also enshrined in treaties, including the *1986/South Pacific Nuclear Free Zone Treaty* (known as the Rarotonga Treaty) and the *2017 Treaty on the Prohibition of Nuclear Weapons.* (So far, New Zealand is one of only two 'Western' parties to the 2017 Treaty, the other being Ireland. However, several Pacific Island Southeast Asian countries are parties or signatories.)

There has been some discussion about the possibility of New Zealand participating in non-nuclear aspects of the AUKUS nuclear submarine project. It remains to be seen whether such participation would be possible practically or politically. (For example, there would likely be significant public opposition to any New Zealand involvement which seemed to connect the country to the nuclear submarine (AUKUS) project.)

Self-Determination in the Pacific

Recognition of the right of Pacific peoples to self-determination has long been a feature of Pacific politics. The only government entities in the Pacific which do not actively support the right to self-determination are those controlled by distant colonial powers like France and, to a degree, the United States, and those which are involved in disputes over sovereignty, as in the case of Indonesia in West Papua.

Aotearoa New Zealand has consistently been a leader in supporting the right to self-determination in the Pacific, both practically and in international forums. Its role as an administering power in Samoa, the Cook Islands, and Niue has been far from perfect. But, these territories achieved independence or self-government speedily and with little controversy. Samoa became fully independent in 1962 — the first United Nations Trust Territory and also the first Pacific Island territory or colony to do so. There had been fears that the Cook Islands and Niue might be too small for them to be able to sustain their own governments. But, they are certainly managing.

The New Zealand Labour Party has always firmly supported the right to self-determination. It was no coincidence that Peter Fraser, Prime Minister during World War II and immediately thereafter, should have taken a close interest in the parts of the United Nations Charter related to creating a trusteeship system to promote and assist colonial territories to achieve full independence.

I was reminded of that when, in 1996, I went to New York to represent New Zealand at the United Nations. It was customary, and often very valuable, to call on other representatives to obtain their perspectives on current issues. I called on the US representative, Madeleine Albright, with that in mind. For some reason, decolonisation was on her mind and she indicated disappointment that New Zealand had often been "on the other side" on decolonisation issues when they came up for debate in the Decolonisation Committee, or C24 as it was sometimes called.

But, in the Pacific Islands region, the right to self-determination has continued to be a sensitive issue with several colonial, or administering, powers unwilling or, at best, slow to recognise the right to self-determination. There seems little likelihood that French colonies like New Caledonia, French Polynesia, and Wallis and Futuna will become independent in the foreseeable future. And, the same can be said regarding American territories like American Samoa. To the surprise of many observers, the Pacific Islands Forum recently admitted New Caledonia and French Polynesia to membership despite their colonial status. It remains to be seen whether this will lessen the Forum's firm support of the right to self-determination.

The issue of self-determination has also arisen when western governments have sought to influence Pacific Island governments to favour their (western) policies vis-a-vis China. For example, Australia strongly opposes any moves that might allow China to build military bases in small island countries, including Tuvalu. While the prime ministers of both Australia and Tuvalu were together at the Forum Leaders' meeting on 10 November 2023, they signed a treaty between their two countries, called the Falepili Union Agreement — *falepili* meaning good neighbourliness. The formal support of both Australia and Tuvalu has yet to be confirmed and, since the original signing, there has been debate in Tuvalu on whether it should proceed.

Under the proposed treaty, a significant number of Tuvaluans will have access to Australia — "to live, study and work" in Australia and "to access Australian education, health and key income and family support." For its part, Tuvalu "shall mutually agree with Australia any partnership, arrangement or engagement with any other State or entity on security and defence-related matters."

Labour Mobility in the Pacific

Labour mobility in the Pacific has often been controversial. The settler countries bordering the Pacific have behaved atrociously at times. When they felt a need for more labour than was available locally, Pacific Island men were sometimes simply taken forcefully, starting of course with 'blackbirding'. Then, when there was more labour available in the settler countries, causing fears that their own people might have difficulty getting work, they behaved equally badly, by seizing and expelling Pacific Islanders following 'dawn raids'.

New Zealand certainly has had much to be ashamed of during the eras of 'blackbirding' and 'dawn raids'. We certainly owe it to our Pacific neighbours to ensure that we do not repeat those two disgraceful periods in our relations with our neighbours.

Recently, substantive and productive consideration has been given to the many challenges that need to be overcome if successful labour mobility schemes are to be devised and introduced. It will, of course, be crucial for Australia, New Zealand, and any other developed countries seeking to employ labour from Pacific Island countries to ensure that Pacific Island views and preferences are fully taken into account — in other words, the exact opposite of the situation in the past when the interests and concerns of the workers' home communities and governments were commonly ignored.

Ultimately, after a regional agreement has been achieved on labour mobility, there is likely to be interest in extending that to additional visa-free mobility among Pacific Island countries and between Pacific Island countries and their developed country neighbours. The existing arrangement between Australia and New Zealand whereby visas are automatically available to all travellers on arrival could provide a precedent.

Improved arrangements are being made for freer travel between and among Pacific Island countries and Australia and New Zealand, and, for obvious reasons, such arrangements are popular in the Island countries. That popularity makes it difficult for Pacific Island governments and leaders to be seen to be opposing freer mobility in the region. But, there are additional issues which would need to be addressed: for example, the possible brain drain consequences for Island countries and, indeed, the possibly severe social, community, and economic impacts of removing significant numbers of people.

Pacific Island people came to New Zealand in the 19th century largely as captives brought to ease labour shortages. More than a century later, a number of recent Pacific immigrants were arrested by police in the course of the 'Dawn Raids' aimed at returning the immigrants to their original homes as they were no longer wanted in New Zealand. Against this background, New Zealand's future immigration policies affecting Pacific Islanders will be watched closely.

Chapter 9

Singapore's Relations with Pacific Island States

Mary Seet-Cheng

Relations Based on Shared Interests

There is a natural affinity between Singapore and the Pacific Island States (PIS). We are all small island developing states dependent on an effective multilateral rules-based order. This international order protects us against the alternative order of 'might is right'. In this current era of big power contestation, we share the Pacific nations' desire to pursue a foreign policy of 'being friends to all, enemy to none'. Singapore and most of the PIS are connected by history, through our common colonial experience and membership in the British Commonwealth. However, today, our links are forged through our strong shared interests as members of the Forum of Small States (FOSS) and the Alliance of Small Island States (AOSIS).

Dialogue Partner of PIF

Singapore's main institutional link to the Pacific Island States is through the Pacific Island Forum (PIF). We have regularly attended the PIF annual Leaders' Meeting since 2012, after we appointed our first Non-Resident Ambassador to the Pacific Island Forum

(NRA to PIF), Mr Verghese Matthews, in 2011. He was concurrently accredited as our Non-resident High Commissioner to Fiji. The designation of our NRA to PIF signalled our support for Pacific regionalism. I was appointed NRHC to Fiji and NRA to PIF in February 2020 after Ambassador Matthews retired. Singapore was admitted as a full PIF Dialogue Partner in January 2022 after the PIF finalised its new guidelines and lifted its moratorium on new dialogue partners. To mark the occasion, our Minister of Foreign Affairs Vivian Balakrishnan attended the 52nd PIF Leaders' Meeting in November 2023 in the Cook Islands, where we were present as a full Dialogue Partner for the first time.

Enhancing Bilateral Relations through Capacity-Building Programmes

The responsibility of our NRA to PIF extends beyond working with the PIF Secretariat to building our bilateral relations with all PIS (PIF members minus Australia, New Zealand, and PNG, as we have resident missions in Australia and New Zealand, and a separate non-resident High Commissioner to PNG based in Singapore). Our focus in bilateral relations with the PIS has been on capacity-building through the *Singapore Cooperation Programme* (SCP). The SCP is a series of training and technical assistance programmes offered by Singapore to developing countries to share our developmental experience. The SCP, established in 1992, was to consolidate, within the Ministry of Foreign Affairs, technical assistance initiatives Singapore has offered since the 1960s and to expand their reach and scope. Over the 30 years of the SCP, more than 5,800 PIS officials (close to 4% of the total SCP cohort of over 150,000 participants) have attended courses in a wide range of disciplines. Since then, we have also organised close to 50 customised bilateral programmes to meet the specific requests of individual PIS countries.

Our SCP has evolved its course offerings to meet the needs and priorities of our development partners. The SCP added new training packages to help the unique challenges faced by fellow

Small Island Developing States (SIDS). It offered new courses to build climate resilience in areas such as climate science, adaptation, and mitigation; disaster risk reduction; green project management and financing; and low-carbon development and carbon markets. SIDS are given priority placement in these SCP courses.

In sharing our development experiences, we have engaged the PIS at various levels and sectors. For high-level political exchanges, Singapore hosted *High-Level Study Visits* (HLSV) *for the Pacific* in 2012 and 2017. Heads of government and ministerial representatives have attended these HLSVs. Beyond sharing our development experience, these visits also allowed our leaders to exchange views with PIS leaders on areas of common interest, including climate change and sustainable development. We plan to host the next run of the High-Level Study Visit soon. To share our urban, water management, and environment development experiences, we have invited Pacific Ministers to attend the *World Cities Summit*, *Singapore International Water Week* and *Clean Enviro Summit,* events which are held regularly in Singapore. Under its *Programme for Foreign Diplomats* launched in 2013, the Singapore Ministry of Foreign Affairs Diplomatic Academy has hosted 25 junior foreign diplomats from the PIS, giving them an opportunity to forge links with their Singapore counterparts. We hope to resume this programme when resources allow.

Singapore has hosted several editions of the *Singapore–Pacific Islands Transport Ministers' Forum* to bring together the Transport Ministers to exchange views on key challenges in the civil aviation, land, and maritime transport sectors. The next run of the Singapore–Pacific Islands Transport Ministers' Forum was held in February 2024 in conjunction with the Singapore Airshow. Since 2005, the Civil Aviation Authority of Singapore (CAAS) has organised in Singapore *annual dialogue sessions with Directors-General of Aviation Authorities from the Pacific SIDS* to provide them with updates on developments in ICAO and the Asia-Pacific and to discuss challenges and opportunities specific to the PSIDS (Pacific Small Island Developing Countries).

Singapore–Pacific Resilience and Knowledge Sharing (SPARKS) Package

To mark our Dialogue Partnership of the PIF and to build upon our sustained bilateral and regional engagement with the Pacific, Singapore launched a new customised *Singapore–Pacific Resilience and Knowledge Sharing (SPARKS) package* (2024–2026) at the 52nd PIF Leaders' Meeting with Forum Dialogue Partners in November 2023. For a start, the SPARKS package will focus on three main areas: *Climate Resilience* — Singapore will offer a customised three-year modular programme from 2024 to 2026, aimed at supporting our Pacific partners in achieving climate resilience, through capacity-building in urban governance and planning; *Cybersecurity* — Singapore will offer placement to our Pacific partners in the Singapore Cyber Security Agency's newly-launched SG Cyber Leadership Programme, which includes topics on cyber diplomacy concepts, international law, and the operational and technical considerations of international cyber policy; and *International Law* — Singapore will offer online courses on international law, covering topics of direct relevance to the Pacific to provide participants with an understanding of how international law can help address challenges posed by climate change and rising sea levels.

Maritime and Aviation Cooperation — Helping the PIS Build Connectivity

We have been active in supporting the capacity-building efforts of the Pacific in the maritime and aviation sectors through our agencies, the Civil Aviation Authority of Singapore (CAAS) and the Maritime and Port Authority (MPA). Being Large Ocean States with vast distances between each other and the rest of the world, building capabilities in connectivity is vital for the development of the PIS.

On the *maritime* front, through our Third Country Training Programme (TCTP) with the IMO, MPA has conducted courses on the implementation of IMO instruments on safety and environmental protection that have benefitted the PIS. To date, the MPA has welcomed more than 180 participants from the Pacific nations under this programme. The MPA Academy also conducts a range of maritime leadership training programmes for maritime and port leaders. To date, we have welcomed more than 500 participants from over 100 countries, including many from the Pacific nations. On the *aviation* front, the CAAS has provided consultancies and on-site training in the Cook Islands, Fiji, the Federated States of Micronesia, Kiribati, Marshall Islands, Palau, Papua New Guinea, Tonga, and Vanuatu, as well as aviation training fellowships and scholarships at the Singapore Aviation Academy (SAA) for the PSIDS. To date, more than 2,200 participants from all PSIDS have participated in the Special Aviation Programme.

Recognising that air transport connectivity will continue to be a key enabler for the Pacific region's sustainable economic development, we have supported flight connectivity between Singapore and the Pacific region.

Singapore is now directly connected to the Pacific Islands through four Pacific airlines: Fiji Airways, Air Niugini, Air Calin, and Alii Palau. Through these direct flights, Singapore is more connected to the Pacific Islands than most PIS are to each other. We hope to have more links as we have liberal Air Services Agreements (ASAs) with several other PIS. They recognise the importance of having direct links with Asia and the world through an international air hub like Singapore.

Close Partnership at the UN and Other International Fora

As fellow SIDS, Singapore and the Pacific Islands share existential concerns such as rising sea levels as a result of climate change. This is why SIDS place importance on multilateral institutions, systems, and the international rule of law, as only global action can meet such challenges. In this regard, Singapore has supported the PIF's longstanding request for a new UN office in the Pacific and the PSIDS' calls for greater debt sustainability. We also agree that for vulnerable small low-lying States facing existential threats due to climate change-induced sea-level rise, the balance of equities under the 1982 UN Convention on the Law of the Sea (UNCLOS) clearly and indisputably favours the preservation of existing maritime zones and entitlements, if they were established in accordance with UNCLOS.

At the UN, Singapore has and will continue to work closely with PSIDS to advance issues of common interest and importance, such as sustainable development, trade and connectivity, financing for development, and ocean governance. As members of AOSIS, we play an instrumental role in pushing for ambitious outcomes at the annual UN Framework Convention on Climate Change (UNFCCC) Conference of the Parties (COP). At COP-28, AOSIS succeeded in pushing for the world to transition away from fossil fuels in energy systems.

Singapore is also a member of the Core Group led by Vanuatu that is seeking clarity from the International Court of Justice (ICJ) on States' legal obligations to protect our climate and the legal consequences for States that have caused significant harm to it. The UN General Assembly resolution on this issue was adopted by consensus in March 2023. Furthermore, Singapore was a participant at the oral hearing at the International Tribunal for the Law of the Sea (ITLOS), following a request by the Commission of Small Island States on Climate Change and International Law (COSIS) for an advisory opinion on the specific obligations of States that are parties to the UNCLOS in relation to climate change.

Singapore collaborated with the PIF during the Intergovernmental Conference sessions to negotiate a new international agreement under the UNCLOS on the conservation and sustainable use of marine biological diversity in areas beyond national jurisdiction ('BBNJ Agreement'). We engaged PSIDS to secure an ambitious Agreement, including the full recognition of the special circumstances of SIDS. As Large Ocean States, the BBNJ Agreement represents an important international agreement to help PSIDS conserve and sustain their ocean resources, given the significant direct and indirect impacts that activities in areas beyond national jurisdiction will have on their waters. We will continue to work with them to secure the swift entry into force of the BBNJ Agreement.

Conclusion

Our relations with the Pacific countries are strong at both the international and bilateral levels. We work closely on many shared interests at various international fora. As a fellow small island state, our SCP programmes provide relevant capacity-building assistance at the bilateral level, which is much valued by the Pacific states. We continually evolve our training offerings to meet their new priorities and as we gain new expertise to share. We will help develop their connectivity with the world through better air links through Singapore. We are particularly pleased that the PIF is now looking beyond the Pacific to forge links with other regions. An MOU to explore cooperation between ASEAN and PIF was signed at the last ASEAN Summit in September 2023. We welcome the ongoing dialogue between the PIF and ASEAN Secretariats, which will add a third dimension to Singapore's relations with the Pacific countries — region-to-region cooperation.

III

BILATERAL DEFENCE AND STRATEGIC RELATIONS

Chapter 10

New Zealand – Singapore Defence Cooperation: A View from Wellington

David Capie

Introduction

As the chapters in this book attest, Singapore is one of New Zealand's most important international partners. On a personal level, New Zealanders feel extremely warmly towards the Lion City. The Asia New Zealand Foundation's annual *Perceptions of Asia* survey consistently ranks Singapore near the very top of the countries perceived as New Zealand's 'closest friend' in Asia. Its 2023 survey ranked Singapore as third 'most important in Asia for New Zealand's future', behind only China and Japan.[1]

But, if the importance of the relationship is instinctively grasped by the New Zealand public, some aspects of the connection have largely flown under the radar. One is the defence relationship, which is both longstanding and close. This chapter explores the contemporary strategic relationship between the two nations, providing a concise overview of cooperation in the defence space. It makes the case that, while the relationship remains strong and the importance of the defence connection is evidenced by its inclusion

---

[1] Asia New Zealand Foundation. New Zealander's Perceptions of Asia and Asian Peoples 2022. Available online at: https://www.asianz.org.nz/our-resources/reports/new-zealanders-perceptions-of-asia-and-asian-peoples-2022/.

as a theme in the 2019 Enhanced Partnership, two challenges have prevented the relationship from reaching its full potential. First, defence ties lost momentum during the COVID-19 pandemic, when closed borders reduced opportunities for training, exercises, and defence diplomacy. Second, a significant capability gap has emerged between the two militaries, which some critics have argued weakens New Zealand's value as a partner. This chapter argues that the defence relationship is strong and New Zealand has a significant base of goodwill to build on, but it will need to invest in the Singapore relationship to demonstrate ongoing value to an important security partner.

Shared History and Shared Interests

New Zealand and Singapore share many important interests across international trade, political, and strategic issues. Both are open trading nations, strongly supportive of international law and institutions. They share a keen interest in maritime security and in the preservation of key norms such as freedom of navigation. And, both are attempting to navigate an increasingly contested Indo-Pacific, maintaining close ties to the United States, but also managing an important if complex relationship with the People's Republic of China.

The New Zealand–Singapore defence relationship has its origins in imperial connections. New Zealand was one of the first parts of the British Empire to support London's plans to build a naval base in Singapore in the 1920s. The base was seen, in part at least, as a "bulwark for the Dominions of the South."[2] About 600 New Zealand personnel, including aviators from no. 488 (NZ) squadron, played a role in the defence of the then-British colony following the outbreak of war with Japan in 1941.[3]

---

[2] McIntyre, W.D. (1971). New Zealand and the Singapore base between the wars. *Journal of Southeast Asian Studies*, 2(1) (March), 2–21.

[3] Nickless, M. Stories from Singapore: RNZAF in World War II. Auckland War Memorial Museum. Available online at: https://www.aucklandmuseum.com/war-memorial/online-cenotaph/features/rnzaf-singapore.

After the war, New Zealand forces remained in Southeast Asia, fighting communist guerrillas during the Malayan Emergency and later countering Indonesian forces during the Confrontation, when a squadron of RNZAF Canberra bombers was deployed to Singapore as a deterrent. In 1969, New Zealand moved an infantry battalion to a base in the young republic, and in 1971 the two countries joined Australia, Malaysia, and the United Kingdom as members of the Five Powers Defence Arrangements (FPDA), through which states pledged to consult immediately in the event of an armed attack on Singapore or Malaysia. New Zealand's infantry departed from Singapore in 1989, but to this day a New Zealand Defence Support Unit (NZDSU) contingent plays an important role in managing the facility at the Sembawang Naval Installation.

In strategic terms, Singapore offers New Zealand a vital point of entry into Southeast Asia. Its location, astride some of the world's busiest shipping lanes, gives it importance well beyond its size. Its significant geographic position is augmented by Singapore's outsized influence internationally and, in particular, in East Asia. Singaporean officials have insights to share about cooperation across ASEAN, emerging trends in regional security, and the interests of great powers, the United States, China, and also India, where Singapore has a broad network of diplomatic posts.[4] Singapore is an active member of the ASEAN Defence Ministers Meeting Plus process — a regional grouping that includes New Zealand. And, it is an important centre for defence diplomacy, hosting the annual IISS Shangri-La Dialogue, which brings together defence ministers from the United States, China, Japan, and around the world — an event that has become a 'must-attend' appointment for the New Zealand minister.[5]

---

[4]On Singapore–US security ties, see Capie, D. (2020). The power of partnerships: US defence ties with Indonesia, Singapore and Vietnam. *International Politics*, 57(2), 242–258.
[5]For a discussion of the value of the Shangri-La Dialogue, see Capie, D. and Taylor, B. (2010). The Shangri-La Dialogue and Institutionalization of Defence Diplomacy. *The Pacific Review*, 23(3), 359–376.

From a Singaporean perspective, New Zealand is a 'natural partner' despite its distance and limited hard power.[6] As small states, the two countries see common value in a world where the law of the jungle is tempered by international rules and institutions. Singapore values New Zealand's support for a 'rules-based order', for the ASEAN-centred architecture, and for the commitment to its defence under FPDA. But, given Singapore's limited strategic depth, the defence relationship with New Zealand also offers practical training opportunities for the Singapore Armed Forces (SAF). Since 1997, some 500 SAF personnel have deployed to New Zealand annually for 'Thunder Warrior' artillery live-firing exercises at the Waiouru Training Area. Although Thunder Warrior is perhaps the most visible example of defence cooperation, the relationship engages all the services under a Defence Cooperation Arrangement signed in May 2009. As well as FPDA interactions, bilateral exercises include Lion Zeal (between the two navies), Lion Heart (special forces training), and Exercise Kiwi Walk (XKW), which involves ground forces.

In February 2017, two Singaporean F-15SG aircraft took part in the 80th anniversary of the Royal New Zealand Air Force (RNZAF). Later that year, a detachment of RSAF F-16 fighters deployed to New Zealand for training and the two countries explored the possibility of a permanent detachment of F-15SGs being based at the Ohakea air base. While a strategic assessment of the proposal was "strongly in favour on foreign policy grounds," a cross-agency report concluded that, overall, the costs and risks outweighed the benefits, and the two countries made a decision not to go ahead with the initiative.[7]

---

[6] PM Lee Hsien Loong, Joint Press conference with Prime Minister Jacinda Ardern, Singapore. 19 April 2022. Available on at: https://www.pmo.gov.sg/Newsroom/PM-Lee-Hsien-Loong-at-the-Joint-Press-Conference-with-New-Zealand-PM-Jacinda-Ardern-April-2022.

[7] Singapore proposal to base F-15 fighter jets at Ohakea Air Base: Further report. Minute of Decision, Cabinet External Relations and Security Committee. 4 December 2018. Available online at: https://www.defence.govt.nz/assets/Uploads/dca2a03a77/Singapore-Proposal-to-Base-F-15s-at-Ohakea.pdf.

In addition to training and cooperation in military education, the two partners have also worked together in operational deployments. An illustration of the close working relationship is the fact that when Singapore announced its first sizeable contribution to a United Nations peacekeeping mission, to East Timor in 2001, its 70 infantry personnel were embedded as part of the New Zealand battalion. Before deploying, an SAF platoon spent a week training in New Zealand. Similarly, when Singapore sent a small deployment on a humanitarian mission to Afghanistan in 2007, personnel were based with the New Zealand Defence Force Provincial Reconstruction Team (PRT) in Bamiyan.[8] The two militaries also worked together in counter-piracy operations in the Gulf of Aden in 2010 and 2011.[9]

In 2011, the defence connection also proved its value when disaster struck close to home. On 2 February, a powerful earthquake shook the South Island city of Christchurch, killing 185 people. A group of Singaporean national servicemen were in New Zealand for a training exercise at the time. The SAF team was quickly redeployed to Christchurch, where they spent three weeks helping New Zealand authorities manage the disaster response.[10] Two RSAF C-130 aircraft were also dispatched to support the delivery of assistance.

Defence and the Enhanced Partnership

If defence has historically been an important part of the bilateral relationship, its salience was given a further boost when Singapore and New Zealand concluded an Enhanced Partnership (EP) agree-

---

[8] Goff, P. (2007). Singapore to join New Zealand in Afghanistan. 7 March 2007. Available at: https://www.beehive.govt.nz/release/singapore-join-new-zealand-afghanistan.

[9] Joint Statement of New Zealand Minister of Defence Jonathon Coleman and Singapore Minister for Defence Dr Ng Eng Hen. 11 September 2012. Available online: https://www.mindef.gov.sg/web/portal/mindef/news-and-events/latest-releases/article-detail/2012/september/2012sep11-news-releases-01873.

[10] NS55 -SAF HADR Operations in New Zealand (2011). Our Singapore Army, 5 October 2022. Available online at: https://www.mindef.gov.sg/web/portal/army/army-news-and-resources/army-news/story-detail/2022/October/NS55_SAF_HADR_Operations_in_New_Zealand.

ment in 2019. The EP identified four 'pillars' where deeper cooperation in the bilateral relationship could be pursued: trade and
economics; science, technology, and innovation; people-to-people
ties; and defence and security. (A fifth pillar on climate change and
the green economy was added during a visit by then-Prime Minister
Jacinda Ardern in 2022.) In terms of specific measures around
defence and security, the EP established an annual Defence
Ministers Meeting and an annual security and intelligence dialogue. It
pledged to "strengthen cooperation in security technology, and cybersecurity," including cooperation on 'Homeland Security Technology'
with an agreement between the New Zealand Defence Technology
Agency and the Singapore Ministry of Home Affairs.[11]

But, if the EP pointed to the potential for even closer cooperation, there have been at least two challenges that have impacted
plans for enhancing the defence partnership. First, no sooner had
the agreement been made than the COVID-19 pandemic border
closures curtailed the regular tempo of exercises that brought
Singaporean forces to New Zealand. Thunder Warrior, a key practical point of engagement, was not held in 2020, 2021, 2022, or
2023. New Zealand's approach to COVID-19 management also
restricted travel by defence personnel, officials, and ministers.
Although CDF Kevin Short met with Minister of Defence Ng Eng
Hen in a September 2021 visit, many FPDA interactions were cancelled or held virtually, and no Shangri-La Dialogue — a key opportunity for ministerial engagement — was held in Singapore in either
2020 or 2021 (New Zealand ministers attended from 2022 when it
resumed).

If COVID-19 was a shock, a second challenge has emerged
over a longer period of time: the growing capability gap between
the two security partners. New Zealand's annual spending of
around 1% of GDP on defence contrasts sharply with Singapore's
defence budget of closer to 3%. This has manifested itself in two

---

[11] Joint Declaration by the Prime Ministers of New Zealand and the Republic of Singapore
on an Enhanced Partnership. 17 May 2019. Available online at: https://www.mfat.govt.nz/
assets/Countries-and-Regions/South-East-Asia/Singapore/Singapore-NZ-Enhanced-
Partnership/NZ-Singapore-Enhanced-Partnership-Joint-Declaration-15-May-2019.pdf.

differently equipped armed forces. As Euan Graham commented, "Fifty years ago, New Zealand had bombers, had fast jets — now it has neither, and it's just only now really starting to reinvest in new capabilities with the P8 maritime patrol aircraft, but otherwise it's a very small force."[12] New Zealand's drawn-out ANZAC frigate upgrade programme saw its two naval combat vessels out of action for several years after 2018, reducing the opportunities for ship visits and training in Southeast Asia. Senior Singaporean figures have quietly raised concerns about the problems facing the New Zealand Defence Force, as it has struggled with ageing platforms, ships unable to go to sea, and record levels of attrition.[13]

Challenges, But Cause for Optimism?

These challenges notwithstanding, there are reasons to be optimistic about the future of the defence relationship.

First, the broader bilateral relationship between New Zealand and Singapore remains strong. Indeed, if it curtailed some interactions, the pandemic also reminded the two countries of their value to one another as they concluded agreements to ensure supply chains remained open and that essential products, including food and medicines, could flow freely.[14] Shared concerns around challenges in regional security, including in the South China Sea, have also become more acute, sustaining a rationale for engagement and strategic dialogue.

Post-COVID-19, high-level visits and some bilateral training opportunities have also resumed. In late 2021, a newly upgraded HMNZS Te Kaha, HMNZS Aotearoa, and an RNZAF P-3K Orion took part in Exercise Bersama Gold 51, marking the 50th anniversary of the FPDA. The ships also transited the South China Sea as

---

[12] Sachdeva, S. (2022). New Zealand's unsung ally. Newsroom, 9 June 2022. Available online at: https://newsroom.co.nz/2022/06/09/new-zealands-unsung-ally/.

[13] For details, see Fisher, D. (2024). NZ Defence Force in crisis — our ships can't sail, our planes can't fly, and soldiers have left in droves. *New Zealand Herald*, 2 January 2024.

[14] Parker, D. (2020). Covid-19 response: New Zealand and Singapore launch initiative to ensure free flow of essential good. 15 April 2020.

part of a Combined Strike Group that included US, Japanese, and British vessels. In late 2022, the Republic of Singapore Air Force participated in TACEX22, an air mobility exercise in southern North Island.[15] In 2023, both HMNZS Aotearoa and HMNZS Te Mana took part in the Bersama Lima FPDA exercise and a bilateral exercise (Lion Zeal) with the Republic of Singapore Navy. The NZDF has maintained a presence in the Singapore-based Information Fusion Centre, hosted by the Singapore Navy, and in March 2021, Wellington agreed to send an NZDF analyst to the new Counter-Terrorism Information Facility (CTIF) — a multinational, open-source, intelligence-sharing operation. A paper to Cabinet argued that "New Zealand's commitment to the CTIF enables us to be a trusted, reliable and valuable partner in a multi-national regional effort."[16]

Second, there are also reasons to believe that Singapore will get greater attention from New Zealand following the election of a three-party coalition led by Prime Minister Christopher Luxon in late 2023. A Ministry of Foreign Affairs and Trade (MFAT) briefing to the new government in December 2023 recommended that as part of a "reset" of New Zealand's foreign policy, there should be a "step up in our engagement with Southeast Asia." What it called the "enduring defence partnership" with Singapore was one of the items singled out as one of the most important capabilities New Zealand brings to the region.[17] Luxon himself has pointed to Singapore as a country that New Zealand can learn much from and one with which he wants a "much deeper" relationship.[18]

Third, there are also early signs that New Zealand plans to address some of the investment issues that have arguably limited

---

[15] RNZAF trains alongside Republic of Singapore Air Force at Base Ohakea (n.d.) Available at https://www.nzdf.mil.nz/media-centre/news/rnzaf-trains-alongside-republic-of-singapore-air-force-at-base-ohakea/.

[16] Counter Terrorism Information Facility in Singapore: Proposal to Continue Participation. Cabinet External Relations and Security Committee, Minute of Decision, ERS-22-MIN-0016. Available online at: https://www.defence.govt.nz/assets/publication/file/CTIF-2022.pdf.

[17] Ministry of Foreign Affairs and Trade (2023). Our Southeast Asia and ASEAN relationships. Cabinet Paper, 5 December 2023. Available online at: https://www.mfat.govt.nz/en/media-and-resources/our-south-east-asia-and-asean-relationship-5-december-2023/.

[18] PM Luxon speaks after Cabinet meeting. Radio New Zealand, 11 December 2023.

defence interactions in recent years. All the members of the coalition government campaigned in support of an increase in the defence budget, with 2% of GDP identified as an important benchmark. Although the new government has pushed for deep cuts in public spending, Defence Minister Judith Collins has stressed that the Defence Force will need additional funds, commenting that New Zealand cannot "free load" when it comes to international security.[19] Whether that talk will be matched with investment in new capabilities remains to be seen, but comments from across the coalition suggest that New Zealand may be at a turning point in the way it thinks about defence and national security. In the meantime, some of the new capabilities purchased in the last five years have also become operational. The P-8A Poseidon maritime patrol aircraft are expected to be deployed in Northeast Asia in support of United Nations sanctions enforcement in the first half of 2024. It will be interesting to watch when they first make an appearance in Southeast Asia.

Finally, for its part, Singapore remains keen to deepen defence ties with natural partners, as the remarkable development of the Singapore–Australia defence relationship in recent years shows.[20] Indeed, as New Zealand looks to deepen interoperability with its ANZUS (Australia-New Zealand-United States) ally, it may be that triangular connections with Canberra and Wellington's closest defence partner in Southeast Asia could become a new feature of the evolving defence landscape.[21]

---

[19] Quoted in AAP (2024). Peters, Collins, to meet Aussie counterparts. *Otago Daily Times*, 31 January 2024.

[20] Graham, E. (2016). The Lion and the Kangaroo. Lowy Interpreter, 24 May 2016. Available online at: https://www.lowyinstitute.org/publications/lion-kangaroo.

[21] Bassi, J. and Capie, D. (2024). Building an Australia-New Zealand alliance fit for the 21st Century. *ASPI Strategist*, 2 February 2024. Available online at: https://www.aspistrategist.org.au/building-an-australia-new-zealand-alliance-fit-for-the-21st-century/.

IV

SINGAPORE AND NEW ZEALAND: INTERNATIONAL TRADE COOPERATION

Chapter 11

Small-State Diplomacy in Action: The Real Origins of the Trans-Pacific Partnership Agreement (TPP)

Tim Groser

The Trans-Pacific Partnership (TPP) Agreement — now the Comprehensive and Progressive Trans-Pacific Partnership Agreement (CPTPP) — is, by any measure, a central part of the emerging global trade policy framework. To the surprise of many, including the author, it survived the decision of the United States to withdraw after US Trade Representative Mike Froman had signed the Agreement in Auckland in 2015 on behalf of the US government. Today, the CPTPP incorporates 12 economies, including leading G20 economies such as Japan, Mexico, Canada, Australia, and the UK, which is its most recent entrant. Six other economies, most importantly including China, the world's second-largest economy, are now applying for membership. What began between Singapore and New Zealand — a conscious strategic decision on the parts of the two countries to try to incentivise this process of Asia-Pacific regional integration in 1999 — is now clearly a major part of the global geopolitical chessboard.

This chapter is an attempt to explain the early negotiating history of an agreement that has gone through a variety of name changes and speculate, hopefully in a constructive way, on the steps that may follow. The TPP (now CPTPP) has its political roots in a shared New Zealand–Singaporean perception of the role of trade policy, not only in terms of their respective commercial interests but also as a vital element in preserving a broader strategic environment in which small, independent states such as Singapore and New Zealand could flourish.

From the start, the role of the United States was central to the thinking of both countries. More to the point, their decision to begin negotiating a bilateral FTA had almost nothing to do with promoting bilateral trade between Singapore and New Zealand but was explicitly intended as a stepping stone to a wider agreement on economic integration in the Asia-Pacific.

Multilateral or Regional Economic Integration?

The decision of Singapore and New Zealand to initiate this strategy did not reflect any misgivings in pursuing multilateral trade liberalisation. However, a 'preferred' approach to achieving any policy objective is one thing; it is quite another to have an *exclusive* approach that relies entirely on the success of the preferred approach. In the case of New Zealand, this strategy had even been formalised in an extensive discussion paper on trade policy issued by the government in September 1993: *New Zealand Trade Policy: Implementation and Directions: A Multi-Track Approach.* This explicitly laid out the fact that New Zealand would seek to advance the integration of its economy with its trading partners through multilateral, bilateral/plurilateral, and unilateral trade liberalisation — in that order of preference.

Singapore and New Zealand were aware that the integration of trade and investment was increasingly being advanced in regional trade agreements and, prior to initiating this FTA, had the experience of signing FTAs with their most important neighbours. New Zealand had negotiated its first comprehensive FTA with its then largest trading partner, Australia, in the early 1980s. This was more to turbocharge reform of the then highly protected NZ economy than to gain access to the Australian market.[1] Similarly, Singapore had entered into an FTA with its ASEAN neighbours in 1992, less for (narrowly defined) 'trade' reasons than to support the broader political objective of strengthening the cohesion of ASEAN.

Trade and Open Society

By far, the most important example of this relationship between open trade policies and open societies is, of course, the EU. Against the background of three wars involving France and Germany (Prussia in 1870) in less than a century, the last of which morphed into the truly global, catastrophic Second World War, two great Europeans, the Frenchman Jean Monnet and the German Robert Schumann, provided much of the vision for a united Europe. It had a very modest first step — the European Steel and Coal Community. Again, through a variety of name changes and increasingly broad membership, this agreement on steel and coal evolved into the European Union. Yes, there were clear trade and economic objectives behind this move, but the incremental steps towards the EU were driven far more by fundamental political and strategic drivers.

For some four decades after the Second World War, and in contrast to most countries' willingness to entertain regional trade agreements, the United States had focussed overwhelmingly on promoting multilateral trade and investment integration as the sole modality to shape its post-war system. But, in the early 1980s, USTR Bill Brock signalled a major shift in strategic direction by indicating that the United States was open to considering bilateral FTAs. This did not escape the attention of Singapore or New Zealand.

The Emergence of 'The Asian Century'

Over the course of the 1980s, the concept of an integrated Asia-Pacific economic area gained traction. The term 'the Asian Century'

---

[1] See, for example, Groser, T, (2020). The CER negotiations — The real backstory, *Policy Quarterly*, 16(4), https://doi.org/10.26686/pq.v16i4.6615.

was coined. A variety of currents fed into this stream. The first key development was the extraordinary re-birth of the Japanese economy after the disaster of the Second World War. This was followed by the rise of 'The Four Tigers' — the high-growth economies of Singapore, South Korea, Taiwan, and Hong Kong.

The very success of this commercial strategy did, of course, contain the seeds of its own destruction. In time, real wages in, say, South Korea or Taiwan would rise to capture at least some of the productivity gains. This, then, would force their economies to move beyond simple, labour-intensive manufacturing, such as footwear, to more sophisticated models of development.

This pattern of development — dubbed 'the flying geese' theory — would then see footloose capital (exporting companies) 'fly off' to other destinations (Thailand or Indonesia, for example) and spread the development process to a wider net of countries in the region. Over time, the benefits were enormous: much higher life expectancy, mass literacy among the populations made possible only by economic growth, better health outcomes, and many other similar positive social indicators. Equally, along this development pathway, there would be exploitation, poor labour conditions, and many people left behind in entrenched poverty. But, as one expert said recently, a *"rising tide may indeed not raise all boats, but a stagnant pond raises none."*[2]

APEC and the Bogor Goals

Policymakers followed, rather than led, this commercially driven vision of an integrated Asia-Pacific region. In 1989, Prime Minister Bob Hawke of Australia proposed in a formal sense the formation of the Asia-Pacific Economic Cooperation (APEC). In 1994, at the APEC Leaders' Meeting in Indonesia, leaders endorsed the concept of the 'Bogor Goals' — the vision of 'free and open trade and investment in the Asia-Pacific by 2010 (for developed economies) and 2020 (for developing economies)'.

---

[2] Alan Wolff, former WTO Deputy Director, Peterson Institute, 23 May 2023.

The 'Bogor Goals' quickly achieved totemic significance in both academic and official circles. However, a small dissident group of professional negotiators[3] with a great deal of practical experience in negotiation thought otherwise. They were not opposed to the objectives of the Bogor Goals — on the contrary, they were strongly supportive of them — but they simply believed that the proclamation of such sweeping objectives without any attempt to develop a realistic political strategy to achieve it was wishful thinking in the extreme. It has been said that a plan not driven by a vision may frequently turn into a nightmare — a vision without a plan is usually hallucination.

The idea that the United States would somehow remove pockets of high-tariff protection (in, say, textiles, cotton, sugar, or dairy), or China (which had not at that stage 'resumed' its seat at the multilateral table and had very high protective tariffs) would similarly dismantle its protective structures, or Japan would achieve free trade (in, say, rice) *without* a negotiation, marshalling the political force of 'reciprocity', was completely unrealistic. Elaborate attempts were made by intellectuals to explain this away, with the tautology of 'concerted unilateralism' being the most creative.

This impenetrable APEC debate over 'modalities' — a word that no sane person would use in public — was fiercely conducted out of the public eye and beneath the radar screen of political discourse. This was central to the strategy of Singapore and New Zealand in launching what we call the TPP or CPTPP. Both countries were, by the late 1990s, prepared to accept that a sub-APEC FTA would be needed to actualise the vision of an integrated Asia-Pacific economic community as encapsulated in the Bogor Goals. 'Reciprocity' had to be loosely harnessed such that it could start with two small economies establishing an FTA[4] and then expanding its membership, with the United States being the ultimate prize.

---

[3] Including, obviously, the author.

[4] It is worth recalling that neither Singapore nor New Zealand had anything other than trivial tariffs left by the late 1990s, so comprehensive was the liberalisation of their import regimes. The 'reciprocity' in their bilateral FTA was almost completely fictional in a quantitative economic sense — as has been the case for all New Zealand's subsequent FTAs.

But, one other key political element entered that strategic calculation: a shared view of the challenges facing their 'first-best' option — the growing signs, by the late 1990s, of stasis in the WTO. This strengthened the case for Singapore and New Zealand to operationalise their Plan B.

The WTO: Darkening Clouds

A little history needs to be recalled at this point. By any standards, the last comprehensive multilateral negotiation of the WTO, the Uruguay Round, was a great success. That success included fixing a foundational mistake made in 1947 which exempted trade in agriculture from the standard operational disciplines.[5] For New Zealand (and many other countries, including Australia and the United States), the development of operationally effective rules and disciplines over world trade in agriculture was a major additional step forward after literally decades of political failure.

Inevitably, those first steps did not meet the ambitions of some of the most aggressive agriculture exporters. A trade-off was made involving a review of market access in the three areas of services, industrial trade, and agriculture a few years later.

However, as negotiators would quickly discover, a negotiation focussed solely on market access, delinked from the numerous other issues that affect both the conditions of access and which could provide political trade-offs to facilitate market access concessions, was deeply problematic. Therefore, a consensus emerged that an entirely new comprehensive negotiating round would be required. With a WTO ministerial meeting coming up in Seattle, this would be called 'the Seattle Round': The author still has in cold storage the celebratory umbrella he received in Seattle on arrival,

---

[5] For technicians, this refers to the prohibition of quantitative market access restrictions, and its exception for agriculture in Article XI:2 (c), and the similar prohibition on export subsidies, and its exception for agriculture (the footnote to Article XVI:4 of the General Agreement).

with the words 'Seattle Round' on it; it has never been opened.[6] The 'Seattle Round' died stillborn.

TPP: The Discussion Paper that Launched the Process

Against this complicated strategic background, the NZ government in the 1990s had been very active in exploring alternatives in the form of various FTAs with different countries, including Singapore.[7] The then Singaporean Minister of Trade (and later Foreign Minister), George Yeo, paid a visit to New Zealand and was asked by the then NZ Minister of Trade, Dr Lockwood Smith, to consider the possibility of an FTA. The author of this paper, as the Principal Economic Adviser to the NZ Minister, was invited to write a discussion paper outlining the strategy. That paper was sent off to George Yeo under the guise of a letter from his NZ Ministerial counterpart.

That paper has never been published.[8] Essentially, the paper began by describing the strategic outlook that both small economies faced in those uncertain times:

- It voiced scepticism that the forthcoming meeting in Seattle would succeed in launching a new, coehensive round of multilateral trade negotiations — although both Singapore and New Zealand would do whatever they could to achieve such a

---

[6] This is not the place to properly analyse the fiasco that occurred in Seattle. It is simply sufficient to recall the phrase that emerged to describe the street riots that closed the Conference — 'the Battle at Seattle'. This was not the first manifestation of anti-globalisation riots: G7 and other major international meetings had been similarly disrupted. For the United States, it illustrated even then how the split in the Democratic Party on trade, between centrists such as President Clinton and his then USTR, Charlene Barshefsky, and the 'Progressives' on their political left, posed an acute danger to US leadership on trade. As the 2016 presidential election unfolded and both candidates walked back from the TPP (which the Obama Administration had signed in Auckland in December 2015), the problem remained.

[7] As the then Principal Economic Adviser to the NZ Ministry of Foreign Affairs and Trade, this was the author's principal responsibility.

[8] The author would be happy to send a copy to any researcher interested.

result. The paper noted the deep-rooted problems within the US Democratic Party over trade, the lack of a fast-track authority, and, more generally, what the paper called "...*the erosion of the domestic consensus that 'trade is a good thing' for the US.*"[9]

- It expressed concern that the APEC was losing momentum in advancing its key economic objective of an integrated Asia-Pacific community and expressed deep scepticism, though not widely shared initially, that the Bogor Goals would, by themselves, drive the process, particularly if the WTO failed to launch a new negotiating round.

- The paper noted the extraordinary proliferation in the 1990s of regional trade agreements, many of which 'lacked strategic coherence.'

Against that summary of the strategic analysis, the paper specifically proposed a sub-APEC FTA, using a phrase that already had some political currency — P5, or Pacific Five.

There was, therefore, nothing particularly original about the proposal: There had been numerous, highly generalised discussions of such a sub-APEC FTA. What matters in political life, however, is not simply to talk about 'moving forward', but to have a plan, based on realpolitik, not wishful thinking, to realise it.

The geometry of the 'Pacific Five' was variable, but it was always centred on the United States. The NZ paper noted the following: "*...it has proved very difficult to advance the idea beyond positive, but highly generalised, discussions... [This] is a reflection of a deeper malaise in the world's leading economy. If we wait for the US to exercise leadership here, we may be waiting a long time. ...The question arises therefore as to whether Singapore and NZ — the economies which are the least reluctant to push forward with the P5 agenda .... could do something to give the idea traction?*"

---

[9]Almost a quarter of a century on, one could use, somewhat bitterly, the French phrase, '*rien n'a changé au fil des années*'.

From New Zealand's point of view, the reaction of the Singaporean government to the discussion paper was decisive. The author, on his way back from chairing a WTO Dispute Settlement Panel, was asked to travel to Singapore. Whisked unexpectedly into the Minister's (George Yeo) office on arrival, the author was delivered a bombshell. The Singaporean Prime Minister had read the NZ paper, instructed his entire cabinet to read it, and they had all agreed to the NZ proposal.

When two countries with virtually no trade barriers and sharing an all-but-identical strategic perspective begin a negotiation, one should expect a very smooth process. And so it was, but it took time to integrate a number of new directions in trade policy, such as a Mutual Recognition Agreement, as opposed to regulatory harmonisation provisions (which rarely work in practice). It was not long before the author had the opportunity to expand the process beyond Singapore and New Zealand. At the APEC Leaders' Meeting in Auckland in September 1999, the author raised the possibility of Chile joining the initiative after NZ and Singapore had concluded their bilateral FTA. The two key Chilean officials, Alejandro Jara and Ricardo Lagos Jnr,[10] expressed immediate interest.

The only threat to this first step towards the TPP came out of (far) left field — literally. Near the very end of the negotiation, there was a change of government in New Zealand and Helen Clark became Prime Minister. There had been intense opposition to the FTA with Singapore from the far left of the NZ political spectrum. The NZ Labour Party, the centre-left party of New Zealand, has a long and credible track record of supporting open trade policies, and the new Prime Minister, Helen Clark, was no exception. She faced down the opposition well to the political left of mainstream Labour Party thinking.

---

[10] Ricardo Lagos Jnr, the son of the former Chilean President, later become President of the Chilean Senate, but at that stage was a senior Chilean economic official. Alejandro Jara would later become a Deputy Director General of the WTO.

TPP: Subsequent Developments

A comprehensive analysis of the establishment of the TPP (CPTPP) awaits a future professional researcher with access to all the official documents. The expansion of the Singapore/NZ initiative into the P4 (Pacific Four, given Australia's unwillingness to participate until the US came on board) and then into the TPP took years and the effort of many people from many countries. For the author, however, there are a few distinctive developments that are worth a brief mention.

The first was the decision of the Obama Administration to mount a friendly takeover of the P4 initiative in 2010 — precisely what Singapore and NZ had tried to achieve a decade earlier as the whole point of their bilateral strategy. The decision of President Obama followed two years of intensive discussions by the author (then Trade Minister, having subsequently gone into politics) and the NZ team of negotiators with USTR Ron Kirk, Mike Froman, President Obama's Deputy National Security Adviser for Economic Affairs (subsequently USTR), and their teams.

The decision of the US in 2010 to join the P4 caused others to request to join the organisation — Canada, Mexico, Australia, Malaysia, Peru, and Vietnam. Canada and Mexico, one could say, almost had no choice. The three North American economies of Canada, the United States, and Mexico are so integrated with each other, originally through NAFTA[11] as well as the dictates of human and physical geography, that Canada and Mexico had to follow the US. The P4 was re-named the 'Trans-Pacific Partnership' Negotiation.

Japan's decision to join, under the leadership of Prime Minister Abe, was also considered extremely important. This was a courageous decision. For one thing, it required confronting the deep resistance in Japan to agricultural liberalisation. It also required the unification of the Japanese governmental system on

---

[11] NAFTA — denounced by President Trump as "*the worst trade agreement ever*" — has been replaced by the USMCA, the best trade agreement ever negotiated. American experts estimate that around 85% of the two agreements are identical.

trade — a single voice at a political level instead of separate presentations by three ministries.[12] Prime Minister Abe appointed a single minister, Akira Amare, to unify Japan's position — something Amare-san did outstandingly well.[13]

The withdrawal of the United States by President Trump is etched in the author's mind. The author had been appointed Ambassador to the United States by Prime Minister John Key and was on the floor of Congress as one of three guests of Devin Nunes, then Chair of the House Intelligence Committee. The other guests were the Australian Ambassador to the US, Joe Hockey (former Finance Minister), and the Japanese Ambassador to the US, Ken Sasae. In an unusually frank speech in public, Ambassador Sasae had stated the following (prior to the actual US Presidential Election but when both candidates, Trump and Clinton, were walking the US back from the TPP): "*If a book on the decline of American influence in the Asia Pacific is ever written — and I hope it never is — its first chapter will be an account of the withdrawal of the US from TPP.*"

In light of the withdrawal of the US from the TPP, I would argue that Ambassador Sasae's deeply uncomfortable observation remains on the table, *not* with respect to security or military matters, where the United States leadership remains indispensable to the region's stability, but with respect to influencing economic integration.

A 'renegotiation' of a small number of chapters of the TPP text, that had been signed by USTR Mike Froman in Auckland, was then conducted with the US absent. A new name (Comprehensive and Progressive TPP, or CPTPP) was coined to facilitate its political management by the pro-trade, centre-left Prime Ministers of Canada and New Zealand, respectively, Justin Trudeau and Jacinda Ardern. Et voilà! Somehow, all those years of work by

---

[12] The Foreign Ministry (*Gaimusho*), the Industry Ministry (*MITI*), and the Agriculture Ministry (*Norinsho*).

[13] Regrettably, this highly effective and highly personable Japanese minister fell victim to one of those impenetrable Japanese political 'scandals' that no *gaijin* can ever hope to comprehend.

Singapore and New Zealand — along, subsequently, with the efforts of hundreds of highly motivated officials and ministers from the other economies — paid off.

The Future?

We shall have to wait and see what the future holds. But, it is possible to identify a few of the major geopolitical issues ahead of this important initiative.

First, the strategic outlook on trade has deteriorated markedly since, say, 2015. There are many outstanding academic analyses charting the shift from the period of 'hyper-globalisation' (roughly 1990–2010) to today's world of 'fragmented globalisation'. It is not the purpose of this chapter to retrace the same ground. Most importantly, the United States appears to have walked away — at least for the time being — from one of the greatest contributions the American people and the American political system have made to the world since 1945: political leadership on trade — a vital component of the 'liberal[14] world order'.

As the conservative intellectual Robert Kagan put it, "*Less than 80 years ago, liberalism outside a few centres of power, was on its death bed...The dramatic change of course after 1945 was not due to some sudden triumph of our better angels or embrace of Enlightenment principles that had been around for centuries. Nor was it the natural unfolding of Universal History in the direction of liberalism. Liberal ideas triumphed because for the first time, they had power behind them: the United States.*"[15]

The United States may have lost the political appetite to engage in progressive trade liberalisation, but its most important partners have not. This, intriguingly, includes the UK. The post-Brexit decision of the British Government to join the CPTPP, on the back of concluding two world-class FTAs with Australia and New Zealand, is one of those rare occasions where it may be justifiable to employ the dreadful cliché — 'a game-changer'. It is a game-changer not

---

[14] 'Liberal' in the European, not domestic American, sense.

[15] Kagan, R. (2018). *The Jungle Grows Back.*

so much because the world's fifth-largest economy has joined, adding further economic heft to the initiative, but because it has utterly changed the nature of the agreement.

The TPP is no longer an Asia-Pacific (or Indo-Pacific) *regional* agreement. It is, at least in principle, the nucleus of some new potential global trade rules. The other new applicants — Ukraine (intriguing from a political, not economic, perspective), Costa Rica, Ecuador, Chinese Taipei, and Uruguay — will add to that dimension, and it seems likely that South Korea and Thailand will at some stage put in applications.

But, above all, the singular development that extends the 'TPP story' into a different dimension is China's application to join. The implications of this are truly global. Moreover, among the most intriguing strategic questions is what the response of the United States will be if the Chinese application gathers momentum: Ignore it? Put massive pressure on the CPTPP participants to block China?[16] Develop the IPEF into a serious alternative that would, if done seriously, potentially make the TPP redundant, using the playbook of converting the NAFTA into the USMCA?[17] Many CPTPP participants, including the author, would welcome the final option. There is, however, currently no political base for this to take place in Washington.

One or two things are clear. First, at the macro-political level, if China finally does join the CPTPP, after what will be a long process of review and negotiation, it will be a simultaneous decision to admit at the same time Chinese Taipei. Second, China is deadly serious about its application. It is a major mistake to believe it will never happen because 'China could never live with the disciplines, particularly over SOEs (State Owned Enterprises)'. Many Chinese

---

[16] That would at the least be breaking new ground: you leave a 'club' because it is 'the worst club ever' (Trump); but trying to blackball aspiring new members? Interesting.

[17] This attracted overwhelming bipartisan political support in the House — 385 in favour, 41 against. The anti-trade forces are totally dominant today, but this is not the end of the matter. The strong pro-Americans among us always recall Churchill's quip that 'the Americans can always be relied upon to do the right thing, after they have exhausted the alternatives' (there are variants of this, though nobody knows if Churchill was joking when he said it).

officials want to join the CPTPP precisely to submit their inefficient SOEs to those disciplines.

Finally, whatever the future of this initiative, it will be influenced by what happens to the WTO — or more to the point, what may not happen. Again, this is beyond the scope of this chapter. What is clear is that the glacial process of the WTO in moving forward on any issue in the past 30 years since the WTO came into effect leaves increasingly large 'gaps' in the framework of global rules.

This is not some minor intellectual point. The absence of effective global rules on trade in digital commerce is one of the obvious lacunae. Once again, Singapore and New Zealand have stepped up to the mark and established the 'DEPA' (Digital Economy Partnership Agreement). Chile and Korea more recently joined. Canada, Costa Rica, Peru, and China have applied to join. There would not be a single Singaporean or New Zealand official or minister with an interest in digital trade who would not prefer to be doing this in the WTO in Geneva; but, at least for the foreseeable future, this is politically beyond reach. It is not just nature that abhors a vacuum — it also applies to trade policy at the strategic level.

Leaving aside the 'mother of all (TPP) issues' — will China join? — it is an intriguing question as to whether an informal dialogue might at some stage develop between the EU and CPTPP, given the strong and shared values of most of the participants. The EU, for all its difficulties in establishing internal consensus, has today become the most important global power upholding the '*acqui*'[18] of the WTO. If we cannot move forward decisively in the WTO (and without the full commitment of the US, we will not), might it be possible to develop new rules together? The sheer weight of the 26 European economies plus up to 18 CPTPP economies (including, possibly, China) suggests that this is more than an academic question.

---

[18] This French term is universally used by professional trade negotiators to describe the entire 'set' of agreements, understandings, and commitments achieved in the past. It means, literally in English, 'acquired'.

This brief negotiating history of the CPTPP, if it indicates anything, points to a dynamic process of countries/economies committed to economic integration and collectively prepared to engage in creative negotiation. It is clear that the journey begun by Singapore and New Zealand in 1999 is not over.[19]

There can be no question that the strategy agreed upon by Singapore and New Zealand in 1999 has been a spectacular political and economic success — even if the pathway has altered many times in many unexpected ways. It does raise a broader question about how small states can work together effectively.

In an outstanding paper[20] written 10 years ago by Vangelis Vitalis, then New Zealand Ambassador to the EU and NATO and now NZ Chief Trade Negotiator, he raised a series of important questions about the foreign policy of small states, using the *History of the Peloponnesian Wars*, written by the great Athenian general and historian, Thucydides, as its framework.

The most recent exploration of the relevance of this ancient yet 'modern' analysis is, of course, the so-called 'Thucydides Trap', brought to prominence by Professor Allison of Harvard University, among the most distinguished American political scientists.

The primary focus of Thucydides' great work, of course, is the competition between the great powers of the period and the distressing pattern of conflict brought about by historical situations where the (then) hegemonic 'status-quo' power (Sparta) is challenged by the 'rising power' (Athens). Summarised brutally and simplistically, it is about the historical tendency of the existing hegemonic power to initiate war with the rising power, simply because it fears that 'war is inevitable' so it is better to fight with their rival now than wait until they become more powerful.

Essentially, this was the decision of the Sparta-led Peloponnesian League in confronting the rise of the Athenian Empire. It involved —

---

[19] Mark Twain, *"History may not Repeat itself, but it does Rhyme."*

[20] *Small Advanced Economies and Foreign Policy: Insights from Thucydides and the Peloponnesian War'*, paper prepared for the Conference of Advanced Small Economies, Copenhagen, November 2013.

in disturbing echoes of today — numerous alliances and 'understandings' with smaller city-states (there were more than 100; the UN today has a little over 200 members). Obviously, projecting 2,500 years from the time it was written, today, this is about China and the United States. Are they, too, destined for war? Is the Island of Taiwan the trigger, as was the attack on the Island of Corcyra for the devastating Great Power conflict 2.5 millennia ago?[21]

As Vitalis points out, *"...Small States need to be active and creative in their interactions with other larger countries including (a) alignment or integration with larger partners or blocs to project influence; (b) develop 'bespoke' arrangements as force multipliers to influence and shape decision making by the major power (c) [promote] their value proposition ... (d) concentrate their resources on issues and areas that matter to their vital national interests."*

Without labouring the point, there is every reason to believe that Singapore and New Zealand, in their action to initiate what we now call the CPTPP, were acting, either consciously or intuitively, as their counterparts in the small city-states had attempted to do during the Peloponnesian Wars.

New Zealand and Singapore have been extraordinarily creative and effective in using small-state diplomatic tools. Yet, it will come to nothing if China and the United States cannot develop a *modus vivendi*. In expressing this view, the author can visualise, maybe even hear, that quintessential realist, Lee Kuan Yew (whom he met several times while accompanying two New Zealand Prime Ministers as their adviser), nodding in agreement from his grave.

---

[21] Trade sanctions were also involved.

Chapter 12

Commentary on Tim Groser's Essay on the TPP

George Yeo

Singapore and New Zealand are kindred spirits. Being small, we survive by clinical analysis of environmental changes and adjusting to them. Having a smaller margin of manoeuvre, we have to be fleet-footed and agile. We cannot afford to be subjective or have an inflated notion of our own importance to the world. When NZ Trade Minister Lockwood Smith suggested an FTA with Singapore in 1999, I was intrigued and asked for a short paper. Tim wrote that paper. It was so well written that I thought I should simply attach it as an annex to the memorandum I tabled to the Singapore Cabinet that recommended the launch of negotiations with NZ. It was a toy agreement, but one which was fully functioning. It became the basic model for many FTAs that both countries negotiated in subsequent years, including with giant economies like the US and China. These FTAs have served us well, especially with the lack of progress in the WTO.

The idea of a TPP as a cross-regional grouping had earlier antecedents. Recognising that the time was right, both countries, together with Chile, agreed to launch negotiations for an FTA with higher standards that anticipated the growing importance of services, standards, and intellectual property in global trade. This was done in 2005. Singapore brought in Brunei as the fourth economy. The TPP would give economic substance to APEC. Despite Indonesia being a developing economy, President Suharto, during the APEC Economic Leaders Meeting in 1994, proposed the Bogor Declaration which envisaged a free and open Pacific for trade and investment. It was blue-sky thinking but an important collective vision. The Bogor Goals led to the proposal for a Free Trade Area of the Asia-Pacific in the long term. The TPP would provide stepping stones to that common future.

The 90s were a halcyon period when we were marching with linked arms to a bright future of depoliticised trade, cross-border investment, and standardisation. Looking back, that period was the final phase of an American peace which was uncontested after the collapse of the Berlin Wall in 1989. China benefited much from that American peace. It joined APEC in 1992. It acceded to the WTO in November 2001. The failure of the Seattle WTO meeting in 1999, however, foreshadowed a great turning point in world history. Although not the main reason for the failure, protests by a wide range of NGOs in Seattle signalled growing opposition to globalisation. Although the Doha Development Agenda was successfully launched in 2001, it got nowhere. As China's economy grew by double digits every year, it became increasingly seen by the US as a challenge to US dominance of the global system. Around 2010, the US decided to 'pivot East' to contain China. The Global Financial Crisis did bring the US and China briefly together within the framework of the G20. China spent large sums to keep up with global demand, which caused huge distortions in its domestic economy. When the crisis subsided, negative US sentiment towards China resurfaced. The US joined the TPP and, to the chagrin of Tim, myself, and others, turned it effectively into an anti-China grouping.

As Tim pointed out in his recollections, it was ironic that in the run-up to the 2020 Presidential Elections, both Hillary Clinton and Donald Trump turned against the TPP. It was left to Japanese PM Abe Shinzo to save it through the CPTPP. Now, in a further irony, it is China that wants to join. We now live in a great transition from an American peace to a dynamic multipolar world where trade and investments are often politicised in strategic sectors. Trade agreements have to adjust to changing geopolitical realities. There is a risk that worsening conflict between the US and China could lead to proxy wars. Singapore and New Zealand should always be on the side of peace. Each exercises a degree of influence in its own circle — Singapore in ASEAN and New Zealand in the region and in the Anglosphere. Neither wants to see a clash between the US and China. Neither wants the world divided into blocs. In a multipolar world, it is entirely possible for the poles to be linked dynamically, more or less peacefully, and for the US to remain *primus inter pares* for a long time even when China's economy overtakes it.

Tim's essay points out the dangers and possible solutions. As always, he has a keen sense of trends and the future.

Aotearoa (New Zealand) from space January 2015. The curvature of the Earth is clearly visible at the top of the picture marked by a vanishingly thin layer of atmosphere. The part of the atmosphere that supports all life on Earth is less than 10 km thick. *Courtesy of NASA. Image supplied by NASA as part of a programme to help astronauts take pictures of the Earth that are of greatest value to scientists and the public making them freely available on the internet.*

View of Singapore. Image captured on 10 May 2021, by MSI instrument, aboard ESA's Sentinel 2A and 2B satellites. We acknowledge the use of imagery from the NASA Worldview application (https://worldview. earthdata.nasa.gov/), part of the NASA Earth Observing System Data and Information System (EOSDIS).

New Zealand PM Walter Nash calls on Singapore PM Lee Kuan Yew on 8 April 1960, in what was a defining visit in the New Zealand - Singapore Relationship. *Courtesy of National Archives of Singapore.*

Prime Minister Lee Kuan Yew and Mrs Lee welcoming New Zealand Prime Minister Keith Holyoake and his wife, Norma, at the Paya Lebar International Airport, 9.4.1964. *Ministry of Information and the Arts Collection, Wellington, New Zealand, Courtesy of National Archives of Singapore.*

CONFIDENTIAL

DEPARTMENT OF EXTERNAL AFFAIRS

CONFIDENTIAL 10 AUGUST 1965
FROM WELLINGTON
TO SINGAPORE 413
RPTD KUALA LUMPUR 539 Immediate
LONDON 2372 "
CANBERRA 721 "
WASHINGTON 574 Priority
NEW YORK P.R. 294 "

— IMMEDIATE —

INDEPENDENCE OF SINGAPORE

Please pass the following message to Lee Kuan Yew from the Prime Minister.

"I have received your message and the texts of the Proclamations relating to the separation of Singapore from Malaysia as an independent and sovereign state with effect from 9 August.

You will know from our discussions that New Zealand strongly supported the concept of a Malaysia established in accordance with the wishes of its peoples. I deeply regret the step that the Malaysian and Singapore Governments have felt it necessary to take. Nevertheless, we accept the decision freely arrived at by the two Governments and will continue to cooperate with them for the peace and stability of Malaysia and Singapore and of the area as a whole.

The New Zealand Government recognises Singapore as an independent and sovereign state.

I warmly welcome your wish that Singapore should remain within the framework of the Commonwealth of Nations. For its part the New Zealand Government would wholeheartedly support this.

It is our desire to maintain diplomatic relations with Singapore and I trust that in due course your Government will see its way clear to accrediting a representative of Singapore to New Zealand.

It is, as you know, the unchanging policy of the New Zealand Government and people to have the friendliest relations with the peoples of the South East Asian area. This is particularly true of the people of Singapore and Malaysia with whom for many years we have had the very closest association. It is in that spirit that the New Zealand Government will puruse its relations with Singapore.

May I offer you and your colleagues in the Government my warmest good wishes for the future."

EXTERNAL

(S. 18326)

Prime Minister
Secretary of External Affairs
Secretary of Defence

REGISTERED

SENT: 0130z, 10 August 1965

CONFIDENTIAL

40,000/6/64—88676 W

PM Holyoake's letter to PM Lee recognising Singapore's independence on 10 August 1965. *Courtesy of Archives New Zealand; ID: R20769149.*

Lee Kuan Yew, PM of Singapore with Rt. Hon. W.E. Rowling during his official visit to New Zealand in April 1975. *Courtesy of Wellington repository; ID: R26278614.*

Prime Minister of New Zealand Helen Clark paying a Courtesy Call on Prime Minister Goh Chok Tong at the Istana; 27.04.2000. *Ministry of Information and the Arts Collection, Wellington, New Zealand, Courtesy of National Archives of Singapore.*

Signing of Agreement between New Zealand and Singapore on a closer Economic Partnership (ANZSCEP) by the Right Honourable Prime Minister of New Zealand Helen Clark and Prime Minister Goh Chok Tong at the Four Seasons Hotel, Singapore, 14.11.2000. *Ministry of Information and the Arts Collection, Wellington, New Zealand, Courtesy of National Archives of Singapore.*

Prime Minister Lee Hsien Loong and New Zealand Prime Minister Jacinda Ardern witness the signing of Joint Declaration, upgraded Agreement on Closer Economic Partnership and four Memoranda of Understanding (MOU) between Singapore and New Zealand at the Istana, Singapore, May 2019. *Courtesy of Ministry of Communications and Information Collection, Wellington, New Zealand, Courtesy of National Archives of Singapore.*

Ceremonial welcome for Prime Minister of New Zealand Jacinda Ardern at the Istana. Pictured: Prime Minister of Singapore Lee Hsien Loong and Prime Minister of New Zealand Jacinda Ardern. *Ministry of Communications and Information Collection, Wellington, New Zealand, Courtesy of National Archives of Singapore.*

Mr Lawrence Wong, then-Deputy Minister of Singapore with New Zealand Prime Minister Christopher Luxon on his visit to Singapore in April 2024. *Courtesy of Ministry of Communications and Information, Singapore.*

Prime Minister and Minister for Finance Lawrence Wong at a meeting with the Pacific Ministers attending the 3rd Singapore-Pacific High-Level Visit at the Istana on 21 May 2024. *Courtesy of Ministry of Communications and Information, Singapore.*

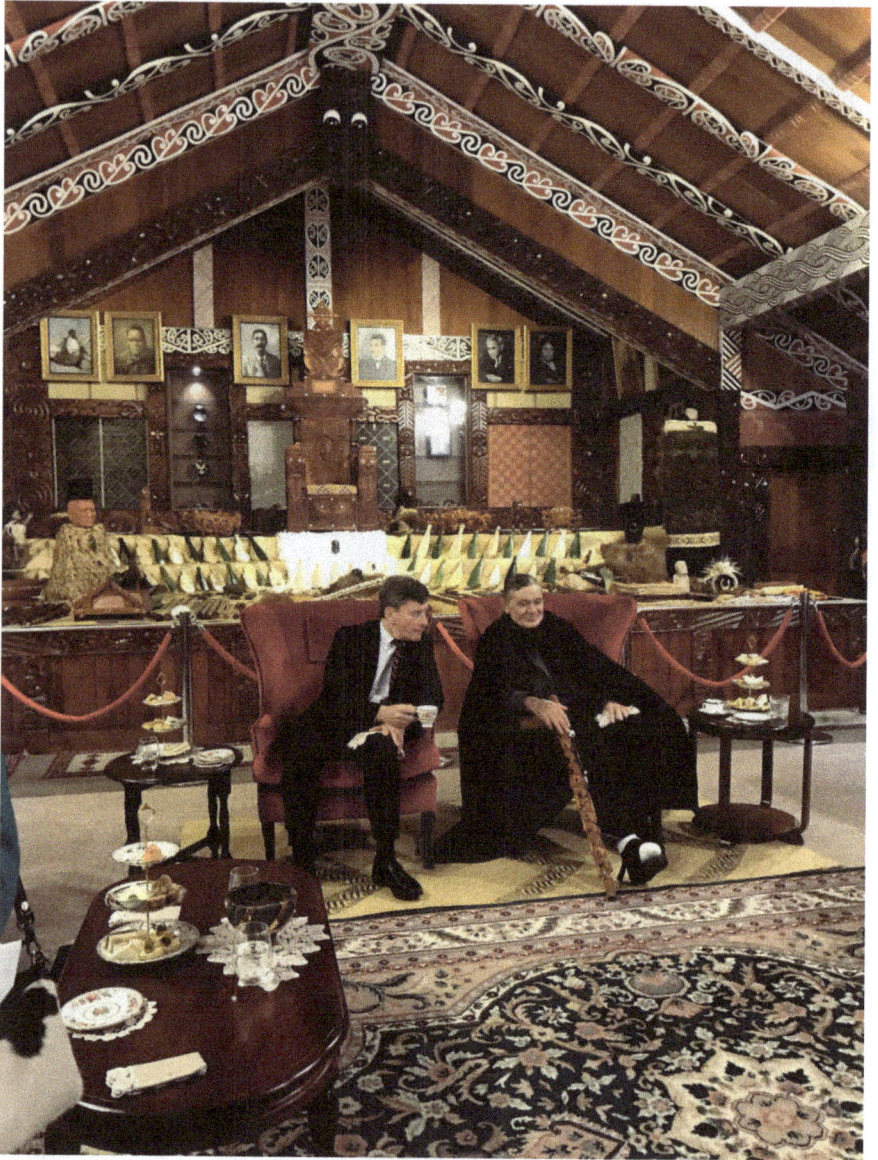

Former New Zealand Minister of Treaty of Waitangi Negotiations, Minister of Culture and Heritage and Attorney-General, Hon Christopher Finlayson KC, during a visit to Māori King, Kīngi Tūheitia. *Courtesy of Hon. Christopher Finlayson KC.*

A southerly storm approaching Baring Head atmospheric monitoring station, New Zealand, July 2023. *Courtesy of Dave Lowe.*

Mayon Volcano, southern part of Luzon, Philippines. Benoit Taisne, Earth Observatory of Singapore.

Pristine Waikawau Bay, Coromandel Peninsula, New Zealand. *Courtesy of Raewyn Peart.*

Richard Taylor sculpts William, one of the Cave Trolls from *The Hobbit. Courtesy of Weta Workshop, Wellington.*

Richard Taylor (right) and Rob Gillies standing with a Dwarven scale double actor during the filming of The Hobbit. *Courtesy of Weta Workshop, Wellington.*

Outdoor evening performance at the Asian Civilisations Museum. *Courtesy of Asian Civilisations Museum.*

New Zealand Museum Te Papa, with external Hirangi banner, 2022. *Courtesy of Jax Myers.*

"The Glory Hoes Present: The Rocky Horror Picture Show" at The Projector. *Courtesy of Becca D'Bus.*

Light to Night Singapore Festival. *Courtesy of Anne-Marie Schleich.*

V

ECONOMIC CHALLENGES AND BUSINESS COOPERATION

Chapter 13

Economic Challenges for Singapore in a Destabilised World

Manu Bhaskaran

Introduction

In this chapter, we assess how Singapore is positioned in a turbulent global setting. After a long period of impressive economic performance, the natural question is whether Singapore can sustain that record. In this regard, we first look at the global environment that Singapore operates in so as to identify the potential pitfalls as well as the opportunities there that Singapore has to prepare for. We then focus on how Singapore's ability to adjust and adapt to such developments has changed and assess the underlying factors that shaped that ability.

Singapore's sustained economic successes have allowed it to emerge as a global centre for commerce, finance, and advanced manufacturing. However, the global and domestic environments have evolved, presenting a multitude of challenges. Domestically, demographic shifts such as an ageing population and low birth rates amplify the existing concerns of low productivity. Rising and almost relentless cost pressures could further impede competitiveness, and escalating geopolitical tensions pose threats to Singapore's small and open economy.

There is no question that Singapore continues to possess robust fundamentals across key areas. But, it has not got everything right. There are emerging weaknesses that pose formidable hurdles. Lagging productivity, together with a dearth of innovation among local firms, stands out as a critical concern. The dwindling presence of local companies compounds the challenge, as heavy reliance on multinational corporations becomes precarious, given their mobility. Striking a balance by nurturing local enterprises, despite cost-related impediments, emerges as a crucial imperative for sustainable economic resilience in Singapore's future trajectory.[1]

Singapore Has Done Well But Now Faces Numerous Domestic and External Challenges

Singapore has delivered a strong economic performance over time

Singapore stands out among economies, having achieved a rare combination of high growth, internal price stability, and a robust external position. It has emerged as a pre-eminent hub in the Asia-Pacific region by continuously evolving. It learnt to overcome the constraints of its small size and lack of scale economies through diversification and free trade. All this enabled it to transition from labour-intensive industries in the 1960s to higher-value manufacturing and capital-intensive sectors in the subsequent decades.

Notably, Singapore has maintained low inflation levels over the past 35 years, averaging 2% per annum from 1981 to 2015. This success is attributed to its exchange rate-centred monetary policy, which has effectively subdued inflation even during economic shocks. The country's strong reserves and prudent fiscal policies contribute to fiscal sustainability.

---

[1] The content in this chapter incorporates material directly sourced from 'Getting Singapore in shape: Economic challenges and how to meet them' authored by Manu Bhaskaran in June 2018.

SG: Gross Domestic Product (2015p)

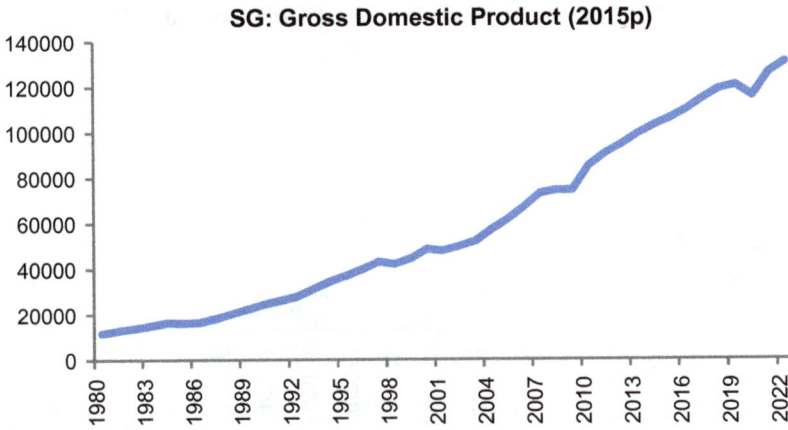

Figure 1.   Singapore's GDP on an upward trajectory.

Source: MTI, OECD.

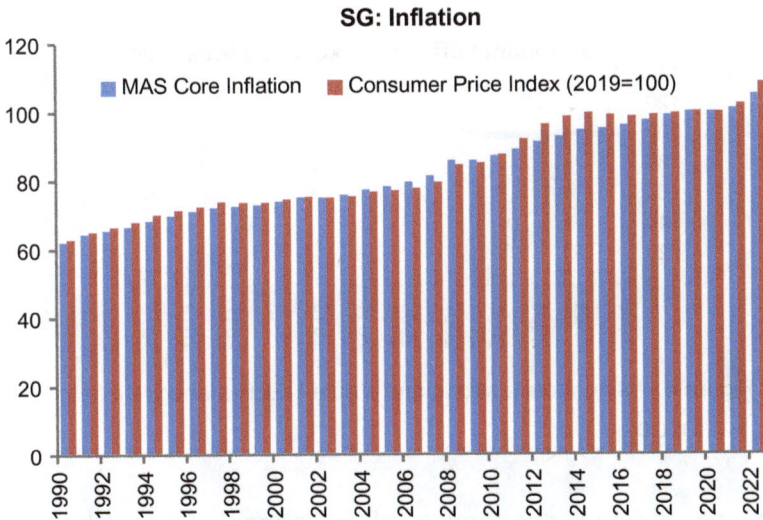

SG: Inflation

Figure 2.   Inflation rose over the years, but is stable.

Source: MTI, OECD.

Several Factors Contribute to Singapore's Economic Prowess

1. *Strategic Location*: Positioned at the southern tip of the Malay Peninsula, Singapore serves as a global hub with direct access

SG: Current Account Balance (% of Nominal GDP)

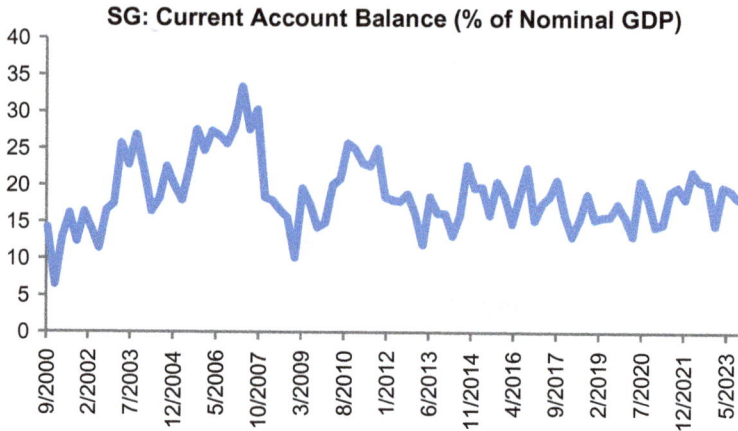

Figure 3.   Strong external position.

Source: MTI, OECD.

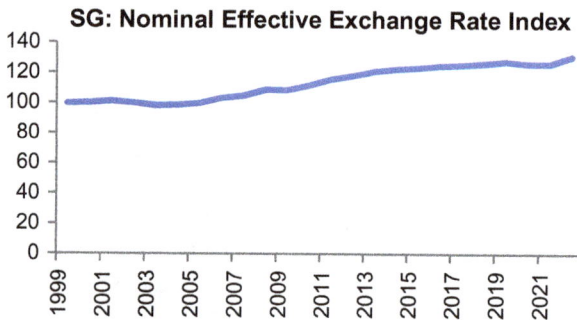

SG: Nominal Effective Exchange Rate Index

Figure 4.   Singapore's strong and stable NEER manages inflation.

Source: MTI, OECD.

to the thriving economies of Southeast Asia, China, and beyond. More than 25 Free Trade Agreements (FTAs) further enhance its market access.

2. *Governance Excellence*: Singapore boasts excellent governance and meticulous planning, resulting in top-notch infrastructure, a favourable regulatory environment, a robust rule of law, and strong economic institutions. This reliability makes it a trusted destination for investors.

Selected Asian Economies: Governance

━━ Singapore   ━━ Hong Kong   ━━━ Japan   ━━ South Korea   ━━ Malaysia

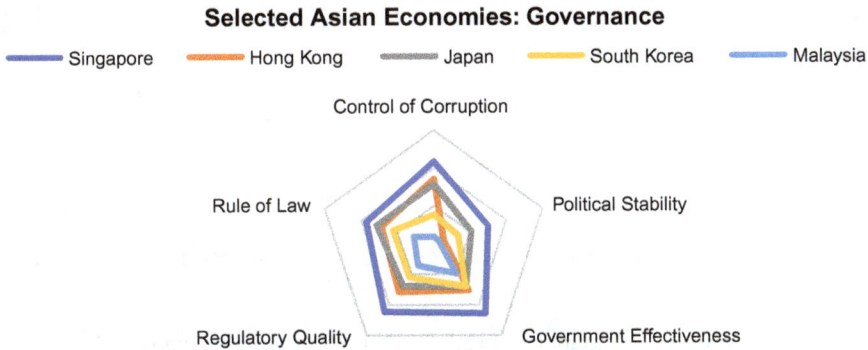

Figure 5.   Singapore's strong governance makes it attractive.

Source: Data from the Global Economy compiled by Centennial Asia Advisors.

3. *Global Opportunities*: These factors have enabled Singapore to leverage global tailwinds, such as globalisation and China's remarkable economic growth, to its advantage.

Having attained one of the highest per capita incomes globally, Singapore finds itself approaching the economic frontier, beyond which it will need to adapt its economic model. The shifting global landscape and evolving domestic circumstances present mounting challenges for the nation. The subsequent sections explore these challenges in greater depth.

An ageing population combined with inadequate productivity growth is a key challenge

Singapore grapples with the challenge of sluggish economic growth attributed to factors such as an ageing population, work-force stagnation, and declining productivity. The nation's fertility rate has undergone a prolonged decrease, falling from 5.76 in 1960 to 1.82 in 1980, and further diminishing to 1.60 in 2000. Despite proactive government measures to encourage childbirth, the fertility rate has continued its downward trend, reaching a mere 1.04 in 2022. Simultaneously, Singapore is experiencing a rapid ageing of its population. In 2010, approximately 1 in 10 Singaporeans were aged 65 and above; a decade later, in 2020, this ratio increased to

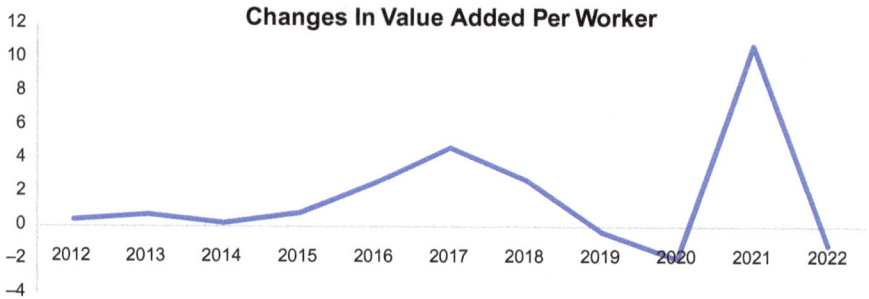

Figure 6.   Singapore's productivity growth remains weak.

Source: SingStat.

about 1 in 6. Projections for 2030 indicate a substantial rise, with almost 1 in 4 Singaporeans expected to be over 65.

The deceleration of growth in the resident workforce exacerbates these demographic challenges. From contributing 4.5% during 1970–1980, the workforce's growth contribution declined to 2.1% in 2000–2010, projecting a further decrease to 0.7% in 2010–2020 and a mere 0.1% in 2020–2030, as outlined in the 2013 Population White Paper.[2] This trajectory may even turn negative if low fertility rates persist alongside more stringent immigration guidelines.

Compounding these demographic hurdles is the failure of productivity growth to offset the deceleration in workforce expansion. Figure 6 illustrates the weak productivity growth consistent through the past decade, compounding the challenges faced by Singapore in maintaining economic momentum.

Global bifurcation limits external-oriented growth opportunities

Singapore's small, open economy flourished during an era of rapid globalisation. This produced flows of goods, services, capital, people,

___

[2] National Population and Talent Division, Prime Minister's Office (2013). A Sustainable Population for a Dynamic Singapore: Population White Paper (Singapore Government, January 2013). https://www.strategygroup.gov.sg/docs/default-source/Population/population-whitepaper.pdf.

and information which sustained Singapore's global hub. Now, however, rising geopolitical tensions, especially between the US and China, threaten to split the world economy into separate spheres, which could drastically slow or reverse these flows. Add in resurgent nationalism, which has led to greater protectionism and an increased focus on national economic security and inward-looking policies, and Singapore has to worry that the synergies from the free flows of trade and capital may no longer suffice to ensure its continued dynamism.

For a small and open economy like Singapore, such geopolitical shifts result in slower growth due to reduced trade and investment opportunities, impacting the country through diminished channels of economic interaction. It is unlikely for globalisation to come to a standstill, but there could be a scenario where the pace of global economic activity decelerates. Such a slowdown is likely to spill over into Singapore, affecting its economic activity in the process.

High costs also weigh on Singapore's competitiveness

Singapore confronts another formidable challenge in the form of soaring costs, particularly for businesses. The 2023 Benefits Trends Survey underscores the pervasive anxieties among organisations, with 55% citing escalating costs as a primary determinant influencing their benefits strategies.[3] This issue extends beyond the macro level, as businesses grapple with an array of cost pressures.

The survey reveals that a quarter of respondents have experienced a substantial 10–20% surge in office rental costs, while 20% have contended with an even more pronounced increase of 20–30%. Notably, this marks the first instance in the past decade where companies are signalling their preparedness to entertain the prospect of relocating from Singapore should the upward trajectory

---

[3] Wtw (2023). Benefits Trends Survey (Wtw, 2023). https://www.wtwco.com/en-sg/insights/2023/02/2023-benefits-trends-survey.

of rental prices persist unabated. SMEs share similar concerns, with cash flow and cost management topping their priorities according to DBS's annual SME Pulse Check survey. Less than half of SMEs express optimism about growth prospects.[4]

Historically, Singapore has been a magnet for foreign investments, leveraging factors such as low corporate tax rates and a stable political system. However, the current surge in costs poses a threat to this advantageous position as it presents businesses with the daunting task of maintaining profitability. This may force companies to reassess their regional footprint. Furthermore, the escalating costs could discourage expatriates from choosing Singapore as their destination, potentially diminishing the country's allure as a hotspot for foreign talent.

The escalating costs in Singapore not only pose a significant challenge domestically but also make it increasingly tempting for foreign investors to explore alternative investment destinations. Compounding this issue is the intensifying global competition, with other countries, particularly China, advancing up the value curve, Indian manufacturing gaining competitiveness, and emerging economies outside the region, such as Mexico, enhancing their competitive standing through impactful reforms. As these countries strengthen their capacities, they are poised to narrow the gap and potentially surpass Singapore in areas where the city-state has historically demonstrated proficiency. There looms a persistent threat of being supplanted by neighbouring countries:

- *Maritime Trade*: Indonesia, under President Joko Widodo's leadership, has embarked on an ambitious plan to challenge Singapore's dominance in the maritime industry. With substantial investments, including the development of strategic ports, Indonesia aims to become a pivotal hub for maritime trade. While Singapore's established status and network effects provide an advantage, Singapore must remain vigilant

---

[4] DBS (2023). DBS survey: Almost half of SMEs are optimistic about business growth this year (DBS, March 2023). https://www.dbs.com/NewsPrinter.page?newsId=lfazyz9z&locale=en.

as Indonesia's transition unfolds, even though it may not pose an immediate and substantial threat.

- *Bonded Logistics Centres*: Indonesia's establishment of bonded logistics centres, coupled with the incentive of waived import duties for goods stored therein, has attracted global corporations. This policy shift has already redirected significant inventory away from Singapore, potentially eroding Singapore's involvement in certain niches of economic activity.

- *Corporate Headquarters Relocation*: As multinational corporations (MNCs) increasingly shift production to emerging Asian economies, the possibility of relocating their headquarters closer to production centres arises. Recent surveys indicate that some Japanese companies in Singapore have either considered or executed the transfer of certain headquarters functions to other countries. Thailand, for instance, has become an attractive destination for regional headquarters after implementing incentives in 2015.

- *Global business hubs*: Various countries around the world are actively competing for the coveted status of being a global business hub. Dubai, in particular, has emerged as a prominent contender, often hailed as a global hub for several compelling reasons. Dubai's strategic geographical location positions it as a crucial player on the global stage. Its world-class infrastructure, characterised by modern transportation networks and state-of-the-art facilities, further enhances its appeal. However, what truly sets Dubai apart is its remarkable diversity in economic activities, which has solidified its status as a multifaceted global business hub. Dubai has successfully established itself as a centre for various industries, including business and finance, tourism, logistics, technology, real estate, construction, restaurants, import–export, and e-commerce. Its prowess in global trade is particularly noteworthy, with the city serving as a major trade hub and re-export capital. This is exemplified by Dubai's exceptional performance in the first half of 2021, where non-oil external trade volumes surged by an impressive 10% year on year, amounting to a staggering 48 million tonnes.

Structural Weaknesses Might Limit Singapore's Potential to Adapt to These Challenges

Singapore demonstrates a constrained ability for the flexible adaptation necessary to prosper in the new global context. The impact of weak productivity is likely to impede the nation's ability to innovate and establish a competitive advantage. Furthermore, the imbalance in Singapore's economy, primarily attributed to the scarcity of local companies, poses a significant risk. The absence of a robust local business presence is precarious, as local companies are essential for the sustainability of the economy. In contrast, foreign companies may opt to relocate their operations when the economic landscape becomes less appealing. Encouraging the growth and retention of local companies is essential, as they are more likely to have the incentive to stay and adapt to evolving economic conditions.

Weak productivity and poor innovation

After attaining independence in 1965 amid challenging circumstances, Singapore's policymakers implemented a series of economic strategies that successfully transformed the nation. The initial focus was on establishing a modern industrial capacity, effectively creating what would evolve into a prominent global financial centre, marked by the development of an Asian Dollar Market denominated in US dollars. As the 1970s unfolded, the prevailing economic model reached its culmination, prompting Singapore to embark on a 'Second Industrial Revolution' to elevate its economy along the value curve. Subsequently, in the late 1980s and early 1990s, policymakers identified and nurtured expertise in high-end electronics, particularly in areas such as disk drives and petrochemicals. The end of the 1990s witnessed another pivotal transformation, positioning Singapore as a leading global wealth management centre.

However, there is growing scepticism as to whether the policy establishment is still capable of such responses. Consider, for example, some of the challenges that Singapore has failed to adequately address or policy misjudgements that have created problems. Singapore has known since at least 1984 that it would face a demographic challenge. More than 30 years later and despite substantial government efforts, the trend of fall in total fertility rates has not been reversed.

Singapore identified productivity as a challenge in the 1980s and set up the National Productivity Board in response. More recently, the Economic Strategies Committee also highlighted the importance of getting productivity right. Despite this, productivity growth has been weak. Singapore's leaders realised the need to boost innovation capacity and have mobilised billions of dollars to fund innovation but the results have been meagre.

Singapore has grappled with a conspicuously feeble level of total factor productivity (TFP) growth, with a compound annual growth rate (CAGR) of −0.7% over the 2009–2019 timeframe, based on our analysis using data from the Total Economy Database. While it is acknowledged that 'mature economies' similarly exhibit subdued TFP growth, with a CAGR of 0.008% during the same period — a trend attributed to the aftermath of the 2008 Global Financial Crisis — Singapore's TFP trajectory stands out for its exceptional downturn into negative territory.

The only dimension of Singapore's productivity performance that remains positive has been labour productivity as measured by real value-added per actual hour worked. This metric grew by 2.8% per annum between 2009 and 2019, achieving the target of 2–3% per annum set by the Economic Strategies Committee. Over this period, Singapore's productivity level, gauged by value-added per actual hour worked, progressed from 31% to 46% as compared to that of Switzerland, a benchmark for economies at the productivity frontier. Similarly, when considering value-added per worker, Singapore progressed from 53% of Switzerland's level in 2009 to 63% in 2019.

Nevertheless, a fundamental challenge persists, rooted in the economy's inherent inability to effectively harness input factors with heightened efficiency.

The reasons behind the lacklustre productivity in Singapore are multifaceted. Productivity has been weighed down by the domestically-oriented sectors. This can be evidenced by distinct divergence in productivity gains between outward-oriented sectors and their

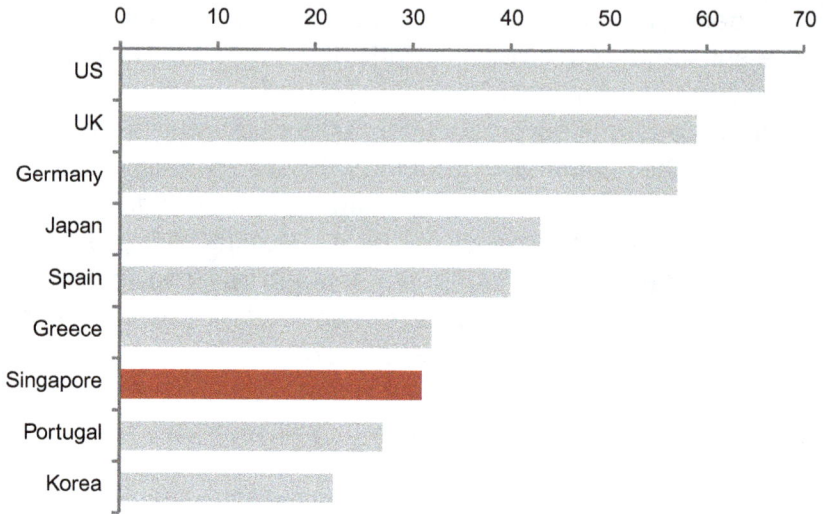

Figure 7.   Real VA per AHW, 2009 (Switzerland = 100).

Source: MTI, OECD

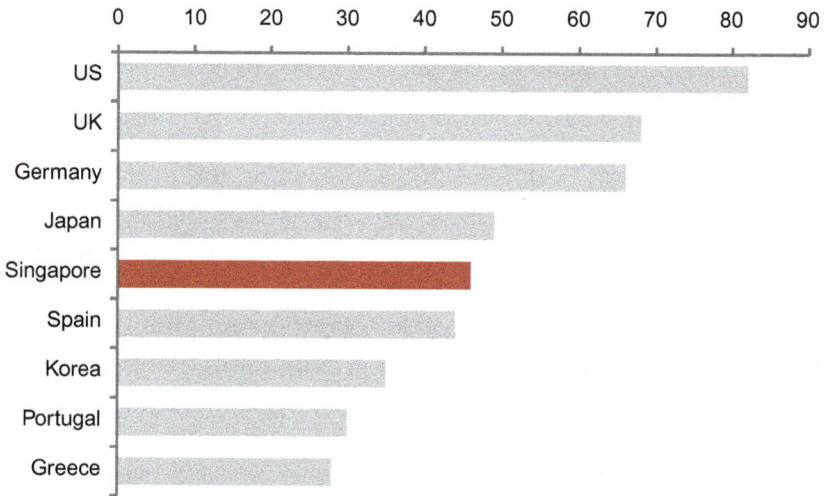

Figure 8.   Real VA per AHW, 2019 (Switzerland = 100).

Source: MTI, OECD

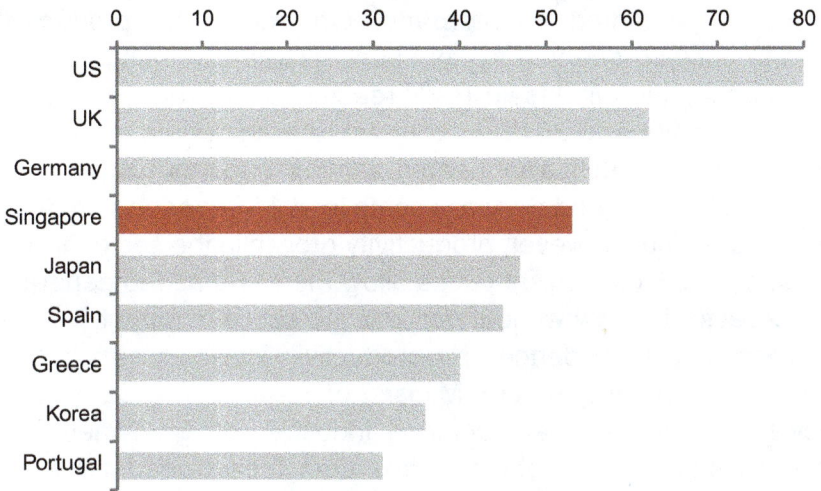

Figure 9.   Real VA/Worker, 2009 (Switzerland = 100).

Source: MTI, OECD

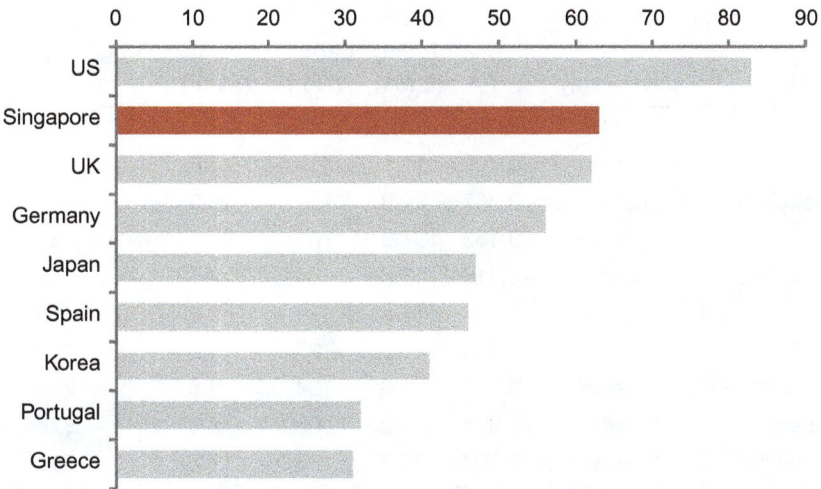

Figure 10.   Real VA/Worker, 2019 (Switzerland = 100).

Source: MTI, OECD

domestically-oriented counterparts. On aggregate, productivity gains in outward-oriented sectors such as Manufacturing, Finance & Insurance, and Wholesale Trade reached an average of 4.0% per annum from 2009 to 2019. In contrast, the aggregate productivity gains of the domestically-oriented sectors such as Construction, Retail Trade, and Food Services come in at 1.7% per annum during the same period. However, productivity growth in the sector is likely overstated as higher asset prices allow the value-added generated by the sector to grow without genuine increases in output.[5]

There is also evidence of a productivity gap between foreign- and locally-run firms. A 2008 Ministry of Trade and Industry report showed that in the manufacturing industry, foreign-owned firms were substantially more productive than local-owned firms and were on average significantly larger than local-owned firms in terms of their value-added, labour, and capital employed.

Productivity gap between foreign and locally run firms

Cluster	Ownership	TFP*	Value-added ($ Mil)	Labour (No.)	Capital ($ mil)	No. of Establishments in 2008
General	Local	−0.018	1.0	19	0.8	3,986
	Foreign	0.208	12.1	116	12.6	110
Electronics	Local	−0.067	22.8	233	49.9	104
	Foreign	0.133	137.0	781	197.8	85
Chemicals	Local	−0.110	3.6	24	2.5	229
	Foreign	0.143	14.8	114	62.8	155
Precision Engineering	Local	−0.030	1.2	25	1.2	2,482
	Foreign	0.257	13.0	134	8.5	278
Transport Engineering	Local	−0.024	6.2	105	2.3	973
	Foreign	0.207	25.3	162	12.2	110

*Note: TFP values are centred on zero and averaged from 2001–2008. Foreign-owned firms are defined as firms with foreign shareholdings of 50% or more.
Source: EDB Census of Manufacturing Activities.

---

[5]The strong productivity performance of the Administrative & Support Services sector was supported by the rental and leasing segment (comprising the leasing of non-financial intangible assets, and the rental and leasing of motor vehicles, equipment, and other tangible goods).

Amid Singapore's remarkable reputation for educational excellence, a perplexing conundrum comes to light: Why has this outstanding educational prowess not translated into the essential skill of optimising factor inputs with heightened efficiency? In the 2018 Programme for International Student Assessment (PISA) assessment that measures the competencies of 15-year-old students in the areas of mathematics, science, and reading globally, Singapore swept the board, coming in second place in all three areas, second only to China in each of them. In the just-released 2022 PISA survey, Singapore maintained its dominant position. There is no doubt about the high quality of human capital in Singapore. It is possible that the education system, for all its strengths, also tends to produce individuals who excel at passing examinations but lack creativity and a willingness to take risks.

This, thus, translates into risk aversion or a lack of entrepreneurialism in the country. A telling example comes from a 2013 survey cited by the OECD, which showed that less than 16% of Singaporean workers have considered embarking on independent business ventures,[6] compared with 40% in Hong Kong and 33% in Chinese Taipei, even though the World Bank ranks Singapore along with Hong Kong as one the best places in the world for doing business. This contradiction limits innovation and the birth of dynamic, high-value enterprises capable of propelling total factor productivity.

Finally, there are concerns over the lack of spillovers from research and development (R&D) into productivity outcomes. While Singapore's gross expenditure on R&D (GERD) as a percentage of GDP aligns with levels seen in developed nations, the anticipated spillover effects on broader economic productivity are not fully realised. As early as 2010, Singapore's GERD had already reached an impressive 2.14% of GDP, placing it in the echelons of

---

[6] OECD (2013). *Southeast Asian Economic Outlook 2013: With Perspectives on China and India.* https://www.oecd.org/dev/asia-pacific/Singapore.pdf.

R&D-intensive nations such as the United States and Germany.[7] This discrepancy, therefore, raises pertinent questions about the extent to which Singapore can effectively translate its robust R&D investment into enhancements in overall economic productivity.

Lack of 'inherent capacity'

Ultimately, the success of an economy is more than simply achieving high rates of GDP growth. For growth to be durable and deliver tangible benefits to its people, it must be accompanied by transformation — expanding the inherent capacity of citizens and the companies that are owned by its citizens to not only create value but to do so in a sustained manner.

Rising sizeable local companies are relatively rare in the Singapore economy compared to the economic heft of foreign multinational corporations. Due to the multinationals-driven, export-oriented strategy that the Singapore government has long favoured, export-oriented manufacturing consists primarily of foreign companies, with local enterprises making up the supporting industry infrastructure.

This is in stark contrast with the manufacturing models seen in Germany, Japan, South Korea, and Taiwan, which incorporate globally-competitive local enterprises such as the Mittelstand in Germany, the keiretsu in Japan, the chaebols in South Korea, and the world-leading semiconductor companies in Hsinchu Science Park, Taiwan. In Singapore, local firms tend to be government-linked companies (GLCs) or Temasek portfolio companies (TPCs).

This presents several risks. First, MNCs are mobile and can swiftly exit the economy, posing a potential challenge. Second, over-reliance on MNCs for driving productivity becomes a concern, especially if local enterprises lag in innovation. Third, attracting FDI may become more challenging in the future. Developed economies

---

[7] Agency for Science, Technology and Research, Press Release: Singapore reports growth in both public and private sector R&D expenditure (n.d.) https://www.nas.gov.sg/archiveson line/data/pdfdoc/20120103002.htm.

are launching multibillion-dollar initiatives to entice production in strategic sectors, making it hard for Singapore to compete at a similar scale. For instance, Germany's negotiations with Intel for a semiconductor plant involve a colossal S$10 billion (US$7.5 billion) in financing support, nearly double the Singapore Ministry of Trade and Industry's projected expenditure for growing the city-state's entire economy in 2023.

A viable approach to address these challenges is to nurture Small and Medium-sized Enterprises (SMEs) in Singapore. The government acknowledges this and has implemented various policies to support SME growth over the years. However, we think that these measures are insufficient. SMEs still grapple with multiple issues, particularly concerning cash flow. Recent reports reveal that cash flow problems, affecting nearly 40% of SMEs, have cast shadows on the ambitions of these businesses. It is imperative to tackle these challenges comprehensively to strengthen the SME ecosystem and bolster Singapore's economic resilience.

What Has Gone Wrong?

As Singapore's economy is so heavily influenced by the outsized role the state plays in it, it is fair to ask whether the weakened capacity to respond might be due to issues in the policy sphere and the nature of government intervention in the economy and society. Part of the problem could be due to narrow performance indicators governing policymaking. For example, in the 2004–2011 period, an excessive emphasis was placed on generating economic growth rather than overall quality of life in guiding the formulation of policies. Moreover, recent major policy initiatives, such as the Committee on the Future Economy in 2017 or the Forward Singapore process in 2023, do not appear to have examined the economy holistically, reviewing the overall structure of the economy and how it has changed. Rather, there appears to be a quick-cut approach, focused on examining a few areas of interest to the leadership.

There has also been an unwillingness to move away from taboos and strongly-held assumptions. It could be argued that generous state-funded infant and childcare programmes and more expansive parental support such as child allowances explain why some northern European countries have managed to reverse the decline in total fertility rates. The Singapore government's initial reluctance to consider such policies, and then to only do so belatedly, probably explains the failure to mitigate negative demographic trends.

Moreover, many observers contend that for Singapore to thrive in innovation, several key areas must be addressed. One critical aspect is the need for a less competitive and more tolerant education system that accommodates late bloomers. It is essential to shift the focus from an overly grades-driven and rote memorisation approach toward fostering critical thinking and out-of-the-box creativity. Attempts have been made to make the grading system less competitive, exemplified by changes to the Primary School Leaving Examination (PSLE) grading system. Now, students are evaluated based on individual performance in PSLE subjects, irrespective of their peers' achievements, aiming to reduce early differentiation of examination results. However, this alone may not be sufficient, as the grades-driven mindset remains ingrained in Singaporean parents. There needs to be a bold restructuring of education, but there does not seem to be much progress thus far.

Conclusion

Singapore's economy, while still robust and possessing considerable strengths, faces growing challenges, especially in a rapidly-evolving world where Singapore's competitors are scrambling to enhance their attractiveness too. Unfortunately, Singapore's ability to adjust effectively to these challenges may have weakened compared to the past.

Going forward, a key area for consideration is to reconfigure policy responses so as to promote successful adjustment. There are several areas that can benefit from more careful analysis of underlying causes and an openness to new ideas. These would include the issue of high business and living costs, how to strengthen the capacity of local companies, and how to address the weaknesses in the innovation ecosystem. It may well be that bolder changes will be needed to overcome these challenges. Whatever it is, Singapore's extraordinary economic performance may prove difficult to sustain unless such a policy rethink is undertaken.

Chapter 14

New Zealand: A Small Economy in a Wide World

Brian Easton

Introduction

Singapore and New Zealand have much the same population — a bit over five million people. They are both affluent economies. Because of their resource base and location, they have rather different economic structures. Yet, the two small economies work together in international fora.

New Zealand experiences most of the challenges that other affluent economies face, such as population ageing, slowing productivity increases, and structural change, especially from dealing with global warming and the information technology revolution. Like many of the others, it also suffers from political inertia when dealing with these changes, and there are the usual short-term pressures requiring macroeconomic management. Among New Zealand's economic particularities, which will not be further covered here, are a proneness to natural hazards and high infrastructural needs reflecting its topography and population density.

This essay focuses on a series of international issues which are particular to the New Zealand economy. It does so, in part, by contrasting it with the Singapore economy.

Comparing Singapore and New Zealand

While New Zealand and Singapore are economies with a similar population size (NZ = 5.2 m; Singapore = 5.9 m in 2023), there are two crucial economic differences.

First, New Zealand's land area is 368 times that of Singapore (268,000 kms^2 vs. 729 kms^2), so there is a lower population density. The United Nations World Population Prospects ranks Singapore's density only behind Monaco, while ranking New Zealand 170 out of 199 countries. (The ratio between their EEZs is roughly 4000 times greater: 4 million km^2 vs. 1067 km^2.)

The difference results in quite different economic structures. Compared to the typical affluent economy, New Zealand has a large natural resource sector based on the land and sea; Singapore's natural resource sector is negligible. As a consequence, if Singapore were located as far away as, say, the Falkland Islands, it would be as poor and as unpopulated as they are.

But, it is not. Singapore is near the centre of the world economy. Almost half (about 46%) of the world's population lives in countries within 4000 kms, producing over a third (36%) of the world's production (GDP measured at purchasing power parity). Both figures are increasing. Australia is the only country of any significant size within the New Zealand 4000 km circle. Australasia has 0.4% of the world's population and 1.1% of its GDP. Additionally, Singapore sits on the Straits of Malacca, a critical link in the international transport network, which has been very important to its development. It is the international hub for the countries which encircle it.

Location is a source of the difference. An OECD (Organisation for Economic Co-operation and Development) report estimated that reduced access to markets relative to the OECD average could contribute negatively to GDP per capita by as much as 11% in Australia and New Zealand. Conversely, a favourable impact of around 6–7% of GDP is found in the case of two centrally-located countries: Belgium and the Netherlands. Singapore was not included in the study, but applying the latter figure to it, New Zealand's GDP would be depressed relative to Singapore by 16–17% (Boulhol *et al.*, 2008).

The structural consequence for the manufacturing and tradeable services sectors is that Singapore is involved with the web of Asian supply chains, whereas New Zealand's manufacturing mainly consists of primary product processing or small localised market supply where importing would be too complicated or costly; its businesses are rarely in the middle of supply chains, which have been one of the most dynamic developments of international manufacturing in recent times. (A nice illustration of the difference between the two countries is that New Zealand is a supplier of milk powder to Singapore, which converts it into infant formula that it distributes throughout its region.)

Historically, New Zealand's main resource-based activity has been pastoral farming, with wool, meat, and dairy products making up about 90% of total foreign exchange earnings. A shrewd summary was that New Zealand was an 'exporter of processed grass' — the processing through livestock and factory. Its comparative advantage was not so much its land — which is not particularly fertile — but a generous supply of sunlight and water. For a variety of reasons, there has been a substantial diversification of the farm sector since the 1960s into forestry, horticulture, and wine.

Additionally, the fishing industry has boomed both offshore (New Zealand's EEZ (Exclusive Economic Zone) — the ninth largest in the world — also has a substantial continental shelf) and with fish farming. Its mineral resources are not comparable to Australia's, but there are not unimportant hydrocarbon reserves (gas plus condensate) around Taranaki in the North Island.

Perhaps the tourist industry should be included among the 'resource-based' industries, given that scenery, as well as novelty, is a major appeal to one of New Zealand's biggest foreign-exchange-earning industries. If the isolation adds to the attractions, it also puts New Zealand a long way from where the tourists live. In contrast, Singapore's tourism arises from its location at the centre of a large population. Its tourist attractions are primarily urban.

The apparently low value-added of the primary sector as measured in New Zealand's GDP is misleading. It purchases inputs from the rest of the economy and there is also substantial processing of pastoral products after the farm gate. So, the sector's proportional contribution to earning foreign exchange far exceeds that of its apparent contribution to GDP. Without its primary sector, New Zealand would be a very different and poorer place. Tourism aside, the same cannot be said of Singapore.

Both economies have the large service sector characteristic of a modern affluent economy. But, Singapore's financial and business sector is a major Asian and world centre; New Zealand's financial and business sector mainly services its domestic market. Singapore's dominance arises from its location and a sound and robust domestic rule of law that has been strengthened recently by Beijing's increasing involvement in Hong Kong's affairs.

New Zealand and Singapore are both affluent, although on conventional measures Singapore is more so. For the latest available year (2022), Singapore's output was US$98,149 per capita measured in US purchasing power dollars; New Zealand's was US$52,242 (or 53% of Singapore's).

This measures production in each country. Singapore's production is boosted by a higher share of foreign investment and daily workers from Malaysia, the remuneration of both needing to be deducted to calculate the effective income of residents. Adjusting for this will still not give parity.

An additional complication using Purchasing Power Parity comparisons is traded exports being measured at average international prices but domestically consumed local production being measured at average domestic prices; in the case of agricultural produce, there can be a substantial difference between the two because of domestic protection of the farm sector, which depresses New Zealand's relative GDP.

(Auckland might be compared with Singapore because it is the New Zealand region with the densest population; it is also its main point of connection with the rest of the world. Auckland's per capita GDP is 20% above the national average. However, Auckland does not have the highest per capita output, with both Taranaki with its hydrocarbon resources and the capital city Wellington reporting higher levels. There is a concern that Auckland's margin should be higher, but the relatively low margin may reflect New Zealand's resource-based economy where most provinces are prosperous.)

It is even more complicated to compare income inequality between the two nations. Unofficial international comparisons are all over the place. One useful measure might be to compare average wages adjusted for living costs. Again, the comparisons are not very reliable, but I have never found one in which the Singapore rate exceeds the New Zealand one in a comparable proportion to the per capita GDP difference. Some, but not all, even have the real value of Singapore wages below the New Zealand one. Certainly, the bottom of Singapore's labour market pays less than New Zealand. Altogether, those data suggest that market income inequality is lower in New Zealand than in Singapore. With its more substantial welfare state, New Zealand's effective disposable income inequality is likely to be even lower.

A substantial difference is that Singapore's exports of goods and services (including re-exports) amount to around 176% of its GDP, while its imports are 148% (in 2019); New Zealand's comparable figures are both 27%. The ginormous Singapore figure reflects its involvement in supply chains because of its near neighbours and location on the Malacca Straits. This is evident in the fact that Singapore's principal exports are electronic components, refined petroleum, gold, computers, and packaged medications, while its principal imports are electronic components, refined petroleum, crude petroleum, gold, and computers. Re-exports accounted for 43% of Singapore's total sales to other countries in 2000. New Zealand's re-export proportion was nearer 4%, although this does not include imports of inputs such as oil and fertiliser, which are vital in the production of exports. It has little intra-industry trade.

International Trade Agreements

Despite their rather different external structures, the two economies have similar external trade strategies. Indeed, Singapore's first international trade agreement still in force is the 'Agreement between New Zealand and Singapore on a Closer Economic Partnership'

(ANZSEP) signed in 2001 and upgraded in 2020. It is New Zealand's second; the first is the 1983 'Closer Economic Relations' (Australia-New Zealand Closer Economic Relations Trade Agreement (ANZCERTA) or CER for short) with Australia, which replaced the 1966 'New Zealand Australia Free Trade Agreement' (NAFTA).

Since 2001, the two countries have worked together on a range of other deals including the following:

2005 Trans-Pacific Strategic Economic Partnership P4 — with Brunei and Chile;

2009 ASEAN Australia NZ FTA — involving 12 countries;

2018 Comprehensive and Progressive Agreement for Trans-Pacific Partnership (CPTTP) — currently involving 12 countries;

2022 Regional Comprehensive Economic Partnership (RCEP) — involving 15 countries.

The sequence represents an evolution which began with ANZSEP. (CPTPP and RCEP might be thought of as a branching.) Australia is also involved with most of them.

Additionally, the two countries are involved in the following sectoral initiatives:

Digital Economy Partnership Agreement (DEPA);

WTO Joint Statement Initiative (JSI) on e-commerce;

Small Advanced Economies Initiative;

Singapore–New Zealand Declaration on Trade in Essential Goods

(The last deserves special mention. The Declaration on Trade in Essential Goods for Combating the COVID-19 Pandemic was signed in April 2020, just after the beginning of the COVID-19 pandemic, indicative of the warm and ongoing relationship between the two countries. Five other countries have since made non-binding ministerial declarations.)

Some of these agreements are 'open plurilateral' — that is, they are designed to allow countries not involved in the original agreement to join (as happened with the United Kingdom joining the CPTTP in 2023).

The commonality of the two countries arises from both being small and being specialised producers in the world economy. Each depends on a rules-based international trading order which favours unrestricted (or very limited restricted) trade. In a free-for-all world, it is too easy for small nations to be bullied. Lee Kuan Yew's comment that whether elephants make love or war, the grass gets trampled, is apposite for New Zealand too.

Perhaps more so for New Zealand. It has a formidable comparative advantage as a processed grass exporter which has been enhanced to competitive advantage by dynamic innovation and effective social institutions. Unfortunately, meat and dairy produce continues to face some of the toughest restrictions on access to other markets. Singapore has not suffered similar restricted access; indeed, its local resource sector is so limited that it has welcomed international supplies of foodstuffs.

Thus, the two countries have a common interest in promoting an open international order and working together to extend it. Because that order is constantly evolving, there is an ongoing need to develop the framework, as illustrated by the four sectoral agreements which do not cover commodities and so are not strictly Preferential Trade Agreements (PTAs or, sometimes, FTAs).

New Zealand's Economic Relationship with China

Inevitably, both countries face challenges with the rising importance of China in the world economy. Here, we focus only on New Zealand and only on the economic relationships — other chapters in the book look at other dimensions.

There are two major aspects to New Zealand's relationship with China: economic over-dependence and the way in which security tensions in relations between China and the United States and its allies impact the economic relationship.

New Zealand is haunted by the dangers of economic over-dependence on a single economy. As recently as 60 years ago, around two-thirds of (mainly pastoral product) exports went to Britain. A decade later, Britain joined what became the European Community, which at the time was commonly seen by New Zealanders as Mummy running off with a continental gentleman — or rogue.

The official and informed view was that Britain should join the community, providing New Zealand's special interests were not compromised. New Zealand had been aware of the possibility of British accession since at least 1961 and had made (successful) efforts to diversify. Between 1965 and 1980, New Zealand exports had shifted from being one of the most concentrated in the OECD by both markets and products to being near the middle.

In 2008, New Zealand entered into a free trade agreement with China — a world first for any developed country. Today, China takes almost a third of New Zealand's exports of goods and services, but it is so deeply interconnected, especially by supply chains, with East and Southeast Asia, that the wider group probably takes nearer two-thirds of New Zealand's exports (depending on how the group is defined, but including Australia).

The dominance of China in New Zealand's trade is extraordinary. It is its biggest market for milk products, sheep meats (for beef, it is only second), fish, apples, wine, and honey (for kiwifruit, it is third). Thirty years earlier, China was not among New Zealand's top ten export destinations for any of these products. These products make up a significant share of New Zealand's exports. They can be particularly difficult to manage, as Australia's recent tensions with China illustrate. (Significantly, these product groups also present political problems in the international economy, most notably widespread barriers to entry for pastoral products.)

New Zealand has welcomed the opening up of China's markets, which has been important to its recent prosperity. However, the ghost of the British experience remains. New Zealand went through periods of stagnation — notably in the 1920s and 1950s — because the British economy, and hence its imports, stagnated. Chinese economic growth is slowing down; that could well have a similar impact on New Zealand.

Export Diversification

New Zealand has vigorously pursued improving access to markets elsewhere — hence the recent trade deals with Britain and the European Union. Others are on the table, especially with India. Negotiations are also continuing with the Pacific Alliance — the Latin American regional group made up of Chile, Colombia, Mexico, and Peru — and with the Gulf states — Saudi Arabia, the United Arab Emirates, Qatar, Kuwait, Oman, and Bahrain. Negotiations with the Russia–Belarus–Kazakhstan Customs Union are currently suspended. There has been a long-term ambition for a PTA with the US, but that is hardly on the table given the US Congress's attitudes; in any case, its political price may be unacceptable to the New Zealand public. Existing trade deals are being upgraded.

As when Britain joined the EC, a major stumbling block in the negotiations has often been the access to dairy products — and, to a lesser extent, access to meat. Protecting its dairy farmers seems to be a sine qua non of a sovereign nation.

Extending market access for New Zealand's primary products will continue to be pursued and may grudgingly happen, but the key to reducing over-dependence on particular markets may be new products sold elsewhere as well as finding non-traditional markets.

Some years ago, I observed that Australia had been losing market share in its export markets and New Zealand had been gaining market share. But, Australia had the stronger total export growth because it was exporting to faster-growing markets.

Guessing which will be the future faster-growing markets is not easy. Who would have expected 50 years ago — as Britain was joining the European Community — the explosive economic growth of East and Southeast Asia? Probably South Asia is a good bet in the near future; possibly Latin America. PTAs for both areas are high among New Zealand's priorities.

Guessing new products can be equally challenging. Fifty years ago, New Zealand was (rightly) obsessed with butter and cheese exports. The dairy focus then moved onto milk powder; today, infant formula looms large. In the future, dairy products for the growing numbers of affluent (and elderly) may become more important. It is not only New Zealand's resource-based exports that will be challenged; there will be new sector exports — notably 'weightless' tradeable services.

Given New Zealand's tradition of state-driven development stance — an integral feature of the nation for over 150 years — it is perhaps necessary to say that the government's role is likely to be limited to extending and monitoring international trade deals and facilitating and supporting trade rather than the widespread interventions — especially protection and subsidisation — of the past.

De-risking

Security tensions between China and the United States and its allies also pose challenges, especially given the increasing international recourse to economic sanctions (typically led by the US). The horror scenarios for New Zealand would be a collapse of the Chinese economy or a conflict between China and the US which involved economic sanctions between them; gradations below either scenario would be difficult enough. (The implications of such scenarios for Singapore are probably even worse.)

Because of such security horror scenarios, New Zealand treads a very careful path in its relations both with China and the US — 'tippy-toe', one might call it. It wants to condemn some of China's actions, but not so forcefully that it will have trading repercussions, as has occurred to Australia. It wants a security relationship with the US which is not too close because of the China dimension — in any case, its public would not support a formal alliance involving a nuclear umbrella — but close enough so that were tensions to rise, New Zealand would have its submissions respected, especially if there were trade sanctions on exports important to New Zealand. (The US unwillingness to offer adequate trade access to key New Zealand exports compounds the issue of loyalties.)

New Zealand will almost certainly pursue the widespread de-risking industrial strategies being practised elsewhere. Unfortunately, the terms 'de-risking' and 'decoupling' are used loosely in popular discourse. The Ministry of Foreign Affairs (2023) provides systematic definitions:

"Decoupling is where a country disconnects, separates, terminates or severely restricts its economic ties with another. It is large scale economic and supply chain fragmentation along geopolitical lines.

De-risking relates to actions to reduce a country's economic vulnerability within its domestic system to a defined external risk. It is aimed to protect sectors and technologies that are of national security interest.

Re-shoring, on-shoring, friend-shoring, and *near-shoring* are all subsets of decoupling and de-risking."

So, de-risking is a kind of decoupling but only for strategic industries. Currently, much of the international focus on de-risking is on advanced technology industries with which New Zealand is not richly endowed. The de-risking focus in New Zealand is likely to be concerned with coping with a multi-year period of widespread economic sanctions which might be triggered by, say, increased China–US tensions. Dealing with disruptions of a shorter-term nature, as occurred from the COVID-19 outbreak, might be categorised as increasing the economy's 'resilience'.

While some proponents of Import Substituting Industrialisation (ISI) would have justified their early post-war strategy in terms of 'de-risking', had the term existed then, it generally did not. New Zealand's strategy of 'manufacturing in depth' shifted production back up supply chains rather than abandoned them. Car assembly did not de-risk the economy because it still depended on CKD packs from overseas for the assembly. ISI's purpose was employment generation.

Significant de-risking is limited for small economies like New Zealand or Singapore. The earlier discussed export diversification is part of the strategy, as is import diversification so that the countries are not dependent on a single, potentially vulnerable, supply chain. In New Zealand's case, the ongoing switching to energy renewables from oil (and coal) imports is for climate change reasons, but it will also reduce its external vulnerability.

While re-shoring and on-shoring may be limited, friend-shoring and near-shoring (notably with Australia) may be important and arise when PTAs are upgraded. More generally, as already mentioned in terms of security relations with the US and its allies, high-quality, friendly diplomatic relations may add a further modicum of protection if trade wars break out.

A Food and Pharmaceutical Security Agreement

I have long wondered whether there was the possibility of an international Food and Medicines Security Agreement which would rule out the application of sanctions to basic foodstuffs and medicines, as well as simplifying support for economies and regions facing crises in their supply (e.g. from a famine or catastrophe). There have been attempts to introduce such measures going back to the League of Nations — the recently agreed Singapore–New Zealand Declaration on Trade in Essential Goods is a step in this direction. It may well be that the world's appetite for such a deal has increased since Russia weaponised its food supply in its conflict with Ukraine. The US is unlikely to be a signatory to any such agreement as its Senate is likely to be opposed even if its President was not reluctant. But, the US might well respect the spirit of a widely supported agreement when it came to applying economic sanctions.

New Zealand as a significant food producer would have a major interest in any such agreement. It would ease pressures on it during a trade war and it would also be valuable in peacetime if it reduced access restrictions to others' domestic food markets. One of the common justifications for those restrictions is domestic food security. An agreement would reduce those security concerns.

Conclusion

While the New Zealand economy internally faces much the same challenges as other affluent economies, its smallness, its physical isolation, and its industrial specialisations have often meant it has had to approach its global connectedness in a quite distinctive way. It has not been able to participate in the middle of global supply chains; it is only at the beginning and end of them. It has not been able to participate in larger economic communities, instead relying on multilateral, plurilateral, and bilateral trade and other economic agreements. Additionally, it has actively supported less official organisations such as the Asia-Pacific Economic Cooperation (APEC) *Aotearoa Plan of Action* (2021). It has done so energetically and innovatively, on occasions taking on a leadership role far greater than New Zealand's significance in the final deal.

It has been able to do this because of good relations with like-minded countries which are also committed to an open rules-based global economy. The most important ally in this has been Australia, its closest neighbour, which is also closest culturally, although both sides of the Tasman Sea would draw attention to their differences. (In security terms, Australia is New Zealand's only ally.) Perhaps more surprising has been the way in which it has been able to work with Singapore, over 10 hours' flying time away.

Nevertheless, the successes in the development of the global architecture to which New Zealand, with Australia and Singapore, has contributed have not diminished the disappointment that pastoral exports, central to the New Zealand economy's prosperity, still face restrictions on access to the markets of many economies which have otherwise embraced open trade.

I am grateful to Alan Bollard, Malcolm McKinnon, and some New Zealand public servants for their comments on an early draft of this chapter.

Bibliography

APEC (2021). *Aotearoa Plan of Action.* https://aotearoaplanofaction.apec.org/.

Boulhol, H., de Serres, A., and Molnar, M. (2008). The Contribution of Economic Geography to GDP Per Capita. *OECD Journal: Economic Studies*, 2008, issue 1, 1–37.

Easton, B. H. (2022). *Not in Narrow Seas; The Economic History of Aotearoa New Zealand.* Victoria University Press, Wellington.

Ministry of Foreign Affairs (2023). *Navigating a Shifting World.* https://www.mfat.govt.nz/en/media-and-resources/release-of-mfats-2023-strategic-foreign-policy-assessment-navigating-a-shifting-world-te-whakatere-i-tetahi-ao-hurihuri/.

New Zealand Productivity Commission (2023). *Improving Economic Resilience.* https://www.productivity.govt.nz/inquiries/resilience/.

New Zealand Productivity Commission (2024). *Improving Economic Resilience: Report on a Productivity Commission Inquiry.* NZPC, Wellington.

Notes

The data is from
https://en.wikipedia.org/wiki/Economy_of_Singapore
https://wits.worldbank.org/Default.aspx?lang=en
https://www.stats.govt.nz/.

Chapter 15

New Zealand and Singapore: Key Areas of Bilateral Business Cooperation

Siah Hwee Ang

Introduction

New Zealand and Singapore share many commonalities. Both are small countries, with a population of just more than 5 million. Both countries rank high on a few of the World Bank Worldwide Governance Indicators in its latest survey in 2022 (The World Bank, n.d.), such as regulatory quality (Singapore 1st, New Zealand 3rd), corruption control (Singapore 4th, New Zealand 3rd), and rule of law (Singapore 3rd, New Zealand 8th). Both countries enjoyed being relatively neutral in international geopolitics and are part of many of the multilateral free trade agreements, for example, the Regional Comprehensive Economic Partnership (RCEP), Comprehensive and Progressive Trans-Pacific Partnership (CPTPP), and ASEAN–Australia–New Zealand Free Trade Agreement (AANZFTA).

Nonetheless, the two countries deviate in terms of their economic base. New Zealand is very much an agriculture-driven economy, with the country also relying on tourism and education as its main exports. Singapore, on the other hand, has moved to advanced technology manufacturing and cutting-edge science research, while relying on its position as a key financial hub.

Singapore's gross domestic product (GDP) was US$374.3 billion in 2021 while New Zealand's was US$247.4 billion in the same year. The respective figures for GDP per capita were US$63,474.90 and US$50,892.10.

Due to their various commonalities, membership of multilateral agreements, and in fact differences in their economic bases, it is not surprising to see business cooperation between the two Asia-Pacific countries. The next section focuses on some key areas of collaboration.

Key Areas of Business Cooperation

Agriculture and Agritech

Through support from both governments, FoodBowl, an Auckland-based hub of the NZ Food Innovation Network (a pilot-scale food processing facility), and FoodPlant, a shared facility for small-batch food production in Singapore, signed an agreement to collaborate to develop capabilities in food innovation and manufacturing across shared facilities (*The Straits Times*, 2022). They also undertake to share knowledge and extend networks. Given that this is a collaboration of platforms, it sets up a lot of other potential collaborations between food businesses from both countries.

A major push around trade in New Zealand has been exporting. Most New Zealand businesses rely on this hands-off approach to conducting business internationally. In recent years, however, the larger New Zealand businesses have been more active in direct engagement in markets, and Singapore represents both a market for New Zealand premium-pitched products and a major hub through which products can be distributed to the wider Southeast Asia region.

Through FoodPanda Singapore, a food and grocery delivery service provider, NZ-based dairy cooperative Fonterra was able to allow consumers in Singapore and Malaysia access to its products within 60 minutes (Fonterra, 2021). Zespri, the world's largest marketer of kiwifruit and New Zealand's largest horticultural exporter, has been able to utilise Freshmart, a Singapore-based fresh fruits and vegetables importer and distributor, to repack and distribute its products. Such is the importance of the Singapore market as a benchmark market that Zespri has opened a Centre of Sales and Marketing Excellence that will act as a hub connecting Zespri's growers (Zespri, 2023).

The allure of the Singapore market has also led Comvita, New Zealand's largest producer of honey and bee-related products, to acquire HoneyWorld, Singapore's largest manuka honey retailer to gain market share in Singapore and strengthen its position in the region. This is a similar strategy to Alliance Group's (NZ-based red meat and co-products company) acquisition of Goldkiwi Asia (Singapore-based marketing and sales company) to allow the Group to have easier access to the Asian market (*National Business Review*, 2017; Stuff, 2017).

Business cooperation in the food space is not restricted to larger New Zealand businesses though. Singapore-based beverage retailer and management consultancy service provider Global One Three One has been instrumental in assisting NZ-based Gin producer Juno gain a market presence in Singapore (Juno, n.d.). New Zealand-based oat milk manufacturer Otis Oat Milk's only international engagement so far is in Singapore, where it sells its milk through Jewel Coffee, a specialty coffee company (Jewel Coffee, n.d.; Juno n.d.).

Logistics

Singapore has the largest port in Southeast Asia and is one the busiest in the world. Logistics connectivity is essential for the city-state to maintain its competitive edge. The continuous search for logistics enhancements would see Singapore businesses internationalise to expand their networks.

In 2017, Yang Kee Logistics, one of Singapore's largest privately-owned logistics companies, acquired Fliway, one of New Zealand's largest independent and locally-owned specialised transport and logistics companies, a few months after the Singapore company's first major move into Oceania with the acquisition of Axima Pty Ltd, a key player in Australia's third-party logistics market. The New Zealand acquisition allows Yang Kee to strengthen its presence in Oceania, citing New Zealand as having "a stable currency and economic outlook, a growing middle class, and a demand for integrated freight and logistics solutions" (*The Straits Times*, 2017a). The business deal also allows Fliway's customers to scale and leverage a larger geographic footprint across Oceania and Asia.

In the food sector, New Zealand-based GVI Logistics and Seafrigo Singapore, a food and beverage logistics company, established a joint effort to operate a fortnightly Auckland–Singapore LCL reefer service to transport chilled and frozen products from Auckland to Singapore (GVI Logistics, 2020).

Healthcare and healthcare services

Two of New Zealand's healthcare service providers have been able to establish partnerships with Singapore's health tech agency Integrated Health Information Systems (IHIS) to provide collaborative services to the Singapore market.

The Clinician, a digital health platform provider, has linked up with IHiS to provide a timely exchange of health data (e.g. patient-reported outcome measures, wearable device data, and communication and educational materials) between healthcare providers and patients for better healthcare experience and outcomes in Singapore (Healthcare IT News, 2021). Orion Health, a healthcare software developer, will deliver a healthcare enterprise service system that allows healthcare systems in Singapore to better integrate (Orion Health, 2017).

Tourism

Skyline Enterprises, a New Zealand-based tourism operator, ventured into the tourism service industry in Singapore by setting up

Skyline Luge Sentosa, in collaboration with Sentosa Development Corporation, a statutory board under the Ministry of Trade and Industry of Singapore, responsible for the development, management, and promotion of Sentosa Island (Skyline Enterprises, n.d.; *The Straits Times*, 2017b).

Green technology

The New Zealand government-funded future energy centre Ara Ake and the tertiary education institution Western Institute of Technology (WITT) entered into a partnership with EcoLabs, a Singapore-based energy innovation cluster, jointly established by Nanyang Technological University, Enterprise Singapore, and the Sustainable Energy Association of Singapore, to work on a Low-Carbon Technology Translation Programme. This involves (1) establishing the Testbeds Framework, Global Co-Innovation Programme, Capability-Building Platform, and Launchpad Programme for NZ energy innovators; (2) helping WITT achieve its 2025 Carbon-Neutral Campus goal by structuring the Testbeds Framework and Global Co-Innovation Programme; and (3) creating a platform for Singaporean cleantech innovators to expand to the NZ market, leveraging local networks and testbed opportunities (Ara Ake, 2022; EcoLabs, n.d.; OpenGov Asia, 2021; Scoop, 2021). This collaboration offers many platforms for Singapore businesses in New Zealand around the low-carbon space, including bringing advanced technology. It creates a backdrop against which many other businesses in New Zealand and Singapore can get involved.

Two venture capital companies — New Zealand's Pacific Channel and Singapore-based TRIREC — entered into a collaborative agreement to identify and support deep-tech start-ups in New Zealand and Australia to create a more environmentally-sustainable future (Pacific Channel, 2023). Such cooperation will no doubt see greater collaboration between businesses of the two countries engaging in the sustainability space.

Fintech-related services

While New Zealand is not a financial hub like Singapore, the country has produced a decent number of small and medium-sized enterprises that are specialised in technology related to finance.

Cogo, a New Zealand-based company specialising in carbon footprint management tools, expanded into the Asia market in cooperation with Moneythor, a Singapore-based digital banking technology firm. Using Cogo's tools, more than 20 financial institutions integrated with Moneythor's digital banking platform to allow their customers to track their carbon emissions and, therefore, understand their carbon footprint based on their spending habits directly via their banking apps. In a separate cooperation, Moneythor collaborated with Bank of New Zealand to allow the bank to foster its customers' financial well-being and diversify its digital banking offering by implementing Personal Financial Management (PFM).

OCBC Bank, a Singapore-based multinational banking and financial services corporation, has partnered with 9 Spokes, a New Zealand-based fintech company with a bespoke tracking and insights tool helping small and medium-sized enterprises enhance business performance and drive growth. In this partnership, 9 Spokes supports OCBC Bank's SME customers in setting up and monitoring their internal operations, while allowing the company to access the Asia-Pacific region (Small Caps, 2018). OCBC also collaborated with Valocity to digitalise its entire valuation workflow, deliver a more streamlined customer experience, and improve collateral risk management via Valocity's platform (Valocity, 2019). Valocity is a New Zealand-based fintech company specialising in automating and streamlining the mortgage-lending and valuation process. NTUC Income, Singapore's general and health insurance provider, also utilised JRNY, a New Zealand insurance tech company, to help simplify the insurance-purchasing process for its customers (Insurance Business, 2019).

This section has provided a few areas of prominent business cooperation between New Zealand and Singapore. Not unexpectedly, cooperation has centred on strength matching the needs of both countries, with illustrated observations in the sectors of agriculture and agritech, logistics, healthcare and healthcare services, tourism, green technology, and fintech-related services. The next section will provide some points on where business cooperation will and should be tracking.

Looking Forward

Both New Zealand and Singapore are small-sized markets by global standards, so the business cooperation observed is unlikely to be just about market access.

New Zealand businesses would see Singapore as a market that is likely to appreciate its premium goods and services. Singapore, however, also provides a testbed for which these businesses can pilot new products and services. Having Singapore as a market for verification will provide quality assurance for other potential markets. Singapore also provides a hub for New Zealand businesses to establish a regional base for expansion into the Southeast Asia region and the larger Asia.

On the contrary, Singapore businesses would see New Zealand as a testing ground for new products and services for Western nations. Singapore businesses would also see New Zealand as a safe place to invest. New Zealand is also a model for sustainability, which Singapore would want to learn from. This attracts Singapore businesses to cooperate with their New Zealand counterparts. Further, New Zealand is starting to get recognised for its science and technology space, and we are starting to see collaboration in this area.

Singapore has a '30 by 30' goal in place around its food sector. The '30 by 30' goal is to build the agri-food industry's capability and capacity to sustainably produce 30% of the country's nutritional needs by 2030 (Singapore Food Agency, n.d.). Given the strength of New Zealand's agriculture and agritech sectors, major New Zealand food players have seen action working alongside Singapore food agencies and businesses. As seen from some of the business cooperation mentioned previously, this goes beyond food security.

It also relates to logistical linkages, food safety, and other sustainability-related areas.

With life expectancy (2021 data: Singapore — 83 years; New Zealand — 82 years) and percentage of population ages 65 and above (2022 data: Singapore — 15%; New Zealand — 16%) in the two nations creeping up (The World Bank, n.d.), healthcare services are starting to attract attention. It is expected that a lot of business cooperation will surround this area in the next decade or so, with strong government backing from both nations as they seek to address issues around the health of the ageing population.

Singapore's location in the Asia-Pacific and its position as a hub have ensured that it is an attractive destination for tourists. New Zealand is also an attractive tourist location for different reasons — its natural, clean, and beautiful environment. This has opened up opportunities for tourism collaboration as both countries have strong presence in the tourism sector. Likewise, significant logistics networks are required for a hub like Singapore, while the distance of New Zealand from the rest of the world warrants attention to good logistics. This should mean greater opportunities for partnerships in this sector as well.

New Zealand is famous for its sustainability approach, both generally and in business. Singapore, deprived of natural resources, has been constantly on the lookout for ways to improve its sustainability, not just in the food sector as discussed, but also in other forms of sustainability that preserve its earned resources and environment while its economy grows. This presents a natural partnership between the two nations, and some observations on this have been presented. But, existing business cooperation would involve a lot more than the examples presented here. We should expect extensive business cooperation in this area in the years to come.

Singapore has a strong base in technology, and fintech companies with links to the financial hub have proliferated for more than two decades now. It is more surprising to see the upsurge of many New Zealand fintech-related companies. But, this is not about New Zealand companies and entrepreneurs being less creative, it is just that New Zealand has not been known to have a fintech-type economy. Nonetheless, pockets of strength in this area exist in New Zealand, and we should expect more collaboration between businesses from the two countries. To highlight the potential, New Zealand's fintech transaction value is forecast to grow by 100.2% in the period 2021 to 2025, while Singapore's figure will increase by 149.3% during this time (Statista, 2022a, 2022b).

Many economies are still in the process of trying to recover from the COVID-19 pandemic. They are relooking at and adjusting their economic steering. At the same time, global geopolitics is starting to heat up, even more so due to the lesson of self-survival that countries learned from the pandemic. New Zealand and Singapore, being smaller and non-threatening in many ways, would find themselves still attractive partners to many other countries. But, at the same time, business cooperation is likely to be more balanced between the two. We should expect business cooperation to flourish moving forward.

Bibliography

Ara Ake (2022). New Zealand-Singapore partnership on low emissions energy demonstration project. https://www.araake.co.nz/news-and-events/news/araake-ecolabs-witt/. (Accessed 1 December 2023).

Comvita (2023). Comvita pays $10m for Singapore's largest mānuka honey retailer HoneyWorld. https://www.stuff.co.nz/business/farming/agribusiness/132476158/comvita-pays-10m-for-singapores-largest-mnuka-honey-retailer-honeyworld. (Accessed 1 December 2023).

EcoLabs (n.d.) Ara Ake and WITT — Low Carbon Technology Testbed Program. https://ecolabs.sg/new-zealand-singapore-low-carbon-technology-translation-program-with-ara-ake/#s-cover. (Accessed 1 December 2023).

Fonterra (2021). Dairy delivery-on-demand. https://www.fonterra.com/sea/en/our-stories/articles/Dairy-delivery-on-demand.html. (Accessed 1 December 2023).

GVI Logistics (2020). AKL-SIN LCL reefer service. https://www.gvi.co.nz/news/singapore-lcl-reefer/. (Accessed 1 December 2023).

Healthcare IT News (2021). Singapore's public health system rolling out The Clinician's ZEDOC platform. https://www.healthcareitnews.com/news/asia/singapores-public-health-system-rolling-out-clinicians-zedoc-platform#:~:text=Singapore's%20health%20tech%20agency%20Integrated, island%20state's%20public%20healthcare%20system.   (Accessed   1 December 2023).

Insurance Business (2019). NZ insurtech ties up with Singapore insurance giant. https://www.insurancebusinessmag.com/nz/news/breaking-news/nz-insurtech-ties-up-with-singapore-insurance-giant-193399.aspx. (Accessed 9 December 2023).

Jewel Coffee (n.d.) https://jewelcoffee.com/collections/milk/otis.

Juno (n.d.) https://junogin.com/sg/.

Moneythor (2022a). Cogo partners with Moneythor to lower the climate impact of customers' spending across Asia. https://www.moneythor.com/2022/02/14/cogo-partners-with-moneythor-to-lower-the-climate-impact-of-customers-spending-across-asia/. (Accessed 9 December 2023).

Moneythor (2022b). Promoting financial wellbeing for BNZ customers. https://www.moneythor.com/2022/05/27/promoting-financial-wellbeing-for-bnz-customers/. (Accessed 9 December 2023).

National Business Review (2017). Alliance buys Singapore marketer Goldkiwi. https://www.nbr.co.nz/alliance-buys-singapore-marketer-goldkiwi/. (Accessed 1 December 2023).

OpenGov Asia (2021). New Zealand collaborates with Singapore in testbed establishment. https://opengovasia.com/new-zealand-collaborates-with-singapore-in-testbed-establishment/. (Accessed 1 December 2023).

Orion Health (2017). Orion Health signs contract for Singapore interoperability solution. https://orionhealth.com/global/media-releases/orion-health-signs-contract-for-singapore-interoperability-solution/#. Accessed 1 December 2023.

Pacific Channel (2023). Pacific Channel and TRIREC announce strategic partnership. https://www.pacificchannel.com/stories/pacific-channel-and-trirec-announce-strategic-partnership. (Accessed 1 December 2023).

Scoop (2021). Energy innovation demonstration 'testbeds' in Aotearoa. https://www.scoop.co.nz/stories/BU2108/S00519/energy-innovation-demonstration-testbeds-in-aotearoa.htm. (Accessed 1 December 2023).

Singapore Food Agency (n.d.) Strengthening our food security. https://www.ourfoodfuture.gov.sg/30by30/.

Skyline Enterprises (n.d.) https://www.skylineenterprises.co.nz/assets/Skyline-Annual-Reports/Skyline-Annual-Report-2022.pdf. (Accessed 1 December 2023).

Small Caps (2018). 9 Spokes crystallises deal with OCBC Bank to service Asian small businesses. https://smallcaps.com.au/9-spokes-deal-ocbc-bank-service-asian-small-businesses/. (Accessed 9 December 2023).

Statista (2022a). New Zealand's economy & society — data and analysis. April. https://www.statista.com/study/28594/new-zealand-statista-dossier/. (Accessed 16 December 2023).

Statista (2022b). Singapore's economy & society — data and analysis. April. https://www.statista.com/study/26071/singapore-statista-dossier/. (Accessed 16 December 2023).

Stuff (2017). Alliance buys Singapore marketing business Goldkiwi Asia. https://www.stuff.co.nz/business/farming/97028436/alliance-buys-singapore-marketing-business-goldkiwi-asia. (Accessed 1 December 2023).

The Straits Times (2017a). Yang Kee Logistics to buy New Zealand company for $52.1m in second major acquisition. https://www.straitstimes.com/business/companies-markets/yang-kee-logistics-to-buy-new-zealand-company-for-521m-in-second-major. (Accessed 9 December 2023).

The Straits Times (2017b). Skyline Luge Sentosa unveils new tracks and chairlift as part of $14m upgrade. https://www.straitstimes.com/singapore/skyline-luge-sentosa-unveils-new-tracks-and-chairlift-as-part-of-14m-upgrade. (Accessed 1 December 2023).

The Straits Times (2022). New $13m shared facility for small-batch food production gives boost to local food innovation. https://www.straitstimes.com/business/new-13m-shared-facility-for-small-batch-food-production-gives-boost-to-local-food-innovation. (Accessed 1 December 2023).

The World Bank (n.d.) https://www.worldbank.org/en/publication/worldwide-governance-indicators.

Valocity (2019). OCBC Bank partners with Valocity to accelerate innovation in mortgage lending. https://www.valocityglobal.com/tr-tr/2019/11/ocbc-bank-partners-with-valocity-to-accelerate-innovation-in-mortgage-lending/. (Accessed 9 December 2023).

Zespri (2023). Zespri's overseas New Zealand industry tours return. https://www.zespri.com/en-NZ/publications/newsroomdetail/overseas-new-zealand-industry-tours-return?fbclid=IwAR0jjm4fbxQc9tQPEUbndplAuople8OJYqW3H2s1O2ubEmQDwC0j3rnMOuA. (Accessed 1 December 2023).

Chapter 16

Four Decades of Bridging Business:
Observations of a Bilateral Insider

Ken Hickson

People matter. As well as the company they keep. No more so than when it comes to bridging a longstanding business relationship between New Zealand and Singapore.

This came to my mind recently when I received a supply of fine NZ food products, delivered to my door by *Kiwi Kitchen*, which was set up in Singapore by former South Island dairy farmer *Kevin Youngman* in 2014. He provides top-quality goods that are sometimes not easy to find on supermarket shelves, catering to Singaporeans, Kiwis, and quite a few expats who favour the authentic flavours of NZ. Of course, he is not the first, but he has created a niche for himself and is a fine example of an enthusiastic NZ businessman not afraid of competition.

This has been going on for the four decades that I have been observing — and involved in — the two-way trade in people, goods, services, and investments between New Zealand and Singapore.

Here are some of the people I see as pioneers in establishing and expanding this business partnership.

Alistair Betts ran *NZ Milk Products* (the international arm of the *NZ Dairy Board*) in Singapore through the 1980s and 1990s, leading a team which not only marketed prized products from pastures 'down under' but helped expand NZ's influence in the region.

He was a leader in the business community, acting as President of the *NZ Chamber* — then called the NZ Business Council — and doing more than most to enhance the growing public–private partnership between NZ and Singapore. Incidentally, Massey University has established the Alistair Betts Scholarship "to honour the memory of Alistair Betts, who, when employed by the New Zealand Dairy Board during the 1980's, pioneered access for New Zealand dairy products through South East and Southern Asia."

Lee Town, who worked alongside Alistair in Singapore with Milk Products in those early days, was also actively engaged in other countries in the region to enhance milk production and processing. He also served on the NZ Business Council in Singapore and for a few years was based in Kuala Lumpur. He was on hand when *NZ Milk Products* (now incorporated into *Fonterra*) established its first Malaysian manufacturing facility, *Susumas*, in 1992. Seven years later, the company began operation of its second plant, *Dairymas*.

Lee Chuan Seng, an active member of the NZ Chamber when I was President in 1990, led the growth of *Beca Asia* — originally known as *Beca Carter Hollings and Ferner*, a NZ firm founded in 1920 — and played a major role in the public and private sectors in Singapore, thereby enhancing the longstanding partnership between the two countries. A graduate of the *University of Auckland*, with a Bachelor of Engineering, he went on to be the first Chairman of the *Singapore Green Building Council* and now serves as Chairman of the *National Environment Agency (NEA)*. The NZ Government honoured him with the NZ-ASEAN Award in 2015 for his services to NZ trade and enterprise.

There are many more names in the 1990 printed directory of the NZ Business Council who need to be praised for their pioneering leadership of the Singapore–NZ partnership.

John Lim led *Cold Storage Holdings* for many years — making sure NZ products appeared prominently on supermarket shelves — and went on to play a major role in the Singapore Institute of Directors.

Lim Chee Onn represented Straits Steamship Land (which became Keppel Land) in 1990. He went on to greater heights in the public and private sectors, even acting *President* at times, as he is a member of the Council of Presidential Advisors in Singapore. Currently, he is the Chancellor of the Singapore Management University (SMU).

Ho Whye Chung, of Kingsgate International Corporation — another active Singaporean NZ Chamber member in 1990 — went on to become a major investor in the hotel and property sector in NZ and Australia.

Ho Kwon Ping (Banyan Tree) and *Mohan Mulani* (Harry's Bar) were among other prominent Singaporeans in the property sector, whose investment interests were reported in past issues of NZ News, which was published by the NZ Singapore Business Council, as it was known in the 1990s before it became the NZ Chamber.

Graeme McDowell, *Grant Lilly*, and *Eric Smitten* all played leadership roles for *Air New Zealand* during a significant period of growth for NZ–Singapore business between 1980 and 2000, and were members of the NZ Chamber as well.

In the early years, Air NZ and Singapore Airlines (SIA) were vigorous competitors. Unsurprisingly, due to its aggressive growth ambitions, it was SIA that established the first direct Singapore–Christchurch service (in 1986). A good example of how airline competition was good for trade and tourism in both countries, backed by the active involvement of key business and government players, New Zealanders and Singaporeans. Now, the airlines of both countries see more sense in co-operation and are, together, members of the global Star Alliance, along with 24 other international airlines.

Besides the other NZ organisations that were actively engaged in Singapore and Southeast Asia — like *Goodman Fielder Wattie, Fletcher Challenge, Bank of NZ,* and *NZI Insurance* — many Kiwi individuals actively promoted business partnership with Singapore through their involvement in the NZ Chamber or through the companies they worked for.

Let's put *Errol Gates, Roger Bowie,* and *Malcolm Rees* in that category, as they all held regional and Singapore roles for *DHL* at different times through the 1980s and 1990s. They supported many business, sporting, and community projects in Singapore, including the *Singapore Business Awards*.

DHL was also responsible for bringing *Sir Edmund Hilary* to Singapore — when he was NZ's High Commissioner to India — to speak at an event for the *Singapore Adventurers Club*, as some members were keen on attempting to climb Mount Everest, which Hillary conquered way back in 1953.

Of course, the late Sir Edmund is also remembered as a bee-keeper, which brings us to another famous NZ export, Manuka honey. Look at the work of *Comvita* — here, in NZ, and else-where — for not only promoting the health and nutrition benefits of Manuka honey but also helping boost the bee population, which is threatened globally, and supporting biodiversity at the same time.

Then, there is *Zespri* — in NZ and in 50 countries — which was first established in 1988 under the name of the *New Zealand Marketing Board* before it formed itself into a co-operative of kiwi-fruit growers in New Zealand in 2000 and renamed itself *Zespri International Ltd.*

All this has helped get our Singapore–NZ relationship to where it is today — sound, sustainable, and secure. But, to maintain this we cannot stand still.

I feel there is a distinct role for NZ to play in global food security and also in directly helping Singapore attain its objective of meeting 30% of its nutritional needs by 2030, easing its reliance on imports and reducing its vulnerability to supply disruptions.

Just as *Fonterra* continues to help countries in the region — with some advice and a helping hand from NZ experts — surely there is more we can do to help Singapore produce more nutritious food for itself. Besides dairy, what about honey production, where a small band of novice beekeepers in Singapore could get a help-ing hand to grow the honey business and help biodiversity at the same time?

Partnerships thrive when we capitalise on opportunities and work together to solve problems. We already have some of the best examples in the world where Singapore and NZ are delivering on many of the UN Sustainable Development Goals (SDGs). But, best of all, we can epitomise SDG 17 — Partnerships for the goals — by strengthening the means of implementation and revitalising the Global Partnership for Sustainable Development.

Collaboration is the key. Let's build on the foundations we have set up. Go higher and faster!

VI

CLIMATE CHANGE, ENVIRONMENTAL AND SUSTAINABLE POLICIES

Chapter 17

Climate Change: The New Normal — New Zealand's Role in Early Climate Change Science and Current Climate Change Policies

Dave Lowe

Introduction

In the 21st century, humans face multiple existential threats including global pandemics, increasing inequality, failure of democracy, and warfare leading to massive infrastructure damage and loss of life. But, this is insignificant compared to the colossal impact that human-induced climate change is poised to unleash on our current civilisation. To have any hope of avoiding a climate disaster, humanity must make deep cuts in carbon emissions reaching 50% of current values by 2030 and net-zero carbon by 2050. If we can achieve this, we will avoid the worst consequences of dangerous climate change for us and future generations.

'Dangerous climate change' has been defined as the point where the Earth's global average temperature exceeds pre-industrial (1850–1900) temperatures by 1.5°C. It is not a precise definition because the Earth's response to climate change driven by greenhouse gases is nonlinear and contains many feedback processes.

Above 1.5°C, an increasing number of 'tipping points will occur, for example, irreversible melting of polar ice sheets and subsequent sea level rise, transformation of the Amazon rain forests into a savannah, destruction of the coral reef, and melting of Arctic permafrost regions.

In 2022, the average global temperature reached 1.15°C above the pre-industrial average accompanied by unprecedented heat waves. According to a study in *Nature Medicine*,[1] these led to more than 60,000 premature deaths in Europe, with especially high mortality rates observed in Greece, Portugal, Spain, and Italy. Many parts of the world suffered deadly storms and flooding events as well as wildfires. In the first half of 2023, widespread flooding events occurred, including cyclone Gabrielle, which caused catastrophic damage and loss of life in New Zealand. Later in the same year, devastating wildfires, extreme weather events, and record temperatures were recorded over large parts of the globe — that year is the hottest ever recorded, more than 1.4°C above the pre-industrial average.

Since the beginning of the Industrial Revolution, widespread burning of fossil fuels and agricultural activity have dramatically altered the properties of the atmosphere. Since then, global atmospheric carbon dioxide (CO_2) increased from 280 ppm (parts per million) to about 420 ppm in 2023, an increase of 50%, and methane increased from about 700 ppb (parts per billion) to almost 1900 ppb, an increase of 170%. This has caused a significant planetary energy imbalance with increasing amounts of solar heat being trapped in the Earth system, especially in the oceans where more than 90% of the excess heat is stored.

The amount of heat stored in the oceans varies with meteorological conditions, including changes caused by a phenomenon in the Pacific region known as the El Niño Southern Oscillation with worldwide implications for the Earth's climate. During the past few years, the oscillation has been in a La Niña phase, where relatively more heat is stored in the oceans. However, in the first half of 2023, the system swung into an El Niño phase releasing excess heat from the oceans into the atmosphere. Extreme flooding events, heat waves, and wildfires are becoming more frequent and intense, a trend likely to continue with El Niño exacerbating an already serious situation leading to more deaths, disruption, and misery as carbon emissions continue to increase.

Atmospheric CO_2 and the Beginnings of Modern Climate Change Science

But, how did it come to this? There is overwhelming evidence that carbon emissions from industry and agriculture are causing climate change. There is no doubt that our actions have dramatically increased the intensity of flooding, heat waves, and other climate change-related events, and will continue to do so at a devastating rate as we continue increasing carbon emissions. How could we be so stupid? We seem oblivious to the dangers caused by our unsustainable lifestyles. We know there is a linkage between driving an absurdly large petrol or diesel SUV and deadly flooding events and the disappearance of Pacific islands, but we do nothing. Somehow, we perceive that our freedom to live a high-emissions lifestyle trumps the right to survival of people living elsewhere.

I began making continuous atmospheric CO_2 measurements in the midlatitudes of the southern hemisphere in New Zealand over 50 years ago. What have I seen during my working lifetime, how has our understanding of human-induced climate change evolved, what is New Zealand's role, and where is the science headed?

Since the end of the last ice age about 12,000 years ago, humans have enjoyed a stable climate on a planet endowed with all the conditions needed for life to prosper and for an advanced civilisation to develop. Since then, the human population increased from an estimated five million to just over 8 billion. For millennia, human communities were small and had relatively minor impacts on their habitats. But, as populations grew, particularly with the advent of the Industrial Revolution 250 years ago, rather than living within the limits of their environment, humans developed economies driven by fossil fuel exploitation and agriculture, using huge tracts of land gained from the destruction of forests.

This led to uncontrolled emissions of CO_2 and methane into the atmosphere, slow at first but accelerating in the second half of the 20th century. When I first began measuring atmospheric CO_2 in New Zealand in 1970, its atmospheric growth rate was less than 1 ppm/year, but in 2023, the rate had more than doubled to about 2.5 ppm/year. Within the space of a single century, humans are driving planet Earth into another geological epoch, the Anthropocene — one with a totally different climate. For the first time in history, a single species is modifying the web of life itself, driving the natural equilibria of the Earth system into uncharted territory.

Many climate change scientists refer to Svante Arrhenius, a Nobel Prize-winning Swedish chemist, as the first person to discuss the harmful effects of adding CO_2 from fossil fuels to the atmosphere.[3] However, in the first half of the 20th century, the implications of widespread fossil fuel combustion were not understood. Humanity faced other crises that appeared to be far more pressing than worrying about the effects that humans might be having on the global environment. The idea that CO_2 from fossil fuel combustion could be leading to the greatest calamity ever faced by the human race was inconceivable. The expression 'human-induced climate change' did not exist.

In the 1950s, a young American chemist, Charles David Keeling, worked on a research project aimed at investigating carbonates dissolved in California groundwaters. He needed to know the concentration of atmospheric CO_2 in the region where his samples were collected. But, there were no reliable data; the few estimates available ranged from 150 to 350 ppm. After months of painstaking work, Keeling produced estimates of about 310 ppm along the USA's Pacific coast. But, what were the global values of atmospheric CO_2? With support from the Scripps Institution of Oceanography in La Jolla, California, Keeling set up a continuous infrared analyser in the late 1950s on Mauna Loa, Hawaii, a mountaintop meteorological station sited at an altitude of 3400 m. This site, remote from local sources of pollution, proved to be ideal for making atmospheric CO_2 measurements representative of the 'clean' Northern Hemisphere.

By the early 1960s, Keeling published two discoveries that would completely change atmospheric science. First, he showed that atmospheric CO_2 reached a peak in April, the onset of rapid northern spring growth, after which it dropped dramatically to a minimum in early autumn when it rose again — a completely-natural phenomenon that had been repeated for countless millennia since the appearance of green plants and photosynthesis on Earth. His second discovery showed that CO_2 was increasing in the atmosphere, a situation that has continued ever since. The measurement series that Keeling began continues to the present day — the 'Keeling curve', arguably the most important set of geophysical measurements ever made. These measurements underpin the current knowledge of modern climate change science, with the ever-increasing curve being a dreadful testament to human folly, indelibly marking the damage done to our only atmosphere.

New Zealand's Role in Early Climate Change Science

Atmospheric CO_2 was increasing in the Northern Hemisphere, but what about the Southern Hemisphere? The two hemispheres are geographically very different with most of the Earth's landmass located in the Northern Hemisphere and most of the oceans in the Southern Hemisphere. Keeling believed that the southern oceans probably had a major role in adsorbing excess atmospheric CO_2 and expanded his measurement series by analysing air samples collected on ships in the Southern Hemisphere as well as in Antarctica. But, what he really needed was a site equivalent to his station in Hawaii where he could make continuous measurements of atmospheric CO_2 in the midlatitudes of the Southern Hemisphere. New Zealand, due to its remote location in the midlatitudes of the southwestern Pacific, was ideal.

But, the high-precision atmospheric CO_2 measurements needed were not easy to make, requiring trained staff, sophisticated analytical equipment, and back-up scientific laboratories. In the early 1960s, Keeling visited New Zealand and met with Athol Rafter, an eminent New Zealand scientist running a radiocarbon measurement laboratory in Lower Hutt. Rafter had already made extensive radiocarbon measurements in atmospheric CO_2 and ocean water around New Zealand. Through a remarkable piece of scientific detective work, Rafter showed that naturally-occurring CO_2 was being diluted by CO_2 derived from the combustion of fossil fuels, with the signal becoming clearer every year. Sadly, by the early 1960s, Rafter's measurements were compromised by yet more human folly — widespread atmospheric testing of nuclear weapons by the USA, USSR, and UK led to the naturally-occurring radiocarbon atmospheric signals being swamped by radiocarbon produced in bomb explosions.

Rafter's laboratory in Lower Hutt had the facilities that Keeling needed to set up continuous CO_2 measurements in New Zealand. It was his pioneering science and New Zealand's geographical position that drew Keeling to the country, marking the beginning of scientific cooperation that lasted well over 60 years.

I was involved in conducting the New Zealand measurements from the outset. After a couple of years of setbacks, I chose a measurement site at Baring Head, a rocky outcrop near Wellington exposed to winds from the Southern Ocean, unaffected by local sources of pollution. This has proved to be an ideal location for measurements, representative of a large part of the southwestern Pacific. The site has produced the longest set of continuous atmospheric CO_2 data in the midlatitudes of the Southern Hemisphere, data vital to the current scientific understanding of human-induced climate change.[4] In the 1980s, the site was expanded to include measurements of atmospheric methane, the second most important greenhouse gas, as well as other climate-changing gases including nitrous oxide produced by agriculture.

When I first began this project in 1970, only a few scientists were working in climate change science in New Zealand. Today, there are hundreds of internationally-recognised New Zealand scientists working on various aspects of climate change, including world-breaking research on paleoclimate, dynamical modelling of the atmosphere, as well as the atmospheric chemistry research that I began decades ago. The atmosphere has no borders; its degradation affects all humanity. Sadly, in many cases, the countries that have contributed least to the problem are the worst affected, for example, Tuvalu and other Pacific Island nations whose very existence is now compromised by rising sea levels.

International Research and Climate Change Agreements

By the late 1970s, measurements of atmospheric CO_2 at Baring Head, New Zealand, and Mauna Loa, Hawaii, were complemented by data from other sites all over the world. Everywhere, the answer was the same: CO_2 was increasing in the atmosphere everywhere. The science was irrefutable: Isotopic and other evidence demonstrated that the sources of the emissions were agriculture and industry, driven principally by increasing fossil fuel combustion.

In the 1960s and early 1970s, concerns from individual climate scientists and international scientific organisations often encountered disbelief from non-scientists. That such relatively tiny quantities of CO_2 could alter the climate of the entire planet seemed incredible. But, following a United Nations-sponsored conference on the environment in Stockholm in June 1972, climate change began to shift from being a solely scientific issue to one of political concern.

In 1975, the World Meteorological Organization funded by the UNEP ran the first meeting of atmospheric CO_2 experts in La Jolla, California, and I attended on behalf of the New Zealand government. This marked the beginning of annual international conferences on atmospheric CO_2. In the 1980s, the UNEP expanded the scope of these meetings to create the Intergovernmental Panel on Climate Change (IPCC). This organisation is tasked with providing comprehensive reviews of the state of climate change science by assessing peer-reviewed publications in internationally-recognised scientific journals.

In 1992, the UN Framework Convention on Climate Change (UNFCCC) developed an international treaty aimed at combatting "dangerous human interference with the climate system." This came into force in 1994 and has become a trusted basis for international negotiations on combatting climate change, including setting limits for greenhouse gas emissions. The treaty was ratified by most UN member states, including Singapore and New Zealand.

Since its inception, the UNFCCC has run an annual series of Conference of the Parties (COP) meetings where all member states can put forward their resolutions on combatting climate change. These include the Kyoto Protocol. I observed Prime Minister Helen Clark signing New Zealand's commitment to this in 2002. It came into force in 2005, ratified by 192 countries. For the first time, legally-binding commitments for greenhouse gas reductions relative to the 1990 emissions were made, with a first commitment period set for 2011. But, these applied only to developed countries, and most, including New Zealand, did not achieve them. India and China were categorised as developing countries, with no goals set on reducing emissions. By 2006, China's emissions had surpassed those of the USA, and India's were greater than those of the EU. For these and other reasons, the Kyoto Protocol failed to stem ever-increasing emissions of greenhouse gases in the 21st century. But, it, at least, marked the beginning of formal international agreements to curb greenhouse gases.

After Kyoto, the UNFCC continued to run annual COP meetings, but despite best intentions, the meetings resulted in disagreement with very little progress towards stemming huge increases in greenhouse gas emissions. By 2007, fossil fuel emissions had reached a staggering 32 billion tonnes per year,[5] four times higher than average annual emissions in the 1950s, when Keeling first alerted the world to the dangers of increasing atmospheric CO_2.

The 2009 COP meeting in Copenhagen drew representatives from most UN member countries, including President Obama from the United States, and made progress towards recognising the split between developing and developed countries. The latter had built their economies using unrestricted access to fossil fuels; developing countries, especially India, argued that this was unfair. They needed to use coal to produce electricity to lift their emerging economies. However, for the first time, agreements required specific carbon emissions reduction pledges from all major economies, including China and other developing countries. Unfortunately, as the meeting progressed, fractures developed, derailing agreements to the point where, despite the pledges, no binding resolution on emissions reductions was made. The final text of the meeting asked the world's nations to adopt a non-binding goal to "reduce emissions so as to hold the increase in global temperature below 2°C, and to take action to meet this objective consistent with science on the basis of equity."

The Copenhagen process also called for the creation of a green climate fund. It set the objective of providing US$30 billion between 2010 and 2012 to support developing countries and proposed increasing the sum to US$100 billion per year by 2020. This equitable solution to the developing/developed country divide would have had a significant impact on carbon emissions, but, despite some progress, this has not been achieved. By 2015, carbon emissions from fossil fuel combustion were 35 billion tonnes per year with atmospheric CO_2 at 400 ppm, almost 80 ppm higher than my first measurements in New Zealand in 1970.

The 2015 Paris Accord[6] is considered by many observers to be the most successful international climate meeting ever held. For the first time, the 195 UN member states ratified the central aim of keeping the global temperature rise to well below 2°C since pre-industrial times and preferably below 1.5°C. This required global carbon emissions to drop 50% by 2030 and reach net-zero carbon by 2050. To reach these targets, countries had to submit Nationally Determined Contributions (NDC). The first NDC submitted by New Zealand for the period 2021–2030 was to achieve emissions 50% below gross 2005 levels by 2030. Many countries made similar contributions. But, the aggregate of current NDC pledges is insufficient to keep temperatures below 1.5°C — fossil fuel emissions have continued to climb, reaching 37.2 billion tonnes in 2022.

Many scientists, climate activists, and international NGOs labelled the Paris Accord as yet another failure in a series of over 25 annual COP meetings. Was it? Despite the increase in carbon emissions since the Accord, the meeting produced positive outcomes. Among these are that the NDCs are flexible and several countries have increased their ambitions for carbon emissions reductions. Indeed, many countries, including Nordic and EU nations, have significantly reduced their emissions. At a city level, Copenhagen will reach net-zero carbon in 2025. And, as a sign that the financial world is taking notice, many international pension funds, banks, and insurance companies are withdrawing their investments from fossil fuel companies. Marking a world first in 2021, a court ordered oil company Royal Dutch Shell to reduce its carbon emissions by 45% by 2050. Since then, there has been a dramatic increase in climate change litigation, especially in the USA.[7]

COP28 was held in December 2023 in the UAE with Sultan Al Jaber, an oil executive, as its president. The talks got off to a good start with an agreement on a 'loss and damage fund' for poor and vulnerable countries reached on the first day. However, although the final text agreed upon at the meeting — directing the world to 'transition away from fossil fuels' — is a historic statement, it leaves room for the continued expansion of fossil fuel exploitation by major interests. Crucially, the COP28 agreement does not include the pivotal wording 'phase out of fossil fuels', showing the huge divisions between the major oil-producing states and almost all other countries seeking a 'climate-friendly' future. Indeed, many oil-producing states, including the UAE, plan to increase their fossil fuel production in this decade, the decade where the science is unequivocal: To have any hope of avoiding dangerous climate change, emissions must decrease by 50% by 2030.

Despite the COP meetings seemingly ineffectual, there is progress. For various reasons, including conflicts of interest by several

UNFCCC member oil-producing states, COP meetings will never have the capacity to force ground-breaking change. But, they have, at least, recognised the perils faced by many vulnerable countries, identified the dangers, and focussed the attention of almost all world governments on the urgent measures that must be taken to prevent catastrophe.

Current Climate Change Policy and Progress in New Zealand

New Zealand is unique among developed nations in that 50% of its greenhouse gas emissions are derived from agriculture. In addition, its population is widely dispersed with limited public transport options, leading to dependence on a relatively large light vehicle fleet; in 2023, there was almost one vehicle per person, one of the highest levels in the world. Transport is the fastest-growing single source of carbon emissions, currently 20% of total emissions. In the 2020s, large plantations of exotic trees, about 600,000 hectares, are due to be harvested, removing a relatively large sink of CO_2 and exacerbating already high per capita emissions. Despite substantial renewable energy sources and a small population, the path to net-zero carbon by 2050 will be a difficult one for New Zealand.

In 2008, the NZ government introduced an emissions trading scheme covering all greenhouse gases. In principle, this tool would regulate greenhouse emissions by setting an increasing price on carbon, linked to international markets. But, because of the importance of the primary industry to NZ's economy, emissions from agriculture were excluded. This omission, considered to be unfair by other industries forced to pay for carbon credits, is one of the factors compromising what should have been an effective economic instrument to reduce overall greenhouse gas emissions. The scheme has been reviewed and amended many times since it was introduced, but, so far, has produced only minimal reductions in NZ's domestic emissions.[8]

In 2019, the government passed the Climate Change Response (Zero Carbon) Amendment Act, providing a framework to develop and implement clear and stable climate change policies contributing to the global effort specified by the Paris Accord. The Act established a bipartisan and independent Climate Change Commission to advise the government on climate change policy and develop science- and economics-based plans to fulfil climate change goals. In 2020, the New Zealand government, followed by many city councils, declared a 'climate emergency', pledging immediate action to tackle the crisis. The announcement was backed by a series of measures aimed at curbing emissions, including decarbonising the public sector by 2025. The government is converting its fleet to electric vehicles and there is a widespread movement to build more energy-efficient buildings, offsetting the remaining emissions so as to create a direct financial incentive for the government to reduce emissions.

In 2021, the Climate Change Commission released its first report with an initial emissions reduction plan, recommending the abolition of new household gas connections by 2025, reducing the number of ruminant animals, and a comprehensive shift to electric vehicles by 2035. The report was endorsed by Prime Minister Ardern, and by mid-2022 the NZ government introduced a 'clean car' feebate scheme, making low-emissions vehicles like electric cars cheaper and high-emissions vehicles more expensive. The scheme immediately increased the sales of electric vehicles, and towards the end of 2023, plug-in vehicles made up about 2.5% of the light vehicle fleet, up from only 0.5% in 2020.

But, these plans have been controversial; for example, gas fitters claimed that their industry was under threat, car sales representatives projected that prices of used cars would rise, farmers pointed out that there were no electric alternatives to widely used diesel utility vehicles on farms, and many were opposed to plans to regulate agricultural emissions. Despite overwhelming imperatives to reduce emissions, such measures have become divisive. Although progress has been made at both government and personal levels, increasing emissions from the light vehicle fleet and methane and nitrous oxide from agriculture remain unresolved issues.

In February 2023, the east coast of New Zealand's North Island was devastated by the impacts of extra-tropical cyclone Gabrielle — the costliest ever in the Southern Hemisphere, resulting in a colossal loss of infrastructure and eleven lives. This followed months of severe flooding and storm events in several parts of New Zealand, events exacerbated by the effects of human-induced climate change. Many New Zealanders question whether a return to 'normal' is possible, recognising that rebuilding in flood-prone areas and areas close to sea level is unviable. Insurers are concerned about the increasing number of expensive claims. A recent poll found that more than 90% of those surveyed expected more frequent and extreme flooding events to occur. In urban centres, private car usage has dropped as more people work at home and opt for ride-sharing services like Uber and public transport. The linkage between ruminant animals, methane and nitrous oxide emissions, and water degradation is widely understood — for these and other reasons, including price signals and health concerns, red meat consumption in New Zealand is decreasing.

There is a widespread understanding that climate change is the single greatest threat facing the country. But, carrying through with actions needed to reduce emissions is another matter — although emissions have stabilised, they are not reducing. Unless immediate and deep cuts are made, the country will not achieve the 50% reduction in emissions needed by 2030 to remain on track to achieve net-zero carbon by 2050.

Summary

We face a climate crisis with tens of thousands of heat-related deaths reported over the past couple of years. Record temperatures were reached in most of southern Europe, large parts of the USA, and China in 2023; that year is the hottest ever recorded. Floods have caused catastrophic losses in countries throughout the world, including New Zealand. The science is unequivocal: Increasing greenhouse gas emissions will lead to dangerous climate change and we are close to triggering changes to the Earth's climate system that will become irreversible.

Reducing greenhouse gas emissions to avert the disastrous impacts of climate change is a colossal undertaking. UN organisations, including the IPCC, have led the way with science-based advice and pathways to achieve this. But, despite evidence-based warnings over the last 30 years, the advice has been disregarded and emissions have continued to increase.

The COVID-19 pandemic caused millions of deaths and much economic damage. But, carbon emissions in 2020 fell by 7% compared to 2019. Had this trend continued, emissions would have dropped 50% by 2030, the amount required to avoid the worst consequences of dangerous climate change, setting us on a path to net-zero carbon by 2050. But, since 2020, emissions have rebounded with new records set in both 2022 and 2023.

The lessons of COVID-19 show that when humans face a global emergency, we can reduce emissions. This requires concerted effort, above all from governments, but also from all of us. Sustainable low-carbon technologies are emerging rapidly; offshore wind is now the cheapest way of producing electricity, there has been a revolution in electric car battery technology in China, and autonomous vehicles and ride-sharing technologies are set to remove the need for individual car ownership with a massive drop in transport emissions.

We have the tools to combat climate change. The challenges are gigantic, but with coordinated international political action and individual willpower, humans are more than capable of building a sustainable future. **We can and must do this.**

References

1. J. Ballester *et al.*, 'Heat-related mortality in Europe during the summer of 2022', *Nature Medicine*, 29, 1857-1866, 2023.
2. D. C. Lowe, 'The Alarmist: Fifty Years Measuring Climate Change', Victoria University Press, Wellington New Zealand, pp 271, ISBN 9781776564187, 2021

3. S. Arrhenius, 'On the influence of carbonic acid in the air on the temperature of the ground' *Philosophical Magazine and Journal of Science*, 41, 237–276, 1896.
4. D.C. Lowe *et al.*, 'The concentration of atmospheric carbon dioxide at Baring Head, New Zealand', *Tellus*, 31, 58–67, 1979.
5. https://ourworldindata.org/co2-emissions (accessed August 2023)
6. https://unfccc.int/process-and-meetings/the-paris-agreement (accessed August 2023)
7. https://legaljournal.princeton.edu/global-climate-change-litigation-a-new-class-of-litigation-on-the-rise/ (accessed August 2023)
8. https://www.motu.nz/our-research/environment-and-resources/emission-mitigation/emissions-trading/lessons-learned-from-the-new-zealand-emissions-trading-scheme/ (accessed August 2023)

Chapter 18

There Has Never Been a More Crucial Time for the Earth Observatory of Singapore

Benjamin P. Horton, Lauriane Chardot, Emma M. Hill, Muhammad Hadi Ikhsan, Siti Rohaya Bte Jantan, Jhoanna Paula Santos Jovero, Andrew Krupa, KY Woo, Rachelle Xin Yang, Choong Yew Leong, and Sang-Ho Yun

Introduction

Research by the Earth Observatory of Singapore is revealing how our planet works, from the Earth's core to the clouds. As rapid changes in the Earth's system bring immense consequences to peoples, natural ecosystems, and infrastructure, continued progress in our understanding of Earth's processes will better prepare society to meet the challenges of a changing Earth.

Southeast Asia Is Exposed to Multiple Geohazards and Climate Change Is Compounding the Problem

Southeast Asia is one of the most dynamic regions on Earth when it comes to geohazards and climate change (Figure 1). Located at the junction of tectonic plates which drive continuous seismicity and volcanic activity, the region has seen a series of destructive earthquakes, tsunamis, and volcanic eruptions. For example, the 2004 earthquake that occurred in Aceh, off the shore of Sumatra in Indonesia, triggered a tsunami that inundated the coasts of Southeast Asia, all the way to Africa, claiming more than 230,000 lives across 14 countries, and strongly impacting the region's economy. The 2017 eruption from Mount Agung, a volcano located in Bali in Indonesia, led to the evacuation of thousands and disrupted aviation across Indonesia and as far afield as Australia.

The region is also affected by a range of climate-related events. Powerful typhoons regularly make landfall in Southeast Asia, such as Typhoon Haiyan in 2013, which devastated the Philippines in particular. Extreme rainfall regularly triggers flooding and extreme heat affects the health and well-being of peoples, leading to severe droughts.

These natural hazards will be compounded by climate change. Global mean temperature is projected to increase by 1.5°C to 2°C

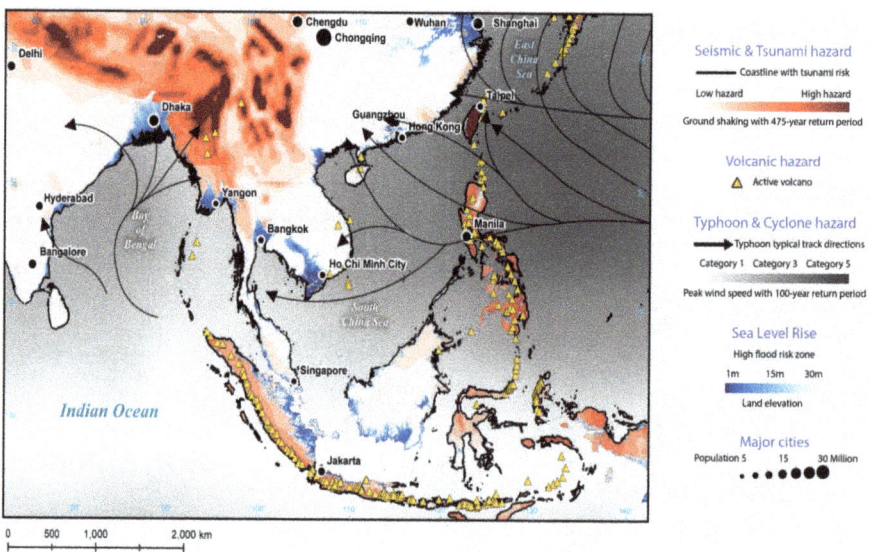

Figure 1. The natural hazards threatening Southeast Asia. *Source*: Earth Observatory of Singapore.

by the mid-21st century or sooner, bringing increases in the rate of sea-level rise, hotter weather, longer monsoon seasons, and increased droughts to Southeast Asia. Low-lying coastal cities will be exposed to sea-level rise and tropical cyclone risk. The region is also expected to see increases in heat and humidity, with extreme precipitation predicted in some areas and droughts in others. Southeast Asian societies are facing a complex challenge due to climate change and they need to implement mitigation and adaptation measures to ensure the sustainability of the region.

Understanding These Environmental Threats and Promoting Resilient and Sustainable Societies Require Local, Regional, and Global Collaborations

Reducing disaster risk and addressing climate change

Promoting the resilience of the region against geohazards and climate change is an urgent but complex challenge. This is because geohazards and climate change are interconnected and because our society is exposed and vulnerable to them. A better understanding of these hazards can allow us to forecast the risk and alert the at-risk communities so that they can respond. At the same time, addressing the region's vulnerability is key, so communities can better prepare for, respond to, and recover from the hazards when they strike.

This requires long-term efforts within and across borders and on many fronts, including scientific research, technological advances, education, and capacity-building. This also requires data to observe the complex processes driving the changing Earth and to help build the models that describe these processes, which can project future outcomes. And, this requires many partnerships at the community level, national level, regional level, and global level, with regular communication with appropriate stakeholders so that knowledge can be transferred and actions undertaken.

Creating a centre for Earth observations, scientific discovery, and knowledge transfer in Southeast Asia

After the shock of the Indian Ocean tsunami in 2004, the Singapore government proposed a world-class research centre that could serve as an international hub for geohazard and climate change to promote a safer, more sustainable Singapore and Southeast Asia. The Earth Observatory of Singapore (EOS) was created in 2008 as a Research Centre of Excellence with the mission *"to conduct fundamental research on earthquakes, volcanic eruptions, tsunamis and climate change in and around Southeast Asia, toward safer and more sustainable societies."* During the following 15 years, EOS would make conceptual, technological, computational, and observational advances in the study of the Earth as an integrated system, with direct applications to ensure a safe and sustainable future for Singapore and Southeast Asia. EOS is now a University Research Institute at Nanyang Technological University (NTU) Singapore and provides fundamental scientific advancement for a better understanding of the value and relevance of Earth science to society.

One of the key centres helping to provide the data needed to drive the geohazard and climate research of EOS and its collaborators is the EOS Centre for Geohazard Observations (CGO). The CGO installs, maintains, and manages EOS's geohazard and climate field instrumentation stations and networks spread across several countries in and around Southeast Asia.

Singapore's strong financial support and the excitement of working in one of the most geologically-dynamic and climatically-vulnerable places on Earth have enabled EOS to attract and support a vibrant group of talented researchers and staff, coming from Singapore, Southeast Asia, and other parts of the world. Faculty members from NTU's Asian School of the Environment and other schools are driving the research and are leading teams comprising researchers of different levels, from PhD students completing their degree to researchers who have worked at EOS for many years and have helped forge connections with neighbouring countries.

The push for interdisciplinary research

Addressing the region's complex and interconnected environmental hazards requires scientists from diverse backgrounds to work together towards the same goal of promoting resilience and sustainability. To this effect, EOS is organised into four scientific research groups:

- The EOS *Climate* Group focuses primarily on tropical paleoclimate and sea-level change, with the objective of understanding drivers of past and present climate variability to better forecast future climate change. This includes work on climate proxy-record reconstruction from geological archives (e.g. cave stalagmite records of hydroclimatic changes); reconstructions of sea-level changes throughout the Holocene (the last 11,300 years) and over recent decades (Figure 2); and coastal

Figure 2. Professor Benjamin Horton and his team in Antarctica in 2023, researching how glacial melt contributes to sea-level rise and impacts Southeast Asia. *Source*: Earth Observatory of Singapore.

hazards from extreme events such as tsunamis and storm surges. The timescales of focus in the Climate Group range from glacial–interglacial cycles (about 100,000-yearlong) through to present-day interannual variations, as well as projections of future changes.

- The EOS *Tectonics* Group studies the active fault systems of South and Southeast Asia, including the boundary between the Indo-Australian and Eurasian tectonic plates along Sumatra, through Myanmar, and up into the Himalayas; and the Manila Trench off the shore of the Philippines. The group is also investigating poorly-understood fault systems closer to Singapore to determine which, if any, pose a significant hazard to the region. By having ready access to data and field sites across these regions, partly through long-term monitoring arrays, the group can compile and analyse uniquely-comprehensive datasets.

- The EOS *Volcano* Group focuses on understanding these enigmatic giants and their early signs of eruptions to help develop techniques that can forewarn decision-makers and at-risk communities, giving them the time they need to activate emergency response plans and mitigation measures. The group applies a wide range of observational techniques, including seismology, geodesy, geochemistry, and petrology, in combination with analogue and numerical modelling techniques, to better understand magmatic processes that lead to volcanic eruptions, the history of eruptions in the region, and signs of volcanic unrest.

- The EOS *Risk and Society* Group is unique in that very few research groups in the world (let alone Southeast Asia or Singapore) rigorously develop their own science-based evidence related to societal impacts, recovery, adaptation, and mitigation to geohazards and climate change. The group tranlates this information to innovative solutions for public policy and governance, science communication, and economic incentives.

Through interdisciplinary work between the separate groups at EOS, researchers in Singapore, Southeast Asia, and around the world, and government and policy stakeholders, EOS aims to ensure a sustainable and resilient future society.

Partnering to achieve impact

Promoting safer and more sustainable societies involves engaging with stakeholders and informing policy as appropriate. EOS has developed partnerships with agencies, businesses, and other institutions to further its mission and address societal challenges. For example, partnerships with regional monitoring authorities such as the Philippine Institute of Volcanology and Seismology and Indonesia's Center for Volcanology and Geological Hazard Mitigation have allowed EOS to advance the understanding of tectonic and volcanic processes of the region, through data collection and joint publications. Partnerships with Singapore agencies such as the Singapore Land Authority have allowed EOS to develop monitoring networks in Singapore which will provide critical data to understand climate change impacts.

Scientific Findings Have Better Characterised the Hazards the Region Is Facing

EOS and its collaborators have achieved many scientific successes in geohazards and climate change that are shaping future research. Highlights include the following:

Geohazards

- The discovery of the longest slow earthquake ever recorded: Mallick *et al.* (2021) found that the catastrophic 1861 Sumatra earthquake was preceded by a 32-year-long slow slip event. The discovery, which changes global perspectives on the phenomenon, suggests that current earthquake risk assessments may not carefully consider the potential for slow slip events to trigger future earthquakes and tsunamis. This study was published in *Nature Geoscience*.

- The realisation that human activities affected the impacts of the Palu earthquake: Bradley *et al* (2019) revealed that the deadly landslides in Indonesia's Palu Valley following the 2018 earthquake resulted from liquefaction in areas heavily irrigated for rice cultivation. This discovery raises awareness of anthropogenic hazards where active faults and irrigation coexist. This study was published in *Nature Geoscience*.
- Understanding diffusion chronometry to constrain the timescales of magmatic processes: Costa *et al* (2020) revealed that diffusion modelling of the chemical gradients in crystals can be used to extract invaluable time information from magmatic systems. This study was published in *Nature Reviews Earth & Environment*.
- Describing the atmospheric waves and global seismo-acoustic observations of the January 2022 Hunga eruption, Tonga: EOS co-authored an international publication that made the cover of *Science* (1 July 2022). The EOS infrasound team was part of an international team that studied the Tonga eruption to reconstruct the eruption and associated tsunami.

Climate change

- The longest reconstruction of sea-level history in Singapore: Chua *et al* (2021) reconstructed the history of sea-level changes dating back 10,000 years ago, using sediment samples from around the country and a core from Marina South, which has pollen showing the presence of mangroves 10,000 years ago. This discovery will help future projections of sea-level rise in Singapore. This study was published in *The Holocene*.
- The first detailed history of rainfall in the Amazon during the past 45,000 years: Wang *et al* (2017) reconstructed the history of rainfall in the Amazon, using cave speleothems that recorded rainfall changes over the last 45,000 years. This discovery ends a long-lasting debate and shows that the Amazon stayed a living forest during the last ice age, despite lower rainfall. This study made the front cover of *Nature* (12 January 2017 issue).

- The quantification of how much coastal cities are sinking, especially in Asia, making them vulnerable to sea-level rise: Tay *et al* (2022) conducted a study showing that many coastal cities around the world are sinking. Among the causes for the subsidence are rapid urbanisation and extraction of underground resources. This study can help practitioners and policymakers better understand and address coastal risk. This study was published in *Nature Sustainability*.

EOS's proportion of publications among the world's most highly-cited journals has grown steadily over the past 15 years.

Reducing Vulnerability and Promoting Resilience to Geohazards and Climate Change

Reducing vulnerabilities in the region and responding to disasters

While hazards cannot be prevented, the risk to communities can be reduced if they are less exposed and less vulnerable to the hazards. Scientists from EOS have derived frameworks and technologies that are helping future adaptation and response strategies. For example, a framework to quantify the benefits of nature-based solutions for disaster risk reduction was proposed by Lallemant *et al* (2021) to compare the benefits of nature-based solutions with that of 'grey infrastructure' when deciding on solutions for reducing disaster risk. Another framework was derived to quantify how certain interventions prevented the occurrence of disasters. It was, for example, applied to quantify how the retrofitting of schools in Nepal prevented loss during the 2015 Nepal earthquakes. Scientists hope to inspire other communities to pursue similar initiatives.

When disasters strike and affect communities, rapid response is critical for rescue and relief efforts. The EOS Remote Sensing laboratory is a recent flagship initiative that was founded in 2021 to support regional and global stakeholders and decision-makers such as the Sentinel Asia consortium, ASEAN Coordinating Centre for Humanitarian Assistance on Disaster Management (AHA Centre), and the United Nations World Food Programme. EOS-RS monitors and maps hazards and disasters, environmental crises, sea-level rise, and climate change using innovative technology in satellite remote sensing (e.g. spaceborne Synthetic Aperture Radar, LiDAR, and optical sensors).

Staying nimble and striving for innovation

To address the evolving environmental changes faced by Singapore and Southeast Asia, EOS scientists innovate and develop innovative technologies:

- Leveraging the wealth of satellite data: EOS-RS drives scientific innovation and improves the understanding of hazards through the development of new algorithms and systems to map hazards and disasters.
- Creating a web-based interactive tool to generate reports of probability maps of ash dispersion: With this tool, EOS volcano scientists aim to help the aviation sector forecast impacted areas and plan long-term strategies to manage ash–aircraft interactions in Southeast Asia.
- Monitoring of climate and sea-level changes in Singapore: EOS climate scientists and the CGO installed sensors in Singapore to monitor sea-level changes which will help constrain future sea-level projections.

Future generations

Recognising the importance of educating future generations to address environmental challenges, EOS was instrumental in the creation of the Asian School of the Environment at NTU which trains students at all levels. The school is thus providing the workforce needed to address environmental challenges in all sectors of society.

EOS also set up a Community Engagement Office which takes a multi-pronged approach to promote a safer and more sustainable society. The office informs the public about EOS research and activities, and inspires actions through content creation and engagement. It also aims to build a local base of Earth science enthusiasts and partner with, for example, the Ministry of Education on several initiatives such as curriculum development, teacher training, and co-creation of exhibitions.

Towards Safer and More Sustainable Societies

Looking ahead, EOS plans to focus on three programmes for sustainable growth and resilience to geohazards and climate change: The SouthEast Asia SEA-Level Program (SEA2), the Integrating Volcano and Earthquake Science and Technology (InVEST) programme, and the Climate Transformation Programme (CTP).

EOS has aligned its strategy with national priorities such as Singapore's National Sea Level Programme and the Singapore Green Plan. At the same time, it is critical to work with other countries from the region and beyond. Indeed, geohazards and climate change do not know borders. To understand the rising seas in Singapore, we need to team up with scientists in the Arctic and Antarctic regions where the ice sheets are melting at an alarming pace (Figure 2). To assess volcanic risk in Singapore, we need to unravel what drives seismic and volcanic activity in the region with our partners. And, to reduce the impacts of these hazards on societies, we need to work alongside all sectors of society to reduce the vulnerabilities, adapt to the changing Earth, and promote a better future for us all.

Bibliography

Bradley, K., Mallick, R., Andikagumi, H., Hubbard, J., Meilianda, E., Switzer, A., Du, N., Brocard, G., Alfian, D., Benazir, B., Feng, G., Yun, S.-H., Majewski, J., Wei, S., and Hill, E. M. (2019). Earthquake-triggered 2018 Palu Valley landslides enabled by wet rice cultivation. *Nature Geoscience*, 12, 935–939. https://doi. org/10.1038/s41561-019-0444-1.

Chua, S., Switzer, A. D., Li, T., Chen, H., Christie, M. A., Shaw, T. A., Khan, N. S., Bird, M. I., and Horton, B. P. (2021). A new Holocene sea-level record for Singapore. *Holocene*, 31, 1376–1390 https://doi.org/10.1177/ 09596836211019096.

Costa, F., Shea, T., and Ubide, T. (2020). Diffusion chronometry and the time-scales of magmatic processes. *Nature Reviews Earth & Environment*, 1, 201– 214. https://doi.org/10.1038/s43017-020-0038-x.

Lallemant, D., Hamel, P., Balbi, M., Lim, T. N., Schmitt, R., and Win, S. (2021). Nature-based solutions for flood risk reduction: A probabilistic modelling framework. *One Earth*, 4(9), 1310–1321. https://doi.org/10.1016/j.oneear. 2021.08.010.

Mallick, R., Meltzner, A. J., Tsang, L. L. H., Lindsey, E. O., Feng, L., and Hill, E. M. (2021). Long-lived shallow slow-slip events on the Sunda megathrust. *Nature Geoscience*, 14, 327–333. https://doi.org/10.1038/s41561-021-00727-y.

Matoza, R. S. *et al* (2022). Atmospheric waves and global seismoacoustic obser-vations of the January 2022 Hunga eruption, Tonga. *Science*, 377, 95–100. https://doi.org/DOI:10.1126/science.abo7063.

Tay, C., Lindsey, E. O., Tong Chin, S., McCaughey, J. W., Bekaert, D., Nguyen, M., Hua, H., Manipon, G., Karim, M., Horton, B. P., Li, T., and Hill, E. M. (2022). Land subsidence intensifies sea-level rise: An InSAR analysis of 48 major coastal cities. *Nature Sustainability*. https://doi.org/10.1038/s41893-022-00947-z.

Wang, X., Edwards, R., Auler, A., Cheng, H., Kong, X., Wang, Y., Cruz, F. W., Dorale, J. A., and Chiang, H.-W. (2017). Hydroclimate changes across the Amazon lowlands over the past 45,000 years. *Nature*, 541, 204–207. https:// doi.org/10.1038/nature20787.

Chapter 19

The Recent New Zealand Experience of Environmental Law Reform

Greg Severinsen and Raewyn Peart

Abstract

In 1991, New Zealand passed the Resource Management Act (RMA). The Act was considered world-leading at the time, but has since been widely criticised for not living up to its potential. Thirty years on, the country undertook a rethink of its core environmental legislation to provide a stronger focus on strategic planning, firm environmental limits, and positive environmental outcomes. This chapter looks at the impetus for the reform, the innovative approaches that were adopted in the new legislation, potential implementation challenges, and its swift repeal when a new government entered office in late 2023.

Introduction

In August 2023, the New Zealand Parliament passed into law the most significant new environmental legislation in a generation: the Natural and Built Environment Act (NBE Act) and the Spatial Planning Act. The labour government's objectives for the NBE Act were, essentially, to better protect the natural environment (including through firm "bottom lines") while providing greater certainty and efficiency for development, to more strongly recognise the rights of the Māori (and the Treaty of Waitangi, which is the

247

country's founding document, signed in 1840 between the British Crown and Māori chiefs), and to simplify what had become a highly complex system (notably, by reducing the number of plans in the system).

The idea behind the separate Spatial Planning Act was to ensure, through the creation of higher-level regional spatial strategies, that the activities of planning authorities under multiple fragmented pieces of law (including separate statutes for land use, infrastructure planning, and funding) could be better coordinated. Overall, there was a sense that the existing RMA with its focus on 'sustainable management' was normatively dated, overly bureaucratic, and had not served the interests of the natural environment or development (Resource Management Review Panel, 2020).

The Resource Management Act 1991

To understand the new laws and what they sought to do differently, it is worth considering where the previous system came from. When the RMA was passed in 1991, it was widely seen as innovative and world-leading. In contrast to most other jurisdictions, it took a highly-integrated approach to environmental management, which was one of the core aims of the law reform process. The RMA replaced dozens of fragmented, and often issue- or resource-specific, statutes and brought together the concept of town and country planning (land use/subdivision controls) and 'environmental' (including discharge/pollution) controls under one framework.

The RMA was also underpinned by a number of other key principles. The first was giving greater recognition to the principles of the Treaty of Waitangi, which under section 8 of the Act have to be "taken into account" in all decision-making. These principles were (and are) non-statutory and have been carefully developed over many years by the courts (*New Zealand Māori Council v Attorney General* [1987] 1 NZLR 641 (CA); *Trans-Tasman Resources Limited v The Taranaki-Whanganui Conservation Board* [2021] NZSC 127). The recognition of evolving principles has allowed jurisprudence move beyond the analysis of the Treaty's actual text (which has been complicated, because more than one version of the Treaty was signed).

Secondly, the Act saw (at least in theory) a move towards 'effects-based' environmental management. Essentially, this meant that decisions were primarily based on the predicted environmental impacts of a particular activity, not blanket requirements for a sector/activity, or what would be the wisest use of resources for public social/economic outcomes. This heralded a shift away from a strong reliance on planning towards a much greater emphasis on environmental impact assessment. The rationale was that, so long as environmental bottom lines were not infringed, the market should be left free to operate unimpeded.

Thirdly, there was greater devolution of decision-making. Local government (regional councils, concerned with most 'environmental' functions, and territorial authorities, concerned mainly with land use) made most decisions at first instance. With the exception of aspects of coastal management, the central government's role was left to the discretion of the Minister, who could develop national direction to guide decisions on plans (which set most policies and regulations) and resource consents (individual project permissions), and 'call in' proposals of national significance to be determined by the Environment Court or bespoke boards of inquiry. But, those interventions were ad hoc. In practice, the first half of the RMA's life saw a dearth of national direction or other central government intervention (Resource Management Review Panel, 2020).

Fourthly, there was a desire for a more open and transparent government as well as robust checks and balances on political power. Government entities were to be treated the same as anyone else (e.g. when applying for consent for public infrastructure projects like roads or electricity generation). As the main check on local government decision-making, the public was given broad standing to engage in planning (and, to a lesser extent, consenting) processes, including relatively-extensive rights of appeal to an independent and specialised environment court. The supervisory role of the court was a cornerstone of the system and, for the most part, one that has proven extremely important in keeping councils in check.

Most of the defining features of the RMA were influenced by the turbulent social and political context of the late 1980s. A wave of enthusiasm for market-led neoliberalism under David Lange's Labour government provided a powerful ideological influence. The unique history of the previous decade played a decisive role too: The National Government of Robert Muldoon (1975–1984) had been much more interventionist when it came to the economy and legislated to allow the government to override environmental laws for nationally-significant infrastructure development. The RMA was part of a pendulum swinging consciously away from what had come before.

Problems with the Resource Management Act: The Impetus for Fundamental Reform

The RMA was undoubtedly an improvement on the previous assortment of planning and environmental laws. However, in 2023, it was a generation old and showing its age. Most importantly, the Act proved unable to halt environmental decline. With some notable exceptions, most environmental indicators had become progressively worse (Ministry for the Environment & Statistics New Zealand, 2022). Despite a clear intention to establish firm environmental limits, these were not mandatory and were very slow to emerge. For most of its life, the RMA's purpose of sustainable management was interpreted as allowing the benefits of development to outweigh its environmental risks, in what was termed an "overall broad judgement" or 'OBJ' approach (Minister for the Environment's Resource Management Act 1991 Principles Technical Advisory Group 2012). Civil society litigation softened this position with a landmark 2014 Supreme Court decision (*Environmental Defence Society Inc v The New Zealand King Salmon Co Ltd* [2014] NZSC 38, [2014] 1 NZLR 593), but even this judgement failed to resolve fundamental issues with the RMA, which allowed the OBJ approach to arise in the first place (Severinsen and Peart, 2018). The reality is that the RMA did not require true environmental limits to be established unless public authorities chose to do so.

The RMA also provides next to no recognition of the importance of climate change mitigation. In fact, for almost two decades, it specifically prohibited most decision-makers from considering the impacts of greenhouse gas emissions on the climate, with reliance placed almost wholly on the market mechanism of an emissions trading scheme (which itself has had significant weaknesses, including the exclusion of biogenic agricultural emissions).

Over the past decade, the RMA has also presided over a period of rapid urban growth, with some attributing to it a failure to release sufficient development-ready land, thereby contributing to unaffordable housing in some centres (Productivity Commission of New Zealand, 2017). The Act has enabled urban change and intensification to be opposed by cloaking 'NIMBY' ('not in my backyard') motives in the language of environmental protection. The RMA's effects-based ethos has lacked the forward-looking stance of an 'outcomes-based' statute seeking environmental improvements.

Moreover, the Act's deliberate rejection of considerations of social equity has meant it has largely failed to address issues of resource allocation and reallocation (especially when it comes to freshwater). Rights to natural resources have mainly been given to those who have applied for consent first and have also favoured incumbent users (Resource Management Review Panel, 2020). This has caused issues with both efficiency and equity.

Commentators have also said that the RMA no longer reflects an appropriate approach to the Treaty of Waitangi — if, indeed, it ever did (Waitangi Tribunal, 2001). In contrast to the Conservation Act 1987, which requires giving "effect to" the principles of the Treaty, the RMA only refers to taking them "into account." Although statutory powers can be transferred to the Māori, this has seldom occurred. Instead, bespoke legislation settling historical Treaty grievances has been relied on to provide the Māori with influence in RMA processes, including legislation recognising legal person-hood for *te Awa Tupua* (the Whanganui River).

Efficiency and agility have been concerns as well. Extensive participatory rights (including merit appeals) mean that plan changes can get bogged down in legal proceedings for many years. An effects-based framework has also meant that plans often fail to provide a clear answer as to whether a particular proposal should be allowed or not, requiring lengthy consenting processes to assess individual applications on their merits.

There has been extensive argument as to whether, and to what extent, blame for such poor outcomes can be laid at the door of the RMA itself. Many problems have undoubtedly been the product of the central government's failure to provide national direction in the form of national policy statements (NPS) or national environmental standards (NES), politicised decision-making by local councils that are elected to represent their communities and not the environment, and a lack of capacity and capability. With respect to the first problem, giving the central government optional powers of intervention has meant that important issues such as biodiversity loss, with New Zealand having 4,000 indigenous species threatened or at risk of extinction (Ministry for the Environment & Statistics NZ, 2019), have been left languishing. An NPS for indigenous biodiversity was only promulgated in 2023 — a full three decades after the enactment of the RMA and (rather incredibly) only a matter of weeks before its replacement statute was passed into law (although this was subsequently repealed).

Reform Gets the Green Light

By the mid-2010s, there was increasing support for the proposition that the Act needed to be fundamentally rethought. For many years, the government did not agree. Effort was instead put into a series of amendments to target particular issues (which added considerably to the length, complexity, and incoherence of the legislation). The RMA roughly doubled in length from its inception.

A series of detailed reports in the mid-2010s by Local Government New Zealand (2015), the Productivity Commission (2017), Infrastructure New Zealand (2015), and the Environmental

Defence Society (Severinsen and Peart, 2018), as well as a change of government in 2017, eventually led to the Minister for the Environment accepting that a fundamental overhaul was needed. In 2018, the government announced a process by which reform would be progressed. It established an independent panel headed by retired Court of Appeal Justice Hon Tony Randerson KC, which in a lengthy report drew on the past work of others and echoed many of their conclusions — most fundamentally that the RMA needed to be replaced (Resource Management Review Panel, 2020).

The Minister quickly endorsed the broad thrust of the Panel's proposals and instructed officials to work up the detailed policy needed to underpin two new pieces of legislation — the NBE Act and the Spatial Planning Act. (A third statute recommended by the Panel, concerned with climate change adaptation, was deemed too difficult to progress in parallel with the others and so was put on a slower development track.)

In November 2022, the two Bills were formally introduced to Parliament, to be considered together through a select committee process. The Environment Committee received more than 3,000 submissions and reported its recommendations via an extensive report in June 2023. The Acts were passed under urgency in August 2023, shortly before Parliament rose prior to the general election.

The NBE Act and Spatial Planning Act

The NBE Act was long and complex. Essentially, it filled the same place in the system as the RMA. It was a regulatory statute which (1) told people what activities could not be undertaken without authorisation (e.g. discharging a contaminant into water or occupying the coastal marine area); (2) established a purpose and set of principles to guide decisions; (3) provided for a cascade of subordinate instruments (e.g. national direction and plans) to be created; and (4) outlined the procedural and institutional architecture within which various authorities were to make decisions.

The Spatial Planning Act was something entirely new (and much simpler). Essentially, it provided a framework for the creation of regional spatial strategies that would sketch out how a region would grow or change over the long term. It was separate from the NBE Act, largely because spatial strategies needed to influence many pieces of legislation (e.g. how infrastructure for transport and water supply is funded under the Local Government Act and the Land Transport Management Act), not just regulatory plans under the NBE Act.

While many features of the NBE Act did not represent a significant departure from the RMA, some things were markedly different. First, and most fundamentally, the NBE Act created new legal concepts called environmental limits (defined as the current state of the environment) and minimum acceptable limits (which must be set and worked towards if the current state of the environment is unacceptably degraded). These were mandatory for particular domains (e.g. freshwater, soil, air, and indigenous biodiversity) to restore ecological integrity. If an activity would infringe a limit, a resource consent could not be granted (unless an exemption was conferred).

The purpose of the NBE Act was also quite different. Its core concept was the Māori expression "te Oranga o te Taiao" (which was given a broad definition in the Act), and when achieving this purpose, enabling use and development was to be *subject to* protecting the health of the natural environment. Effectively, this meant that the overall broad judgement interpretation under the RMA (balancing the benefits and costs of development) would not have been possible under the NBE Act.

Secondly, the Act provided a more comprehensive (or at least more wide-ranging) list of 'outcomes' that authorities were required to provide for. It was no longer to be just about mitigating the adverse effects of environmental harmful activities. Authorities were required to work towards a better future and had to pursue synergistic outcomes between development *and* environmental improvement by setting mandatory targets.

Thirdly, the central government was obliged to play a more proactive role than under the RMA, including by providing a more integrated national direction. Ministers were required to prepare a single integrated National Planning Framework rather than issuing separate NPSs and NESs when politically expedient to do so.

Fourthly, the Act was (intended to be) simpler. There were directions encouraging plans to provide more certainty of outcome, meaning that fewer activities would require consent, and those that did would be subject to clearer requirements. In addition, there were to be fewer plans. Councils within a region would have been obliged to work with each other (and the Māori), via a single regional planning committee, to produce one integrated plan rather than the multiple district and regional plans required for each region under the RMA.

Fifthly, the Treaty of Waitangi and the interests of the Māori were more strongly recognised than in the RMA. This was most obvious in the clause dealing with the Treaty itself, where there was an explicit obligation to "give effect to" its principles. But, it was also woven throughout the fabric of the legislation, for example, in the Act's purpose (the Māori concept of te Oranga o te Taiao), numerous references to tikanga, the establishment of a National Māori Entity to monitor Crown compliance with the Treaty, and in the power of the Māori to appoint members to regional planning committees.

Repeal of the New Legislation and Challenges for the Future

The NBE Act was by no means perfect from an environmental perspective. For example, while environmental limits are a positive legal concept, better outcomes on the ground would have been dependent on politically influenced decisions about precisely where they were set. Also relevant is the extent to which exemptions to limits would have been granted, which seemed reliant on political will. The long list of outcomes also invited a balancing exercise and degree of political prioritisation (e.g. between the climate benefits of fast-growing exotic forestry and the biodiversity benefits of indigenous carbon forests), which risked downward pressures towards environmental limits rather than improvements above them.

However, for now, those challenges are academic only. The 2023 general election saw the right-of-centre National Party brought to power, in a coalition with the more firmly-right-wing ACT Party and the populist New Zealand First Party. Coalition agreements put the new legislation on the chopping block, driven by concerns about red tape, the role of the Māori and non-Western concepts, and impacts on the farming sector. Wholesale repeal (with the exception of a fast-track process for consenting) occurred swiftly in December 2023. The RMA is, once again, the relevant legal framework. At the time of writing, there are also proposals for ministers to effectively consent to proposals under separate fast-track legislation, marking a return to the even more problematic settings of the Muldoon era that caused the RMA to be created in the first place. Moreover, there are plans to dilute much secondary legislation made under the RMA for freshwater and biodiversity protection.

The new government has also signalled a longer-term plan to rethink and replace the RMA with something quite different: a new planning act and a separate natural environment act. Those reforms are to be based on an underlying principle of the defence of private property rights. If that libertarian approach is legislated for, it seems likely that a future left-leaning government would, in turn, cast such reforms on the policy bonfire and yet again return to the RMA or NBE Act (after all, the latter is now 'ready-to-go' after a half-decade of policy work). Like many aspects of New Zealand society in 2023, fundamental resource management laws now seem increasingly at risk of lurching from left to right and back again. This mirroring of political ideologies in new environmental legislation is a marked change from the past, where tinkering with the RMA has defined the last 30 years of environmental politics. Such a seesawing approach will do little to provide certainty for business or nature, and may further fracture what little potential remains for bipartisan cooperation.

Environmental policy in New Zealand is now heading in a very different direction, and most debate will be focused on the risks of the new government's 'development-friendly' approach. But, it is worth thinking about the implementation challenges that would have faced the short-lived NBE Act, since a variant of it may return to the statute book in future years. The RMA was widely perceived to have failed because it was poorly implemented; local authorities were expected to prepare plans with constrained financial capacity and capability, and the central government failed to provide meaningful direction for matters that were of national significance.

Adequately funding councils and the Māori to perform their statutory functions (e.g. preparing new plans) and establishing a robust evidence base to support them (e.g. measuring the current environmental state to set environmental limits) would have been crucial to the success of the legislation. In particular, there was a risk that development proposals for large infrastructure (e.g. roads, electricity generation) would be effectively locked in via regional spatial strategies under the Spatial Planning Act before there was sufficient information to establish comprehensive environmental limits under the NBE Act that they might infringe. And, there could be a temptation for the central government to provide the bare minimum of guidance via the National Planning Framework (e.g. when it comes to 'framing' rather than 'setting' environmental limits), risking a repeat of the uncertainty for councils that defines the RMA.

Making sure councils in a region (sometimes with quite different priorities and political platforms) worked effectively together via regional planning committees would also have been challenging, along with ensuring core environmental protections were not politicised, such as when exemptions to limits are granted or significant biodiversity areas identified on private land.

Even though the NBE Act would have grappled more proactively with questions of resource allocation than the RMA, it offered only high-level guidance (through principles of sustainability, equity, and efficiency) that would no doubt have caused difficulty in practice when it came to reallocating rights to scarce resources like freshwater. Uncertainty about whether preference should be given to the Māori in allocation was exacerbated by the much stronger Treaty clause, especially since similar challenges have arisen under the same wording in the Conservation Act.

The transition pathway from the old to the new would also have been challenging. This was expected to take up to 10 years, and most aspects of the NBE Act would have only 'switched on' once new combined plans were made region by region (which made the Act quite straightforward to unwind). Early litigation and case law would have been important to provide test cases that clarified the law. There were many new concepts in the NBE Act that would have required careful interpretation.

Because significant harm has already occurred to the environment, turning things around will rely on the practical ability of decision-makers to make things better (e.g. through funding, replanting, pest control, and potentially the courage to take people's existing rights away), not just prevent further damage. As the Parliamentary Commissioner for the Environment (2023) has stated, "Changing the law alone will not necessarily improve the state of the environment. To do that requires the marshalling of expertise and financial resources, and placing regulatory powers in the hands of those best placed to exercise them." Alongside legislative reform, institutional reform is key.

If implemented properly, however, the NBE Act and Spatial Planning Act would have had the potential to be a significant improvement on the RMA. Plans would have provided businesses with more certainty about what is and is not allowable; fewer expensive consenting processes would have been required; and plans would have been more robust and agile. On the other hand, development interests would have been expected to comply with tougher environmental safeguards; there would have been untested legal concepts to navigate; and there was the uncomfortable prospect of consent holders having to relinquish their rights if they breached limits.

The reform story in New Zealand is by no means yet fully told, and the country is in for some turbulent years ahead. Irrespective of where reform goes next, there is already a rich story that will be of interest to other jurisdictions grappling with the risks and opportunities of deep environmental law reform.

Bibliography

Department of Conservation (2020). *Biodiversity in Aotearoa: An Overview of State, Trends and Pressures.* (Department of Conservation, 2020).

Infrastructure New Zealand (2015). *Integrated Governance, Planning and Delivery: A Proposal for Local Government and Planning Law Reform in New Zealand.* (Infrastructure New Zealand, 2015).

Local Government New Zealand (2015). *A "Blue Skies" Discussion About New Zealand's Resource Management System.* (Local Government of New Zealand, Wellington, 2015).

Ministry for the Environment (1991). *Report of the Review Group on the Resource Management Bill.* (Ministry for the Environment, Wellington, 2023).

Ministry for the Environment (2023). *Ōtūwharekai/Ashburton Lakes Lessons-Learnt Report: A Case Study Examining Ongoing Deterioration of Water Quality in the Ōtūwharekai Lakes.* (Ministry for the Environment, Wellington, 2023).

Ministry for the Environment & Statistics New Zealand (2019). *Environment Aotearoa.* (Ministry for the Environment & Statistics New Zealand, Wellington, 2019).

Ministry for the Environment & Statistics New Zealand (2022). *Environment Aotearoa.* (Ministry for the Environment & Statistics New Zealand, Wellington, 2022).

New Zealand Māori Council v Attorney General [1987] 1 NZLR 641 (CA).

Parliamentary Commissioner for the Environment (2023). *Submission on the Natural and Built Environment Bill and the Spatial Planning Bill.*

Productivity Commission of New Zealand (2017). *Better Urban Planning.* (Productivity Commission of New Zealand, Wellington, 2017).

Resource Management Review Panel (2020). *New Directions for Resource Management in New Zealand.* (Resource Management Review Panel, Wellington, 2020).

Severinsen, G. (2019). *Reform of the Resource Management System: A Model for the Future — Synthesis Report.* Auckland: Environmental Defence Society.

Severinsen, G. and Peart, R. (2018). *Reform of the Resource Management System: The Next Generation — Synthesis Report.* Auckland: Environmental Defence Society.

Trans-Tasman Resources Limited v The Taranaki-Whanganui Conservation Board [2021] NZSC 127.

Waitangi Tribunal (2001). *Ko Aotearoa Tenei* (Wai 262).

VII

THE CREATIVE SECTORS

Chapter 20

For the Love of Making — Reflections of a New Zealand Creative

Richard Taylor

When my wife Tania and I entered the creative industries in 1987, it couldn't have been a better time to have started off in this amazing career. Reflecting on it all these years later, I am struck by how important the 'luck of timing' was to our story.

On first arriving in Wellington in 1984 to undertake our studies, we assumed that we would see out our three years of education and quickly make our departure, bound for brighter lights; such was the drab and grey quality of the city we found, but maybe something was lurking under the briny waves of Wellington harbour, or possibly brooding just over the foothills of the city's perimeter, waiting for the right moment to grab us and hold us to this place? Perhaps there was some perfect mix of alchemy percolating, ready to explode in chemical wonder, lighting this dim little city with a vibrant-hued creative flame that would burn for a further three decades.

At the time, there was a proliferation of small, independent film and TV production houses in Wellington, so we quickly discovered sources of work perfectly attuned to the type of stuff we loved to make: robots and monsters, creatures and aliens, puppets and miniatures — oh, and politicians. How exciting! It was possibly inevitable, therefore, that our work would come to the attention of a young filmmaker making New Zealand's first-ever alien splatter movie. It was while we were making puppets for *Public Eye (circa 1988)*, the Kiwi version of the UK's beloved satire, *Spitting Image*, that *Peter Jackson* became aware of our work and popped over to see us. Beginning with *Meet the Feebles* in 1989 and Kiwi Classic, *Brain Dead*, then on to *Forgotten Silver* and *Jack Brown Genius*, through *Heavenly Creatures*, *The Frighteners*, and a seven-year spell on the *Hercules* and *Xena* TV series, this period of crackling creative energy in our capital was like nothing we could ever have imagined. And, it was happening right across the country. New Zealand had found its creative mojo and it seemed that nothing was going to stop the technicoloured rainbow of creativity that was lighting up the skies from Cape Reinga to Bluff.

After *Heavenly Creatures*, Tania and I would ultimately go on to form a partnership with Peter Jackson, and other friends from the local Wellington film industry, to co-found the *Wētā Companies*.

Of course, the chance to work on the *Lord of the Rings* (LOTR) was a once-in-a-lifetime opportunity. Initially, I described it as if teetering towards the edge of a precipice, such was the weight of expectation on myself, Tania, and our young team of technicians, considering the lack of experience we had preceding this opportunity. But, at some point, you have to leap, confident in the fact that grit, self-determination, capability, and confidence in yourself and those around you will arrest your fall — before you slam to the bottom of a cliff. We opted to look after five different departments, ultimately producing 48,000 separate items for the trilogy of films over seven years. Only one-eighth of our Kiwi team had ever worked on a film or TV show before and the average age was 22 years old. We had half a dozen film technicians join us from overseas, with most of these being young and relatively inexperienced.

The phrase I used early on with some of our team was that "regardless of how pale or how fine a thread you are given, if you don't weave it into the tapestry with care, precision and heightened creative intent, the tapestry will be in some way threadbare" — so, basically, we were only as good as our weakest link, so let's all pull together and achieve the near impossible and produce work that we can be proud of. And, fans the world over will hopefully enjoy and ultimately respect the creative decisions made through the work that we provided at Wētā Workshop.

The best part of *LOTR* for me though was the ability to share in this project with a large and diverse group of young NZ creatives who were empowered to indelibly make their mark through these extraordinary films that Peter Jackson had enabled for us all. Our team worked tirelessly for 7½ years and, ultimately, we were nominated for *five Oscars* and won four, and then *3 BAFTAs* across varied divisions. This speaks to the 'Jack and Jill' of all trade mentality and the can-do attitude of the Kiwi film technician/creative.

On *LOTR*, we had 3½ years of pre-production, which gave us the valuable time necessary to self-train, plan, pre-fabricate, and be prepared for the intensity of the shoot because a lot of the work required was already built by the time we got to the first day of filming. We continued to design and construct all the way through the years of filming, safe in the knowledge that we had prepared and planned well for the most part on this monumental project. However, on *The Hobbit* 10 years later, this wasn't the case, unfortunately. Due to a series of circumstances out of anyone's control, the pre-production time was shortened significantly, and 7 weeks out from the first day of the shoot, we started in earnest to produce the items required for the *trilogy* of films. The challenge here was that we were building almost in the minute of the object's requirement — often finishing things with an hour to spare before it was needed on set. Sadly, for me, this meant that I couldn't be as involved in the film shoot as I had been on *LOTR* because of my necessity to stay focussed on the manufacturing side of what we had been contracted to deliver. Regardless, our team of 300+ pulled together and we were able to deliver exceptional work to the brief, and we are proud of everything produced for these three films. Interestingly, for *LOTR*, we built 72 miniatures (or bigatures as we liked to call them due to their massive scale of construction). On *The Hobbit* — due to the decision to shoot in 3D — there was no requirement for miniatures, which was incredibly disappointing as this is a craft that

I specifically love and it had always been a traditional part of the filmmaking process when doing fantasy or sci-fi movies.

Obviously, there was a massive economic benefit for the city of Wellington and New Zealand as a whole due to these two trilogies. Great acknowledgement has to be given to the Director, Writers, Producers, the Studio, and the Tolkien estate who enabled these enterprises to be undertaken here. The economic benefit has been felt across the country well beyond the original film crew/production, and the resulting tourism imprint has remained strong after all these years. We have recently celebrated the 20th anniversary of *The Return of the King*, and we did a number of activities to celebrate; there is still an intensely-passionate fanbase desiring to be part of the ongoing glow of these amazing films.

In the early 2000s, Tania and I partnered with Martin Baynton, who would become a very dear friend of ours. Together, we started a children's television development and production company called *Pūkeko Pictures* — such was our desire to produce beautiful, meaningful children's programming within New Zealand for kids here and all over the world. The first show we made was called *Jane and the Dragon*, based on the much-loved set of children's books that Martin had created. The series told the story of Jane — a girl born into a medieval court, destined to become a lady in waiting, but who would rather be a knight! While out on the funding trail looking for the capital to be able to make our show, we ended up visiting *Singapore*. On this first trip, we met the Singaporean Economic Development Bureau, or *EDB*. The folks at the EDB helped us out with a portion of our funding in exchange for a very novel return — hosting Singaporean university students at our animation facility in Wellington. In all, we had 15 students join us, training on the job. Upon going home, they more than returned the value of the capital injection by taking back to Singapore knowledge, inspiration, and creative empowerment gained at Pūkeko, in the city of Wellington, and setting out on their own entrepreneurial journeys.

It was a wonderful success all around: *Jane* got made and was distributed to more than 40 countries, spawning an ardent fanbase worldwide, and Singapore received a group of young and vitalised students who had been inspired by the creative flurry of our country and our company. As a result, the EDB invited me to travel to Singapore to do a series of lectures and workshops over the span of a couple of years, speaking to the country's senior business executives and industry leaders. The Singaporean government, led by presidential initiative, had concluded that it was high time that the country started tapping more fully into its own creative potential, having successfully achieved world-leading capabilities as a business and technology hub. The government had been keeping a close eye on the expanding creative capabilities of our small country, which had gained much attention thanks to the filming of *The Lord of the Rings* at the time. They felt there was inspiration to be found in our country's creative journey. The ability to take part in these speaking sessions and workshops is one of the highlights of my career and I remember those visits very fondly. Needless to say, Singapore is now one of the most vibrant creative countries in the world and continues to go from strength to strength.

So, what had happened at home to spur our country's creative explosion? What was in the water in the late 80s that started this incredible creative surge in New Zealand that has spanned the past 30+ years? It is an oft-expressed sentiment that as a tiny country we have always achieved beyond what would be expected from so small a population. Whether in sports, quality and quantity of food production, or quality of social services, we have often led by example and achieved astounding things that we have good reason to be proud of. And, it wasn't that our creative industries had been totally invisible up to this point — no New Zealander from those years could forget *Goodbye Pork Pie*, one of the greatest Kiwi flicks, and many other wonderful films, or the superiority of the New Zealand Symphony Orchestra, the world-class performance capabilities of our opera and ballet, or the strength of multiple individuals waving the creative Kiwi flag across the world. Even against that backdrop, there was a change that occurred in the 90s and early 2000s that lit up our country on the creative voltmeter. When you are in the thick of it all, it is difficult to take that 30,000-foot view and look down on what is happening around you, but sitting here reflecting on all that has unfolded, it is evident to me that we, as a population of just 4 million at the time, started to think differently about how important our creative signature was and how we must try to indelibly stamp our cultural mark on the world stage.

There was a familiar refrain echoing in the minds of many colleagues of my generation, accompanied by the image of the well-meaning but concerned parent: 'There's no future in the arts, son. There's just no value to be gained from doing that art-thing as anything more than a hobby, dear. You need to think about a "real job."' Children growing up in New Zealand were bucking that advice and aspiring to enter the creative industries. Maybe its success breeds success, as parents became more confident in the fact that their children will be able to find a commercially-viable and fulfilling career in any number of the eminent creatively-driven industries within New Zealand. I have always held the perspective that, other than Mother Nature, (and a very limited number of technical and scientific endeavours), almost everything we touch in life has in some way been influenced by a creative hand — the knife and fork we use; the books we read; the digital interface on our computer; the clothes we wear; the car we drive; the house we live in and everything in it; the music we listen to; the content we watch; the theatre, opera, and dance that inspire us; all have been designed, created, illustrated, written, evoked by, or dreamed into being by creative minds and hands. Therefore, it could be argued, with due deference to my parents' generation, that there has always been a career waiting for Kiwi kids to discover within the creative sectors of New Zealand. It is therefore so exciting to meet groups of young people who are so focused on making their mark through their creative endeavours, armed with a complete conviction in their capabilities, believing they can change the world and all who interface with their chosen art form.

So, where are we today as a country, when we consider our creative place in the world?

The next generations of creatives emerging from their family homes, polytechnics, and universities of New Zealand have grown up as digital natives, with capabilities far beyond anything I could have imagined when I entered the workforce 40 years ago. The speed at which a commercial artist now needs to work to meet expectations within an intensely-competitive market, where 'exceptional' is considered the norm, is nothing short of staggering. And, new countries are entering and dominating the creative markets every year.

As an example, it is perhaps worth noting the phenomenon that is the entirely Chinese-made films, *The Wandering Earth* movies, based on the books by Lui Cixin and directed by Frant Gwo. Frant and his producer Gong Geer visited us eight years ago to ask if we could give them advice on how they might go about creating an ambitious science fiction film for the Chinese market. At the time, they didn't have experience with projects of the scale and complexity demanded by any that sought to compete with the best of the US film industry, but as history now shows, they went home and produced the highest-grossing sci-fi movie in China. Jump forward a mere five years and I would argue that in technical capability, visionary ideas, and artistic beauty, the sequel, *The Wandering Earth II*, rivals anything being made outside of China. All testament to an empowered, technically-brave, and immensely-astute group of *young Chinese filmmakers* intent on putting content into the world that is as superior as anything being made by any industry anywhere in the world.

New Zealand today is truly playing in a global market, where there is fierce competition from emerging creative world powers. Our expectations of ourselves need to rise, and we must undertake every effort to deliver nothing short of the exceptional in the creative sectors. If we wish to remain part of an international creative sector, we must rise to the challenge, and this challenge is one that we must take up across generations, both those who are already in the sector and those who are incoming. It follows, then, that if we are going to demand so much of the new Kiwi kids entering the industry, who might bring with them the needed vitality, inventiveness, new perspectives, and entrepreneurial spirit, they must be properly supported. That means the best tutors, cutting-edge learning environments, and the ability to access the full breadth of inspiration from both New Zealand and international creative thought leaders. *Passion*, *enthusiasm*, *tenacity*, and *talent* are essential, but they must also be coupled with policies that allow Kiwis to stay on a level playing field by matching the efforts undertaken by other countries. Film incentive schemes and other focussed endeavours that can help young New Zealanders forge their way are vital and necessary tools to be used to help our creative sector stay viable and relevant within a rapidly-changing global industry.

There is also no doubt that we are going to see swift and significant changes in the coming years due to the now ever-present AI realities. AI is already being employed to generate work traditionally done by artists and creative technicians. As robotics advances and AI takes a deeper hold on almost all aspects of modern life across the planet, it becomes imperative that the emerging creatives of New Zealand are equipped to navigate their way through this shifting landscape with a focus on becoming masters in their ability to unleash their own creative worth through these new media.

In line with this, and in reference to the industry that our company predominantly works in, we have seen fundamental shifts in the consumption of screen media. Who could have thought 20 years ago that at an audience would be satisfied consuming seconds-long 'blip' media on cell phones over the immersive, curated experience of watching a story told by a master filmmaker in a darkened cinema? Rather, we now have a future audience myopically focussed on their black mirrors, sitting on the public transport, couches, and bedroom furniture of the world, watching funny cat videos, influencer content, and media specifically designed to be consumed in quick, bite-sized chunks on a screen smaller than the palm of your hand. Measured using the metric of 'likes' or viewership numbers, it is hard to argue against the potential reach and power of such new media. Many of the traditional measures of creative and technical success are being supplanted by different forms of entertainment, whose generational longevity in the marketplace is flying past, and then dying, at lightning speed; such is the accelerating nature of our media consumerism. Therefore, our new generation of digital natives, faced with an ever-accelerating, rapidly-evolving creative sector, will need to be highly versatile, significantly adaptive, made of GRIT, and spontaneously creative in their approach.

When I contemplate the prerequisites that set an emerging artist on the right trajectory of success, I distil them into four key demands. Irrelevant of global competition and expectation, the changing nature of technology, consumer appetites, and the fast-paced nature of change in this dynamic industry, an aspiring young creative mind must have a

love of oneself,
love of what one does,
love of who one does it with,
and love of who one does it for.

Armed with these four tenets, an unabashed enthusiasm to just be 'exceptional', and that traditionally *tried-and-true* critical component of just being a tenacious Kiwi, we can continue to carry our country forward. It is my hope that this will help define the new generation of artistic endeavour, and that it will beam like a spotlight from our small home, here in New Zealand, and be visible around the world.

Chapter 21

Showcasing the Vision of the Asian Civilisations Museum

Kennie Ting

Introduction

The Asian Civilisations Museum (ACM) is located in the historic Empress Place Building, which stands along the banks of the Singapore River and dates to 1867. The building was simply referred to as the Government Offices in the colonial period, and it housed almost the entire colonial administration at the time, including the Secretariat, Treasury, and Public Works Department. Post-independence, the building continued to host a range of government offices and departments, including, most notably, the Immigration Department. It became the new site of ACM after the museum's relocation from the Old Tao Nan school building in 2003. Initially positioned as an ethnographic museum, ACM's curatorial approach was geographically-oriented: its collections were displayed in permanent galleries dedicated to East Asia, West Asia, South Asia, and Southeast Asia. The intent was to educate the Singaporean public about the history of the great Asian civilisations that make up the island nation's ancestral cultures.

Port Cities and Cross-Cultural Connections

Between 2013 and 2020, ACM went through extensive renovations, gallery revamps, and a total refresh of its curatorial mission and approach. The new ACM became the first museum in the region (and one of the first in the world) to shift from a geographical to a thematic approach in displaying its collections. Drawing on Singapore's nature as a cosmopolitan, multicultural, multireligious port city, today's ACM reframes and presents Asian art, history, culture, and design from the perspective of grand, transnational themes. Its mission is to foster an understanding of the diverse heritage and cultures of Singapore and their connections to each other and the world. This thematic approach emphasises networks and flows of people, ideas, belief systems, and artistic traditions, rather than national and regional borders and boundaries.

Galleries on the first floor of the museum tell the story of maritime trade and feature the museum's collections of Asian export art — luxury goods and works of decorative art that were made in Asia and traded to the rest of the world. A highlight is the historic Tang Shipwreck, which features a rare cargo of gold, silver, and ceramics made in China for export to the Middle East in the 9th century. On the second floor, the galleries explore the theme of faith and belief, and feature sacred and ritual objects representing almost all the major systems of faith in the region. Finally, the third-floor galleries present materials and designs, and feature the museum's exquisite collections of historic dress and textiles, jewellery, and ceramics.

Many of the objects that visitors encounter at the museum are cross-cultural in nature — blending east and east, and east and west — reflecting Singapore's identity as an essentially hybrid, or mixed, culture. The museum's key message is that Asia, like Singapore, has always been cross-cultural. No culture or religion has ever existed in isolation, but rather cultures have always interacted with and mutually enriched each other. The museum thus plays a very important role in building bridges between nations, cultures, faiths, and communities.

In alignment with its broader cross-cultural vision, ACM regularly presents special exhibitions that are multilateral in nature, bringing together collections from multiple nations and sources, in an exploration of core themes of trade, port cities, and hybridity. In 2016, it presented the first-ever special exhibition dedicated to the material culture of cosmopolitan Asian port cities. *Port Cities: Multicultural Emporiums of Asia, 1500–1900* featured objects from ACM's permanent collection, as well as objects on loan from museums and private collections in Portugal, Japan, the Netherlands, the Philippines, Singapore, and more. The exhibition re-examined Asia's recent history from the point of view of the sea, suggesting how in the course of encounters, conflicts, and negotiations between European and Asian cultures on Asian soil, new, hybrid communities and forms of art emerged.

In 2019, ACM presented *Raffles in Southeast Asia: Revisiting the Scholar and Statesman*. Co-curated with the British Museum and featuring objects on loan from museums and collectors in Indonesia, Singapore, the UK, and the Netherlands, the exhibition explored the trade history of the British and Dutch in Java in the 19th century. The intention was to provide a nuanced view of Singapore's legendary founding father, Sir Thomas Stamford Raffles, in the lead-up to his arrival in Singapore in 1819. Most recently, in 2023, *Manila Galleon: From Asia to the Americas* examined the sometimes-forgotten history of the Pacific trade between the Philippines and Mexico, by way of immense galleons that for 250 years shipped the treasures of China, India, and Southeast Asia from the port city of Manila to the Americas. Five years in the making, the exhibition features objects from the ACM's collection, as well as objects loaned from the Philippines, Mexico, Peru, and the USA. Among the various historical narratives explored are those of the emergence of a global economy based on the silver bullion from the Americas, fuelled by demand in China; the spread of chocolate, chilli peppers, and other produce from the New World westward to Asia; and how trade and cultural exchange precipitated new forms of decorative art in the regions involved.

Innovation in Tradition

After its complete refurbishment in 2020, ACM was formally repositioned as Singapore's 'National Museum of Asian antiquities and decorative art', with a strong focus on aesthetics and Asian art histories. This facilitated a second major paradigm shift in the museum's curatorial direction — ACM was now a museum of art (rather than ethnography), displaying objects of great beauty that represent the best of Asia's artistic traditions. As part of this repositioning, the museum's curatorial scope was extended to include objects from the present day, allowing it to display contemporary fashion and design alongside the historical collections.

This new, contemporary focus has allowed ACM to explore innovation in the space of tradition, throwing the spotlight onto artists and designers both past and present. This journey began in 2019 with the opening of *Guo Pei: Chinese Art and Couture*, which saw works by Chinese couturier Guo Pei shown alongside objects from ACM's historical Chinese art collection. The exhibition was curated with the intention of introducing mainstream audiences to the broad scope of Chinese art history, with sections dedicated to the basics of imperial, export, and folk art. The highlight was a golden-yellow gown, dubbed the 'omelette dress' in the media, that was worn by pop star Rihanna to the 2015 Met Gala in New York. The exhibition went on to become one of the museum's most successful exhibitions, drawing almost 200,000 visitors over the course of three months.

Guo Pei's success encouraged the museum to embark on a series of exhibitions celebrating 'Asian Masters'. *Life in Edo | Russel Wong in Kyoto*, featuring Singaporean and international celebrity photographer Russel Wong, opened after the completion of renovation works in 2020. The exhibition displayed contemporary photographs of Kyoto alongside *ukiyo-e* woodblock prints by Japanese masters. In 2022, ACM presented *Batik Kita: Dressing in Port Cities*, an exhibition featuring traditional batik textiles from the museum's collection and contemporary pieces by local and regional batik designers — including an extensive section on renowned Indonesian batik designer Josephine Komara and her label, BINhouse. Both exhibitions were a success, drawing more than 100,000 visitors each despite taking place during the COVID-19 pandemic.

The most recent instalment in this series celebrating Asian Masters was *Andrew Gn: Fashioning Singapore and the World*, in 2023. This was the first major exhibition in Singapore to feature a contemporary Singaporean fashion designer, as well as the first at ACM to feature only contemporary works of fashion without any historical objects placed in dialogue. In a generous and unprecedented move, Paris-based Andrew Gn decided — months before the exhibition opened — to donate over 300 gowns and dresses to the museum from his extensive archives. Every piece on display entered ACM's permanent collection. This donation represented ACM's first full, and as yet largest, collection of contemporary material, and was followed by a public announcement that the museum would formally begin to collect works of Asian and Singaporean contemporary fashion and design.

Co-curating with Communities

The COVID-19 pandemic precipitated the third and latest development in ACM's curatorial approach. Travel restrictions between 2020 and 2022 resulted in planned exhibitions being cancelled or postponed. Given that exhibitions and collections could not travel to Singapore, ACM pivoted towards collaborating closely with local communities of culture, faith, and creative practice.

In late 2020, just after Singapore emerged from lockdown, *Faith Beauty Love Hope: Our Stories, Your ACM* brought together ACM colleagues from across all departments in the museum, members of the ACM board, ACM's volunteer guides and docents, and even our security guards, who picked objects from the collection that most resonated with them personally in the middle of the pandemic. These objects were exhibited with labels that consisted not only of historical information but also personal reflections. The exhibition was designed to provide solace, hope, and inspiration for visitors during a very difficult time.

Faith Beauty Love Hope also led to the museum's first collabo-ration with Singapore's Inter-religious Organisation (IRO), wherein local religious leaders selected objects from the collection and shared their own personal reflections on the object, the pandemic, and their faith. These were recorded and released as short educa-tional videos on social media. Since then, ACM has worked more closely with communities of faith in a variety of ways, including the curation of permanent displays and special exhibitions. Most recently, the 2022 exhibition *Body & Spirit: The Human Body in Thought and Practice* saw us explore themes of the body and cos-mos, health and wellness, and mind and matter across the many faiths and cultures of the Indian Ocean. Alongside works from the permanent collection, the exhibition featured sacred objects on loan from faith communities and places of worship in Singapore.

2020 also saw ACM embarking on a collaboration with the larger design community and industry in Singapore, most notably with the Singapore Fashion Council (SFC) and LASALLE College of the Arts, part of Singapore's new University of the Arts. The col-laboration with SFC entailed support for *Singapore Stories*, an annual fashion design competition. ACM opened its vaults to local or locally-based fashion designers, who were challenged to create new capsule collections inspired by its collections or by Singapore's multicultural heritage — to innovate in the space of tradition. The works of the winners of this competition are collected by and dis-played at the museum.

ACM also collaborated with the Fashion Studies Department of LASALLE in the presentation of an annual pop-up exhibition, *#SGFASHIONNOW*, which showcases the works of established, emerging, and experimental Singapore fashion designers. The cura-torial approach was again novel, with the exhibition co-curated by students pursuing a Bachelor of Arts (Honours) Degree in Fashion Media and Industries. The students select the designers to be fea-tured, propose the exhibition curatorial narrative and exhibition design concept, and then work for six weeks at the museum to take their curatorial vision to fruition, with the full support of ACM's curato-rial and exhibitions teams. First launched in 2021, three editions of

#SGFASHIONNOW have since taken place. The 2023 edition — featuring 27 Singapore fashion designers — opened in Busan and Seoul in South Korea, becoming the first-ever special exhibition featuring contemporary Singapore fashion to travel abroad.

The value of these collaborations has been to bring new kinds of perspectives and ideals, and new groups of audiences to the museum, particularly younger visitors who would otherwise not have visited. This approach has also allowed ACM to demonstrate the direct impact it has on people and communities — notably in the fostering of community pride in cultural heritage, and in the profiling and championing of local talent and the local design scene.

Taken as a whole, ACM's commitment to presenting exhibitions that are a mix of international and community-oriented shows debunks prevailing notions that these are dichotomous concepts. The museum's community-oriented exhibitions address universal themes and issues, and boast exhibition displays and scenography that rival some of the best institutions in the world. In the meantime, ACM has also made efforts to involve the community in the curation of its international exhibitions — *Manila Galleon* featured a large-scale art installation created by volunteers from the Latin American and Filipino communities in Singapore.

Summary

A focus on presenting both the traditional and the contemporary subverts notions of 'old' and 'new' being at two opposing ends of a spectrum. Heritage and historical objects ground explorations of the contemporary, allowing visitors to better understand the roots of popular culture today. At the same time, contemporary objects that draw inspiration from tradition bring in new audiences, broadening discussions of historical and heritage narratives. In pursuing and achieving its new curatorial vision, ACM has, thus, reframed the notion of 'civilisations' in its museology (and in its name), refashioning it from a static, academic, and backward-looking objectification of the past to a dynamic and inclusive engagement of past, present, and future.

Today's ACM strives to be a museum for our times — one that creates and presents ground-breaking perspectives on Asia's global connections, usings world-class collection of Asian art.

Bibliography

Asian Civilisations Museum (2017). *ACM Treasures: Collection Highlights.* Singapore: Asian Civilisations Museum.

Chong, A. and Murphy, S. A. (eds.) (2017). *The Tang Shipwreck: Art and Exchange in the 9th Century.* Singapore: Asian Civilisations Museum.

Lee, P. *et al.* (2016). *Port Cities: Multicultural Emporiums of Asia, 1500–1900.* Singapore: Asian Civilisations Museum.

Murphy, S. A., Wang, N., and Green, A. (eds.) (2019). *Raffles in Southeast Asia: Revisiting the Scholar and Statesman.* Singapore: Asian Civilisations Museum and the British Museum.

Onn, C. *et al.* (2020). *Life in Edo | Russel Wong in Kyoto.* Singapore: Asian Civilisations Museum.

Onn, C. and Chong, A. (eds.) (2024). *Manila Galleon: From Asia to the Americas.* Singapore: Asian Civilisations Museum.

The Korea Foundation and Asian Civilisations Museum (2023). *Runway Singapore #SGFASHIONNOW.* South Korea: The Korea Foundation.

Ting, K. (2019). *Singapore 1819: A Living Legacy.* Singapore: Talisman Publishing.

Ting, K. (2021). *Asian Civilisations Museum. Director's Choice.* London: Scala Arts & Heritage Publishers Ltd.

Yoong, J. (2019). *Guo Pei: Chinese Art and Couture.* Singapore: Asian Civilisations Museum.

Yoong, J. (2023). *Andrew Gn: Fashioning Singapore and the World.* Singapore: Asian Civilisations Museum.

Chapter 22

Our Place:
The Museum of New Zealand
Te Papa Tongarewa

Courtney Johnston

The story of Te Papa is one of continuous reinvention.

The history of New Zealand's national museum begins in 1865 with the founding of the small Colonial Museum in Wellington, near where New Zealand's Parliament buildings are now.[1] Over the next 50 years, the museum expanded, and in 1936 the museum and the country's new National Art Gallery were co-located in a new neo-classical building.

By the 1980s, this building was straining to hold the collections, staff and visitors. While much loved by those who did visit, the museum did not reflect New Zealand's increasingly diverse society. The government established a project board to undertake nation-wide consultation on a new national museum. At the heart of the project were three principles: the museum would be inclusive of all New Zealanders; in telling all New Zealanders' stories it would be a narrative-based, rather than a collection-based, museum; and it

---

[1] Te Papa has a series of predecessors. The Colonial Museum was founded in 1865; became the Dominion Museum in 1907; the National Museum in 1972, and the current name 'Museum of New Zealand Te Papa Tongarewa' was instated by an Act of Parliament in 1992.

would be bicultural, reflecting the partnership between tangata whenua (*indigenous Māori*) and tangata Tiriti (*all other peoples*).

Te Papa's formation was heavily influenced by the landmark *Te Māori* exhibition, which toured North American museums from 1984 to 1986 and then visited New Zealand's four largest cities.[2] The exhibition revolutionised how taonga Māori (*artefacts/treasures*) were displayed in museums. Museums had historically presented taonga in static "Māori halls" as artefacts of the past, whereas *Te Māori* showed Māori culture as living, dynamic and forceful. The exhibition was accompanied by Māori kaumātua (*elders*), performers and artists who cared for the taonga and conducted tikanga (cultural protocols). When *Te Māori* was presented in Wellington, a gathering of kaumātua called for influence over the care of their taonga.

In 1992, the Museum of New Zealand Te Papa Tongarewa Act was passed, uniting the national art gallery and national museum, and creating Te Papa as a forum in which the nation may present, explore, and preserve the heritage of its cultures and knowledge of the natural environment, in order to better understand and treasure the past; enrich the present; and meet the challenges of the future.

The new institution was given the responsibility of representing and appealing to New Zealand's changing society. Te Papa was one of the first mainstream institutions in New Zealand to be known primarily by its Māori name. The museum was built on bicultural practices, including having its own functioning marae (traditional gathering place); a co-leadership model with a Kaihautū (*Māori leader*),[3] alongside the chief executive; and centering Māori language, knowledge systems and cultural practices in the museum's way of working.

A new philosophy of mana taonga[4] was also introduced, originating from the museum's Māori advisory group. Mana taonga

---

[2] 'Te Māori', New Zealand Foreign Affairs and Trade, https://www.mfat.govt.nz/en/about-us/mfat75/te-maori/

[3] Kaihautū: traditionally, the person who gives the time for paddlers in a waka (canoe), also used to describe a leadership role.

[4] Migoto Eria, 'The mana of taonga and what it means for museums in New Zealand', 12 September 2018 https://blog.tepapa.govt.nz/2018/09/12/the-mana-of-taonga-and-what-it-means-for-museums-in-aotearoa/

recognises the important role whānau and hapū (*family groupings*), iwi (*tribe*), and communities have in enhancing the understanding and care of collections. Mana taonga is at the core of Te Papa's work with individuals, groups, iwi and communities to co-develop exhibitions, programmes and collections.

Inaugural chief executive Dame Cheryll Sotheran and Kaihautū Cliff Whiting co-led the development of the new museum. The design of the new building was heavily debated and the innovative storytelling was rejected by some traditionalists, but the goal of attracting 700,000 visits in the opening year was met in just three months, and Te Papa drew more than 2 million visits in its first year.

Today, collaboration remains core to Te Papa's success. Diverse examples of collaboration include:

- The long-running Iwi in Residence programme, by which iwi tell their story and present their taonga in their own way at the museum. Te Papa acts as the platform — the goals, approach, the stories and the tikanga are set by iwi.
- Co-collecting programmes are crucial for ensuring collections represent the stories and experiences of New Zealanders. Recent examples include a tapa workshop in Tahiti with contemporary Pacific tapa makers, connecting with a book of tapa samples collected on Captain James Cook's voyages, joining new knowledge with old.
- Te Papa's support of the television series *National Treasures*, where museum curators interview members of the public about their unique historical objects and their personal stories, accompanied by a pop-up exhibition at Te Papa.
- A partnership with Wellington-based Wētā Workshop, on the highly successful *Gallipoli: The Scale of our War* exhibition (visited by over 4 million people at Te Papa) and international touring exhibition *Bug Lab*.
- Significant touring exhibitions with international partners, including *Terracotta Warriors: Guardians of Immortality* (2018) and *Surrealist Art: Masterpieces from Museum Boijmans Van Beuningen* (2021).

Te Papa's remit as a national museum is significant, and includes holding the government mandate to repatriate Māori and Moriori ancestral remains from international collections. Working with a Māori advisory panel and iwi representatives, more than 850 ancestors have thus far been returned. The museum also has a role supporting the approximately 450 museums, galleries and whare taonga in the country with professional advice and training.

Collection development and research are also vital aspects of Te Papa's work, with its contribution to taxonomic research and understanding of Aotearoa's biodiversity being particularly notable. Te Papa researchers have identified over 2,500 new species since the museum opened in 1998, and scientific staff regularly take part in expeditions and research collaborations.

Te Papa emerged from a dynamic period of Aotearoa New Zealand's history, with a clear direction to create a museum of all New Zealanders. It has achieved this by empowering communities to record and share their stories through the museum. Linking the past, present and future, Te Papa symbolises the ever-evolving understanding of national identity in this unique place.

Chapter 23

The Arts as a Value-Creating Ecology in Singapore

Hoe Su Fern

Introduction

Across the globe, cities like Singapore, Auckland, and Wellington have been racing to brand themselves as creative cities, pursuing policies that aspire to harness the arts as a strategic urban (re)development asset and place-branding tool (Scott, 2006; Evans, 2009; Pratt, 2010; Grodach, 2017). Although there has been a significant body of research analysing this global race amongst cities, there is a relative scarcity of literature providing a holistic understanding of how such global state aspirations impact and interact with the local arts ecology, especially in cities from the Asia-Pacific region.

This chapter aims to provide a deeper understanding of the evolving state of politics and practices of the arts ecology in Singapore from 2012 to 2023. This period was selected primarily because Singapore's most recent cultural policy — the Arts and Culture Strategic Review — was officially released in 2012, and has since introduced changes and shifts that have yet to be adequately documented and analysed. However, this chapter is not intended to be comprehensive in nature.

This chapter has two key objectives. First, it will critically interrogate the nature, extent, and implications of the Singapore government's efforts in utilising the arts as a pragmatic and expedient resource to become a globally-competitive creative city. While the Singapore government has long relied on developing hard infrastructure such as museums and performing arts centres as a means to become a globally-competitive city-state, this chapter will demonstrate how there has been a marked shift from a more vertical, developmental, and regulatory approach to a more localised, inclusive, horizontal, and stimulating modus operandi since 2012. Secondly, this chapter will consider some of the key points of tensions and discontinuities arising from Singapore's pursuit to become a global creative city in order to highlight how formal governance structures are linked to and complemented by non-government actors, informal sites, and everyday practices. Together, they contribute to the cultural dynamism and sustainability of the arts sector. Importantly, this approach provides a more nuanced, holistic, and extensive understanding of the linkages and interdependencies amongst the various actors, elements, and subsystems that comprise the arts in Singapore.

Methodologically, this chapter uses locality-based ethnography to provide a situated and 'thick' analysis that is sensitive to the context-specificity of the arts sector in Singapore, as well as attends to the nuances of the layered micropatterns, the localised relations, and the interdependent networks of diverse actors that comprise the arts. In particular, this chapter will analyse the arts through the framework of ecology. This framework is inspired by systems thinking, which approaches the phenomenon under study as a complex web consisting of multiple components and subsystems that interrelate and are interdependent.

This chapter is organised as follows. The first section will provide a background context of how the strong governance system has shaped the development of the arts ecology in Singapore. The second section will show how the current government's focus on local audience development has led to a quantitatively-hyperactive arts sector and the subsequent tensions. The third section will discuss the government's shift towards a more horizontal approach to developing the arts and elucidate the interdependencies between the various actors, sites, and practices in sustaining the arts in Singapore. This chapter will conclude by arguing for the significance of understanding the arts as a 'value-creating ecology' that is relationally interdependent.

Understanding the Operating Environment: The Strong Role of State Governance and Cultural Policy in Singapore

When considering the operating environment of the arts in Singapore, the dominant role of the state in Singapore and its strong system of governance cannot be denied. The arts have always been recognised as an important expedient resource to the pragmatic Singapore government. This is evident in how the Ministry of Culture was one of the first ministries established by the ruling People's Action Party (PAP) when self-governance was attained in 1959. Like other post-colonial countries, the arts were identified as a means to create and promote a new sense of national identity (Mulcahy, 2017). Lofty ambitions aside, it is worth noting that the Ministry of Culture was only accorded a budget of S$2 million for its first year of operations, compared to S$21.9 million for the Ministry of Education and S$27.4 million for the Ministry of National Development (Chong, 2018, p. xxi). This vast disparity in budget allocation highlights how the position accorded to the arts by the Singapore government is at once central and at the same time peripheral.

This positionality is further demonstrated in how it was only in the mid-1980s that the Singapore government started to invest heavily in the arts. The most seminal catalyst for this was the release of Vision 1999 in January 1985, which was a national policy aspiring to transform Singapore into a city of excellence by 1999. Vision 1999 was a government response to the economic growth and the ensuing increase in the standard of living in Singapore. With this change in socio-economic status, quality-of-life issues were prioritised, including the need to rejuvenate Singapore into a vibrant cityscape with a 'cultivated society'. Vision 1999 claimed that the existence of arts activities and facilities would enable this transformation of Singapore into a culturally-vibrant society.

Since Vision 1999, the state has played a robust role in developing the arts in Singapore. This strong role of the state was formalised and asserted through three strategies: (i) the release of publicly-available cultural policy documents since 1989, (ii) the formation of government agencies such as the National Arts Council (NAC) in 1991, (iii) and the establishment of government-owned and -managed infrastructure for the arts like the creation of a museum cluster in the central area of Singapore, which included a new contemporary art museum — the Singapore Art Museum — that opened in 1996 (Hoe and Chong, 2018).

This robust role of the government has enabled a steady increase in government funding over the years, as shown in Figure 1.

This significant financial investment has led to government expectations that the arts address and deliver an expansive range of outcomes from urban regeneration to economic revival and

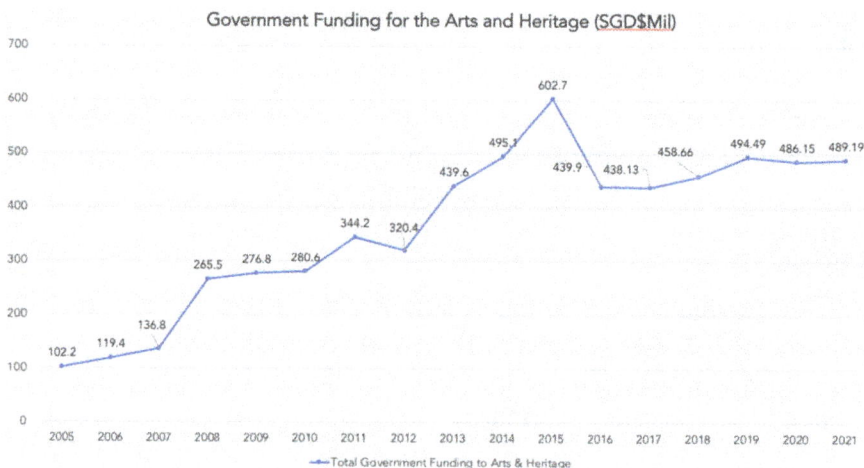

Government Funding for the Arts and Heritage (SGD$Mil)

Figure 1.   Graph depicting the total amount of government funding for the arts and heritage sectors.

Source: Ministry of Culture, Community and Youth (2023).

social inclusion, oftentimes at the expense of art-making and artist interests. This instrumentalist treatment of the arts has led Terence Chong to argue that to understand the arts in Singapore is to understand the "bureaucratic imagination of the arts," a term he uses to describe the "selective and rudimentary application of art and its imagined qualities" by the politicians and bureaucrats as "a creative solution to perceived socio-political or economic challenges" (2014, p. 20).

In 2010, the Arts and Culture Strategic Review (ACSR) was initiated to chart the next phase of arts and cultural development in Singapore, particularly in terms of reassessing how the arts could play a stronger role in strengthening the 'software' aspects of 'our people and society'. The final report was released on 31 January 2012 to guide Singapore's arts and cultural development from 2012 to 2025. The overall ACSR vision was to transform Singapore into "a nation of cultured and gracious people, at home with our heritage, proud of our Singaporean identity" (Ministry of Information, Communication and the Arts, 2012, p. 15). To achieve this vision, the ACSR aimed to meet two quantitative targets. The first was to double the percentage of Singaporeans who attend at least one arts and culture event every year, from 40% to 80%, and the second was to increase the percentage of Singaporeans actively participating in arts and culture activities, from 20% to 50%. Here, increasing access and participation in the arts are seen to have transformative effects on society, including "enriching the lives of Singaporeans," "strengthening Singaporean ties," and "promoting social cohesion across population segments" (Ministry of Information, Communication and the Arts, 2012, pp. 8–11).

This highlights the ASCR shifting the focus towards harnessing the social benefits of the arts for the local population (Hoe, 2018b). With this prioritisation of the local population, the ACSR has led to a substantial shift in focus towards audience development and engagement.[1] This is evident in the ACSR's tagline: "arts for

---

[1] Briefly, audience development refers to broadening the reach of and diversifying the demographics of the audiences to the experience, while audience engagement refers to the deepening of the impact of the arts experience for the audience.

everyone, everyday, everywhere." This focus on audiences has persisted in the two strategic roadmaps released by the NAC to guide the implementation of the ACSR: Our Sg Arts Plan (2018–2022) and Our Sg Arts Plan (2023–2027). Both Plans recognise the central importance of audiences and "growing the appreciation, participation and consumption of the arts at every life stage (National Arts Council, 2023, p. 20).

The next section will elaborate on this shift in focus and demonstrate how this has resulted in a hyper-active arts sector. It must be noted that despite this shift in focus, there remains an identified need for continued investment in state infrastructure for the arts, especially in terms of refurbishments and upgrades to existing cultural institutions. According to the ACSR, funding for "infrastructural support for major national cultural institutions" would be required so that they can become globally-recognisable cultural icons and sources of national pride for Singaporeans (Ministry of Information, Communication and the Arts, 2012, pp. 62–63). Institutions that benefited include the then-21-year-old Singapore Art Museum (SAM), which began a revamp in 2017 at a budget of S$90 million, the addition of a mid-size theatre to the Esplanade at a cost of S$30 million, and the transformation of the Singapore Philatelic Museum into a Children's Museum that reopened in December 2022.[2]

Growing Audiences through a Quantitatively-Hyperactive Arts Sector

In order to meet the ACSR goals, there has been significant state investment to develop audience-centric programmes. A key strategy was to increase the number of arts programmes, especially non-ticketed, free arts programmes, to lower the barriers to entry for audiences. This includes offering free entry to all national museums and heritage institutions from 18 May 2013 and develop-

---

[2]As of 1 January 2024, the Singapore Art Museum at Bras Basah Road has yet to be reopened, although the revamp was originally slated for completion in 2021 with an announced postponement to 2023. On 11 August 2021, it was announced that the Singapore Art Museum would occupy a two-storey space at Tanjong Pagar Distripark from 2022.

ing large-scale arts festivals. A related strategy is to embed these arts programmes throughout the island, especially in neighbourhoods and non-traditional arts venues.

This has resulted in a quantitative growth in the arts sector in Singapore, particularly in the number of arts activities produced (Figure 2) and the amount of arts attendance (Figure 3). Although COVID-19 led to a momentarily decrease in 2020, the arts sector quickly resumed activity. In fact, arts journalist Ong Sor Fern has used the term "revenge arts programming" to describe the intense increase in arts programming since the relaxation of social distancing measures (Ong, 2022).

At first glance, this hyperactive arts sector might appear to be a positive development. With a lack of robust public discussion on the value of art, there is a temptation to equate value with audience numbers or to consider that the art is worth funding only if there are eyeballs and/or footfall. Yet, on a look closer, there are some worrying indicators. As indicated by Figure 4, the rise in arts attendance has been powered by non-ticketed events, particularly

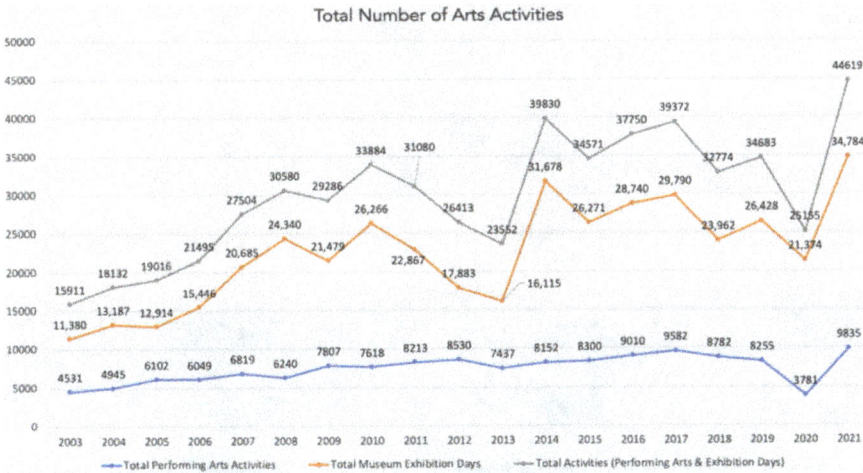

Figure 2.   Graph depicting the total number of arts activities, with a breakdown between the total number of performing arts activities and the total number of museum exhibition days.

Source: Ministry of Culture, Community and Youth (2023).

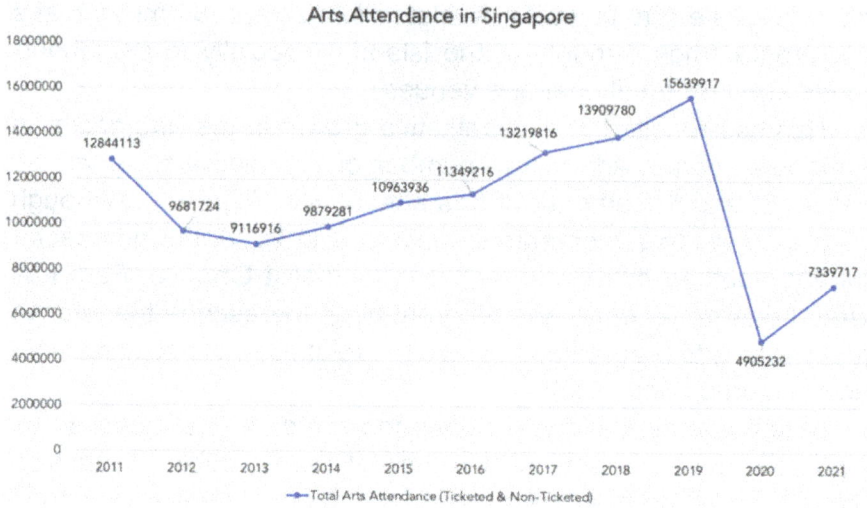

Figure 3.   Graph depicting arts attendance in Singapore.

Source: Ministry of Culture, Community and Youth (2023).

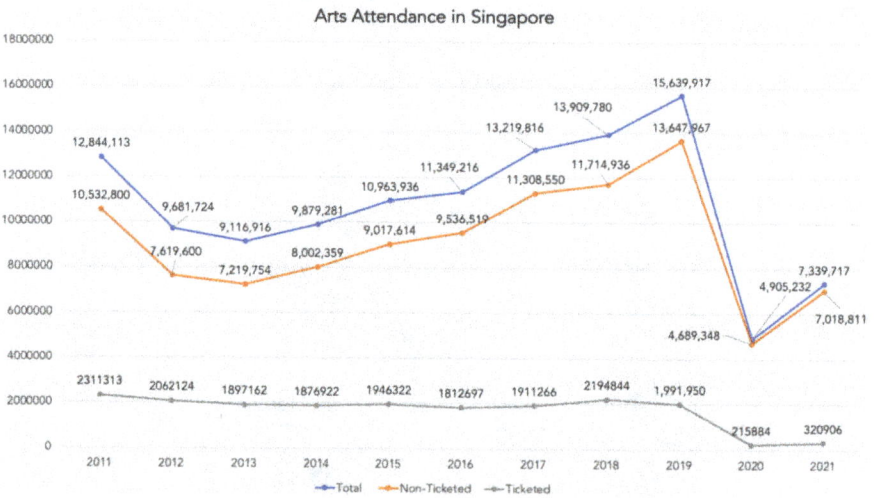

Figure 4.   Graph depicting the breakdown of arts attendance in Singapore.

Source: Ministry of Culture, Community and Youth (2023).

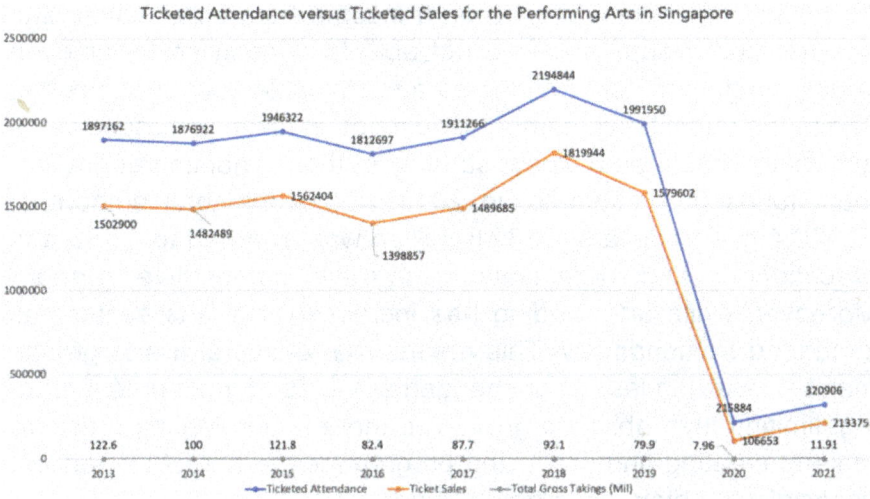

Figure 5. Graph depicting the disparity between ticketed attendance, ticket sales, and gross earnings.

Source: Ministry of Culture, Community and Youth (2023).

large-scale government-initiated events like the Singapore Night Festival.

Apart from this disparity between non-ticketed and ticketed attendance, another disquieting area of concern is the ability to earn income from ticket sales as demonstrated in Figure 5. There are more non-ticketed performing arts activities produced, which results in a corresponding higher number of audiences for non-ticketed versus ticketed activities. For instance, in 2019, the total attendance for performing arts activities was more than 5.7 million, but ticketed attendance in 2019 only reached nearly 2 million audiences. Although this number is the second highest since 2013, ticket sales amounted to only about 1.58 million audiences and total gross takings fell to S$79.9 million from S$92.1 million in 2018. This highlights the difficulty of earning income through ticket sales in Singapore.

Apart from the inability to earn income from ticket sales, arts workers and groups are also not able to depend solely or even largely on government funding as a sustainable source of income. Again, the quantitative numbers must not be taken at surface value and there should be a closer scrutiny of the distribution of government funds. For example, in 2013, out of the total amount of S$320.4 million dollars, S$32.6 million was awarded to 1,150 arts practitioners and organisations through competitive grants.[3] Moreover, while arts funding has increased, the arts sector has expanded tremendously. This means that artists and arts groups may be receiving less or unchanged amounts of government funding, limiting their ability to grow. Yet, there is unrelenting pressure to keep creating and producing programmes to attract audiences, especially to obtain government funding.

Overall, these issues indicate the limitations of arts development that is government-centric. While government funding for the arts in Singapore has remained relatively stable, the development in the arts ecosystem does not necessarily equate to improved and more equitable working conditions or lessen the precarity inherent in work in the arts. Nevertheless, it must be noted there has been increased government acknowledgement of the need to address the precarious work in the arts, particularly with the establishment of the NAC's Arts Resource Hub initiative in 2019 that aims to support arts freelancers. The next section will explore the government's shift towards a more horizontal approach to stimulating the arts in Singapore, and the ensuing conjunctions and disjunctions between various actors, sites, and practices in sustaining the arts in Singapore.

Beyond Numbers, Scale, and Spectacle: Sustaining Survival through Interdependencies

Apart from a shift towards a more localised approach as seen in the prioritisation of developing the population into arts audiences, there

---

[3]As a comparison, the National Gallery Singapore received almost S$14 million in government grants.

has been a move towards acknowledging that the arts constitute a process that occurs and thrives through an interdependent system of activities, thereby leading to a much more inclusive, horizontal, and stimulating modus operandi.

A case example would be Singapore Art Week (SAW), a pinnacle event driven by the NAC in partnership with the EDB and the STB. Its origins stem from a desire to leverage the buzz of Art Stage Singapore, an art fair that was launched in 2011 with the backing of the EDB, STB, NAC, and NHB.[4] According to the EDB, the aim was to create a globally-renowned art fair that would "strengthen Singapore's standing as a platform for international art businesses and expand into Asia and beyond" (*Business Times*, 2011). Helmed by Lorenzo Rudolf who had experience with Art Basel, the first edition of Art Stage attracted 121 galleries and 32,000 visitors (Huang, 2016a). It was widely reported that the momentum of the art fair managed to cause positive spillover effects, particularly in terms of an increase in tourism numbers and spending on hospitality and food.

By 2013, there was a bumper increase in art exhibitions and arts programmes being organised in January. With more than 50 arts programmes, the STB was prompted to publish "a comprehensive 56-page Art Week Guide to help art lovers navigate their way around town" (Shetty, 2013). This marked the beginning of SAW. With Art Stage being promoted as the glitzy anchor event, the third edition of SAW had a surge in arts programming, featuring almost

---

[4] However, it must be noted that SAW's true origins can actually be further traced back to the "National Day Art Exhibitions" that started in 1969 and ran till 1985. The aim of this annual exhibition was to provide a platform to showcase artworks by local artists and increase local support for these artists. From 1986 to 1993, this was replaced by the "Singapore Art Fair." In 1995, NAC developed the "Singapore Art Fair" into "Singapore Art," which became a biennial national art show showcasing local art and artists. In 1999, this was renamed to "Nokia Singapore Art" due to Nokia Corporation becoming the key sponsor. Nokia's involvement expanded the art show into a two-month long visual arts festival that involved multiple venues as well as fringe and affiliate programmes. However, after two editions, "Nokia Singapore Art" was discontinued. In 2005, NAC launched the "Singapore Art Show," which was meant to be a biennial month-long, non-ticketed event showcasing "pieces by Singaporeans for Singaporeans" (Chow, 2005). There were no further editions after 2009.

100 programmes including activities such as neighbourhood walk-ing tours, a family-friendly carnival, and music parties. The devel-opment of SAW as a festival with a variety of programmes reveals how the Singapore government has recognised that the arts require both cultural actors and economic actors, and the flows of resources and knowledge between them.

It must be noted that SAW was briefly disrupted in 2019. Rudolf made the decision to cancel Art Stage 9 days before it was sched-uled to take place due to "the very difficult market situation in Singapore as well to an unequal competition situation on site" (ArtReview, 2019). Rudolf was referring to how SAW had changed its anchor event to S.E.A. Focus, a boutique art fair, showcasing galleries and artists from Southeast Asia that was supported by the NAC. However, Art Stage had been facing declining footfall and sales since 2016.

This abrupt cancellation meant that the 45 participating galler-ies were left stranded, alongside their artists and artworks. However, different players from the arts nimbly stepped forward, providing access to resources and services to the galleries left at their wit's end. One key resource platform that was quickly estab-lished was 'ARTery' a pop-up event organised by Art Outreach Singapore, a non-profit organisation that promotes visual literacy in Singapore, with support from Marina Bay Sands. Around 14 of the 45 galleries who signed up for Art Stage participated in 'ARTery', while other galleries found support from other local spaces and services.

Today, SAW remains a hallmark event. The 12th edition in 2024 featured two art fairs — S.E.A. Focus and ART SG — alongside more than 150 arts programmes across two weekends in January. This quantity was possible because of SAW's open invite for pro-gramme listings. This openness means that many of the arts pro-grammes listed as part of SAW are initiated from the ground by arts spaces and workers who recognise the valuable benefits and opportunities of being part of a large-scale festival, including build-ing connections and developing audiences. This horizontal inclu-siveness enables a breadth of diverse arts programmes to be included, from collaborations with corporate partners like 'Creative Intersections' — an 'art-meets-retail' activation that invites artists to collaborate with brand partners located at Funan Mall — to community art exhibitions in the heartlands and experimental platforms like the 'Islands Time-Based Art Festival' (ITBA) that presented live performance pieces by emerging artists alongside established ones.

Therefore, although SAW may be a state-initiated, output-driven event that thrives on spectacle, it also illuminates how artists and organisations do not exist in isolation but are embedded within a framework of relations in a social world. In particular, the 2019 edition affirmed how the interrelations amongst diverse actors enable regenerative conditions of possibility for creative work, especially in terms of providing forms of support as well as encouraging collaboration and cooperation.

A key dimension of nurturing conditions for the arts is the spatial context. In recent years, the Singapore government has recognised the need to stimulate creativity through the development of conducive spatial conditions for artistic production. As noted by Mommas, cities pursuing a creative economy have recognised the need for a "conscious creation/stimulation/nourishment of sources of creativity and innovation" (2004, p. 521).

Gillman Barracks was established in 2012 at a cost of S$10 million, as a joint effort by the NAC, EDB, and industrial landlord Jurong Town Corporation (JTC) to create "a vibrant centre in Asia for the creation, exhibition and discussion of contemporary art, and will strengthen Singapore's position as a contemporary art destination" (Economic Development Board, 2012). According to Eugene Tan who oversaw the development,[5] Gillman Barracks was a necessary intervention by the government "to step in to address the failures of the open market" to develop a successful arts cluster

---

[5] In 2013, Tan left EDB to become the director of the National Gallery Singapore (NGS). In 2019, he also became the director of the Singapore Art Museum (SAM). On 13 March 2024, apart from these directorships, he was further appointed Chief Executive Officer (CEO) of NGS, CEO of SAM and head of the Visual Arts Cluster (comprising the two museums and STPI).

that would become an "international destination and marketplace for contemporary art in Singapore" (Tan, in Chia, 2012).

Gillman Barracks officially opened on 15 September 2012, with 13 art galleries. From October 2013, the NTU Centre for Contemporary Art (NTU CCA) — an arts research centre — became the anchor tenant occupying four buildings in the cluster. However, negative media coverage surfaced within a year of its opening. The constant issues covered include the departure of galleries and the lack of footfall (Huang, 2013, 2016b; Shetty, 2015). The NAC and EDB remedied some of the issues, introducing improved wayfinding and increased food options and programming to cultivate audiences. In 2014, 'Art After Dark' was launched — a series of free, late-night events with pop-up activations including music, performances, food, and drink. In 2016, the NAC and EDB jointly set up the Gillman Barracks Programme Office to strengthen programming and better integrate the cluster with the arts ecosystem in Singapore.

In 2020, it was announced that the NTU CCA would cease operations at Gillman Barracks after March 2021. In 2022, the Singapore Land Authority assumed management of the space (instead of the NAC and EDB), with aspirations to rejuvenate the area into a "vibrant creative lifestyle enclave" that would offer a wider range of programmes such as farmers' markets. This was justified based on the need to "optimise land resources" and "unlock greater value from state properties" to benefit the wider community (Singapore Land Authority, 2022). Concurrently, Tanjong Pagar Distripark started to be promoted as an arts cluster, especially with the area being a key location for Singapore Art Week with the SAM having opened an extension there (Toh, 2021; Sim, 2022).

The negative media coverage of Gillman Barracks and the land management changes highlight an inherent lack of understanding of the operations of an arts cluster comprising private art galleries and the importance of justifying land optimisation through quantitative metrics such as footfall. What has been lesser publicised is the number of art galleries that have persisted in staying on in Gillman Barracks. Many of the remaining galleries have been there since 2012.

The NAC's expeditious shift towards promoting another area as an arts cluster raises questions about short-term horizons, the long-term sustainability of space for the arts, and opportunities for arts spaces to cultivate deep roots with the communities and neighbourhoods they are sited within. Evidently, despite the overall growth of the arts sector, arts workers in Singapore continue to face challenges, especially the precarity of space and a top-down obsession with land optimisation. In an island city-state where most of the land and existing arts infrastructure is state-owned, the finiteness of space for the arts — literally and figuratively — remains a key challenge. Although there is an expansive variety of arts infrastructure in Singapore today, most of these spaces tend to be consumption- and audience-oriented. The use of state-run infrastructure also comes at a cost — there are great expectations for the users and tenants to deliver multiple instrumentalised outcomes, such as place vibrancy (Hoe, 2020). Additionally, there has been a long history of the closure of arts spaces, from government-run spaces like the Telok Ayer Performing Arts Centre and The Substation at 45 Armenian Street to artist-initiated spaces like soft/WALL/studs and independent music venues such as Home Club, Decline, and White Label Records (Hoe, 2021).

Nonetheless, there continue to be ground-up initiatives to hold and make space for the arts, especially for artistic experimentation, process, and friendship. These initiatives are important because top-down or institutionalised planning and policies for the arts are in and of themselves not sufficient to comprehensively support the development of the arts and their complex dynamics.

One such initiative is The Projector, which opened in 2014 as an independent cinema space at Golden Mile Tower. The Projector took over the former top floor of Golden Theatre, which was once the largest cinema in Singapore when it opened in 1973 with its 1,500-seating capacity. To help finance the renovations as well as the purchase of two digital projectors, The Projector launched an online crowdfunding appeal. Today, The Projector has become a valuable platform supporting indie, arthouse, and local films. In particular, it programmes extended runs for Singapore-made films, so as to grow audiences and box-office sales. Also, as a means to overcome the lack of a permanent lease for the space, The Projector has activated several disused spaces into pop-up cinema spaces.

A cherished part of The Projector is the provision of a social space and inclusive cultural programming, which has garnered a reputation for hosting a diverse range of programmes from poetry slams to 'bad-movie' bingo nights, live music gigs, and pub theatre experiences.

An instance of The Projector's inclusiveness of alternative programming is 'The Glory Hoes Present', a series of queer film experiences that was started in 2017 by The Glory Hoes, an artist collective. Hosted at The Projector, these experiences include 'no-judgement, no-holds-barred film screenings' of cult queer films that include elements such as makeovers, sing-alongs, drinking games, and post-screening dance parties. Fundamental to The Glory Hoes ethos is the screening of films that have a queer resonance and/or sensibility. Another significant aspect is the encouragement of audiences to be open to differences and to challenge social norms.

Besides being vital complements to the state-initiated programmes, The Projector highlights the importance of having open spaces where differences can be encountered and negotiated, and where artistic process and experimentation can take place. According to Ginette Chittick, a DJ who plays frequently at the Intermission Bar, The Projector is a "non-judgemental" space where artists feel "comfortable and safe" to show work (Vincent, 2019). The Projector has also been committed to ensuring continued access to these spaces.

Other noteworthy ground-up spaces that have made room for experimentation and process-driven projects include 136 Goethe Lab by The Goethe Institute, Starch which is self-funded and run by artist-curator Moses Tan, and dblspce, an incubator space in Peninsula Shopping Centre offering a residency and mentorship programme. There are also occasional pop-up interventions. An example is 'An Eminent Takeover' in 2014, where artists were given freedom by the owners of Eminent Plaza to use the rooms and walls of the mall as they liked for a month before the building was demolished. A more recent pop-up is 'Open GR.iD'. GR.iD mall sponsored 16,000 square feet of space to be transformed into a pop-up co-sharing and co-making platform for multidisciplinary artists and collectives to make art, exchange ideas, and 'just be' for two months in 2024. The intent is to socialise risks and motivate experimentation so as to encourage diverse and complementary sets of cultural practices while building solidarity amongst arts workers.

Apart from spaces, there have also been more alliances and mutual aid initiatives to build solidarities. One example is the #WaterlooStKakis, a neighbourly alliance amongst four arts organisations four arts organisations located on Waterloo Street, together with the Arts and Culture Management Programme from Singapore Management University. The alliance was formed due to a shared desire to lessen the precarity of the arts spaces by working together to increase visibility and value as a creative cluster vital to the Waterloo Street neighbourhood.

Despite their improvisational and precariously-impermanent states, these platforms are important for artistic experimentation as well as strengthening care and solidarity. These are what Ava Kromberg calls possibility spaces, which she describes as accessible and inclusive spaces that promote an environment of "generosity, conviviality, and the messiness of coexisting differences, as well as an openness that allows new ideas and forms to take shape in favour of habitual responses or patterns" (2010, pp. 214–215). As local architect William Lim reminded us, we must recognise the city as being in a vital "state of incompleteness, with spaces that are indeterminate and open to continuous unforeseen changes and unplanned growth" (2012).

Conclusion

Today, the arts in Singapore are a unique constellation composed of both private and public entities, comprising a range of artistic strategies from performance to installation, craft, and music raves that are navigating processes of state expectations, multiple modernities, cross-cultural fertilisation, and co-opetition. Together, they constitute a networked field of interdependent relations, or what Hearn, Roodhouse, and Blakey call a "value-creating ecology" (2007). They use this term to describe how value creation in the arts is not a simple one-way linear process but involves continuous networks of relationships, reiteration, feedback, co-creation, and co-opetition.

Importantly, although the arts and creative sectors are never stagnant and do not stay still, understanding the arts as a 'value-creating ecology' productively redirects our attention to the complex shifting nuances and relations of the art-making process, and the need to recognise the incommensurable interdependencies and relations at play. These interdependencies, especially amongst diverse actors, are critical for the long-term sustainability of the arts. There is a need to consider the sustainability of the arts, as the arts today are facing unprecedented challenges, precipitated by the global COVID-19 pandemic crisis and exacerbated by urgent challenges including long overdue calls for social justice, ever-burgeoning structural inequities in health, wealth, and social trust, increasing levels of political polarisation, and the catastrophic consequences of climate change. Ultimately, I hope this chapter offers a useful reference for a growing and multifaceted conversation about the complex conditions of artistic production in Asia-Pacific cities like Singapore.

Bibliography

ArtReview (2019). Art Stage Singapore cancelled a week before opening. *ArtReview*, 16 January. Available from: https://artreview.com/news-16-january-2019-art-stage-singapore-cancelled-a-week-before-opening/. (Last accessed 10 December 2023).

Bromberg, A. (2010). Creativity unbound: cultivating the generative power of non-economic neighbourhood spaces. In Edensor, T., Leslie, D., Millington, S., and Rantisi, N. (eds.), *Spaces of Vernacular Creativity: Rethinking the Cultural Economy* (pp. 200–213). London: Routledge.

Business Times Singapore (2011). Art Stage Singapore makes its bow. *Business Times Singapore*, 13 January.

Chia, A. (2012). Engineered for the arts. *The Straits Times*, 16 February.

Chong, T. (2014). Bureaucratic imaginations in the global city: arts and culture in Singapore. In Lim, L. and Lee, H. K. (eds.), *Cultural Policies in East Asia* (pp. 17–34). London: Palgrave.

Chong, T. (2018). Introduction. In T. Chong (Ed.), *The State and the Arts in Singapore: Policies and Institutions* (pp. xv–xxxviii). Singapore: World Scientific Publishing.

Economic Development Board Singapore (2012). Media Release: Gillman Barracks Art Galleries to Open September 15. Available from: https://www.nas.gov.sg/archivesonline/data/pdfdoc/20120831001/gillman_barracks_art_galleries_to_open_september_15.pdf. (Last accessed 10 December 2023).

Evans, G. (2009). Creative cities, creative spaces and urban policy. *Urban Studies,* 46 (5&6), 1003–1040.

Grodach, C. (2017). Urban cultural policy and creative city making. *Cities,* 68, 82–91.

Hearn, G., Roodhouse, S., and Blakey, J. (2007). From value chain to value creating ecology: implications for creative industries development policy. *International Journal of Cultural Policy,* 13(4), 419–436.

Hoe, S. F. (2018a). Global ambitions: positioning Singapore as a contemporary arts hub. In Chong, T. (ed.), *The State and the Arts in Singapore: Policies and Institutions* (pp. 351–386). Singapore: World Scientific Publishing.

Hoe, S. F. (2018b). The Arts and Culture Strategic Review Report: harnessing the arts for community-building. In Chong, T. (ed.), *The State and the Arts in Singapore: Policies and Institutions* (pp. 447–472). Singapore: World Scientific Publishing.

Hoe, S. F. (2020). Laden with great expectations: (re)mapping the arts housing policy as urban cultural policy in Singapore. *City, Culture and Society,* 21, 1–7.

Hoe, S. F. (2021). The Substation: How many more canaries in the coal mine. *Arts Equator*, 20 February. Available from: https://artsequator.com/the-substation-armenian-street/. (Last accessed 10 December 2023).

Hoe, S. F. and Chong, T. (2018). Nurturing the cultural desert: The role of museums in Singapore. In Chong, T. (ed.), *The State and the Arts in Singapore: Policies and Institutions* (pp. 241–265). Singapore: World Scientific Publishing.

Huang, L. (2013). Turning arts cluster into a dynamic marketplace. *The Straits Times*, 15 July.

Huang, L. (2016a). The dollars and sense of Art Stage Singapore. *The Straits Times*, 20 January.

Huang, L. (2016b). Growing pains for Singapore art market. *The Straits Times*, 10 May.

Lim, W. (2012). *Incomplete Urbanism: A Critical Strategy for Emerging Economies.* Singapore: World Scientific Publishing.

Ministry of Culture, Community and Youth (2023). *Singapore Cultural Statistics 2022.* Singapore: Ministry of Culture, Community and Youth.

Ministry of Information, Communication, and the Arts (2012). *The Report of the Arts and Culture Strategic Review.* Singapore: Ministry of Information, Communication and the Arts.

Mommaas, H. (2004). Cultural clusters and the post-industrial city: towards the remapping of urban cultural policy. *Urban Studies,* 41(3), 507–532.

Mulcahy, K. (2017). Combating coloniality: the cultural policy of post-colonialism. *International Journal of Cultural Policy,* 23(3), 237–253.

National Arts Council Singapore (2018). *Our SG Arts Plan (2018–2022).* Singapore: National Arts Council.

National Arts Council Singapore (2023). *Our SG Arts Plan (2023–2027).* Singapore: National Arts Council.

Ong, S. F. (2022). Year of revenge arts programming. *The Straits Times,* 17 December. Available from: https://www.straitstimes.com/life/arts/year-of-revenge-arts-programming. (Last accessed 10 December 2023).

Pratt, A. (2010). Creative cities: Tensions within and between social, cultural and economic development: A critical reading of the UK experience. *City, Culture and Society,* 1(1), 13–20.

Scott, A. J. (2006). Creative cities: Conceptual issues and policy questions. *Journal of Urban Affairs,* 28(1), 1–17.

Shetty, D. (2013). Feast for the eyes. *The Straits Times,* 15 January.

Shetty, D. (2015). Setback for art cluster. *The Straits Times,* 11 April.

Singapore Land Authority (2022). Gillman Barracks to be rejuvenated into a vibrant creative lifestyle enclave with enhanced infrastructure, innovate F&B and lifestyle offerings. Available from: https://www.sla.gov.sg/articles/press-releases/2022/gillman-barracks-to-be-rejuvenated-into-a-vibrant-creative-lifestyle-enclave-with-enhanced-infrastructure-innovative-fnb-n-lifestyle-offerings. (Last accessed 10 December 2023).

Sim, A. (2022). As Tanjong Pagar Distripark rises as an arts cluster, whither Gillman Barracks? *The Straits Times,* 16 March. Available from: https://www.straitstimes.com/life/arts/as-tanjong-pagar-distripark-rises-as-an-arts-cluster-whither-gillman-barracks. (Last accessed 10 December 2023).

Toh, W. L. (2021). NAC to revitalise Tanjong Pagar Distripark as an arts cluster. *The Straits Times,* 20 January. Available from: https://www.straitstimes.com/life/arts/nac-to-try-reviving-tanjong-pagar-distripark-as-an-arts-cluster. (Last accessed 10 December 2023).

Vincent, S. (2019). Singapore's only independent cinema. *GLOBE,* 14 February. Available from: https://southeastasiaglobe.com/the-projector-singapore/. (Last accessed 20 December 2023).

VIII

AGEING SOCIETIES

Chapter 24

Ageing Successfully in Singapore

Kanwaljit Soin

Blue Zones

Popularised by *New York Times* bestselling author Dan Buettner, a Blue Zone is a region with a high concentration of centenarians or 100-year-olds. The Five blue zones that have been studied by the author are Okinawa, Japan; Sardinia, Italy; Nicoya, Costa Rica; Icaria, Greece; and Loma Linda, United States. The people in these zones not only live longer but seem to remain healthy and happy even in advanced old age by embracing cultural habits that just so happen to support healthy ageing around eating, exercise, sleep, and socialising.

However, what surprised quite a few people (both ordinary Singaporeans and experts) was the showcasing of the Blue Zone series on Netflix in late August 2023 where Singapore was named as the sixth blue zone. However, Buettner called Singapore a "Blue Zone 2.0": a manufactured Blue Zone — a place where the government has instituted policies designed explicitly to promote longevity — as opposed to one where people (in the other Blue Zones) have embraced longevity through tradition and culture.

The Minister for Health, Ong Ye Kung, added to the Blue Zone conversation by expressing the hope that Singapore would one day become a Blue Zone 3.0. To attain that goal, much work lies ahead. But, the journey has begun.

Lifespan and Health Span

Even though Singapore has one of the highest lifespans at 84 years, the average Singaporean still suffers 10 years of ill health before death. This is the gap between lifespan and health span. The Global Burden of Disease 2019 study ranked Singapore first globally for both life expectancy and healthy life expectancy, ahead of Japan.

Lifespan is the amount of time that passes between when you are born and when you die. Health span is basically how long you live in good health. But, in order to define that, you need to define what good health is.

Living a long life with conditions like severe dementia or chronic pain indicates that your lifespan is lengthy, but your health span has ended. Therefore, 'health span' will always be shorter than or equal to 'lifespan' but never longer.

Most people want to increase their lifespan as much as they can. Living longer is meaningful only if the extra years are healthy, so it is health span that we want and not just lifespan.

In this essay, I would like to trace the journey Singapore has taken from when it realised that it was becoming an ageing society to the present where it is aspiring to become a longevity society. This mindset shift is timely.

Population Ageing in Singapore

With people living longer lives and with falling fertility rates, we are going to have a society that consists of smaller cohorts of younger people and larger cohorts of older people. The number of people over 65 is more than the number of people under 15. To be able to cope with this demographic challenge, the focus has to be on converting an ageing society to a longevity society.

An article from *The Lancet* on this subject has this to say: "An ageing society focuses on changes in the age structure of the population, whereas a longevity society seeks to exploit the advantages of longer lives through changes in how we age. Achieving a longevity society requires substantial changes in the life course and social norms, and involves an epidemiological transition towards a focus on delaying the negative effects of ageing."

Singapore's resident population was 4.07 million at the end of June 2022. The city-state is one of the fastest ageing countries in the world and is going through an unprecedented and dramatic demographic shift. A newborn in Singapore today can expect to live 20 years longer than a newborn in 1960. The number of centenarians doubled from 700 in 2010 to 1500 in 2020.

In 2026, Singapore will become a superaged society with 21% of the population above 65. By 2030, 1 in 4 adults will be over 65 compared to 1 in 31 in 1970. This is a very rapid speed of ageing, and thus society has less time to adapt to this change. Singapore's demographic transition has numerous implications for public policy in many areas which include retirement and health care systems, elder-friendly infrastructure, active ageing programmes, and aged care.

Early Policy Responses to Population Ageing in Singapore

Socioeconomic development and population ageing go hand in hand. The time to invest in ageing is early in that cycle, and so Singapore started its deliberations in the 1980s, but most progress has been made from 2015 onwards.

From the 1980s onwards, a series of government committees were established to formulate policy responses to the challenge of ageing. A brief recap of the history helps us see the evolving perspective of the policymakers in addressing this issue.

A *Committee on the Problems of the Aged* (1982–1984) was formed to study the implications of an ageing population and the ensuing concerns. The Committee called for the customary retirement age to be raised from 55 to 60 and to raise the age for the withdrawal of retirement funds in stages. At that time, the Committee acknowledged that the best guarantee of care for older people comes from the family, and so the report placed special emphasis on the need to foster filial piety among the young.

In 1999, an *Inter-Ministerial Committee on the Ageing Population (IMC)* was established to mount a coordinated national response to the challenges of an ageing society. It sought to realise a vision of 'Successful Ageing in Singapore', with a high degree of preparedness for its challenges and opportunities.

By this time, the nature and earlier expectations of 'filial piety' proposed by the committee of the 1980s began to shift as can be seen in the approach established by the 1999 IMC, which encouraged the concept of 'Many Helping Hands' — where the community, family, and older persons work together in partnership to ensure the well-being of the aged. The role of the State is to set out the policy framework and provide the infrastructure and resources necessary for the other sectors to play their part.

Then, we had the 2004–2006 *Committee on Ageing Issues (CAI)* when a new and urgent emphasis was placed on maintaining a high quality of life for a new cohort of older people — the baby boomers who would reach 65 years of age by 2010. This cohort would be healthier due to rapid advances in medical science and much more educated and economically well-off compared to those of the 1970s and 1980s. Within a window of only a few years, the varied needs and aspirations of this baby boom generation would have to be catered to.

After that, in 2007, *the Ministerial Committee of Ageing (MCA)* was established to coordinate and plan strategies across multiple government agencies to respond to the challenges and opportunities of a rapidly-ageing society.

National Blue Print for Ageing in 2015

In 2015, the MCA introduced the *Action Plan for Successful Ageing*, a national blueprint to enable Singaporeans to age actively and confidently. Launched after a year-long society-wide consultation, the S$3-billion-dollar *Action Plan* has more than 70 initiatives in 12 areas, including health and wellness, education and learning, employment, income sufficiency, protection for vulnerable seniors, housing, transport, public spaces, social inclusion, volunteerism, health care and aged care, and research.

Since this action plan was formulated, Singapore has been moving towards a more holistic view of ageing, health, and care, along with policies and systems related to these.

Nestled within the comprehensive *Action Plan for Successful Ageing*, there is a policy shift towards a population health approach with the introduction of *Healthier SG*.

Healthier SG

Healthier SG is a national strategy anchored on preventive care, which empowers individuals to take steps towards better health with the support of their family doctor and community partners. One of its focuses is nudging behaviour towards good health.

Healthier SG is also building up a national system to support aged care in communities. For this task, Healthier SG works together with the Agency for Integrated Care (AIC), which is the designated single agency to coordinate the delivery of aged care services and enhance service development and capability-building across both the health and social domains.

Consistent with the preferences of many older persons who want to age in place, the service delivery system for Long-Term Care (LTC) emphasises home- and community-based care. This is also a means to deliver value at lower cost by reducing utilisation of institutional care like nursing homes.

Many Helping Hands

The ageing policies formulated so far work in line with the *Many Helping Hands* approach, a long-established principle in the country that calls for individuals, families, communities, civil society, the private sector, and government to all play a role in ensuring the well-being of older people.

It affirms the primacy of the family but also encourages the participation of community-based voluntary welfare organisations and grassroots organisations to help in delivering services.

Unfortunately, 'family' is a codeword for women. I will elaborate more on this when I discuss the gender implications of ageing.

Action Plan for Successful Ageing (Refreshed)

In 2023, the *Action Plan for Successful Ageing* was refreshed.

This refreshed plan focuses on the three key thrusts of *Care, Contribution,* and *Connectedness*, referred to as the '3Cs'. The 3Cs focus on redefining ageing as a positive force, turning 'silver into gold', and ensuring that the conversation on ageing centres on empowering older people, amplifying opportunities, fostering resilience, and building an inclusive society.

Let us look at each of the 3Cs and their mission.

1. Care: to empower older people to take charge of their physical and mental well-being through preventive health, active ageing programmes, and care services to stay healthy and pursue their aspirations.

Under the Care thrust, the AACs (Active Ageing Centres) are a key initiative. There are currently 119 AACs and the number is expected to double to 220 by 2025. These are go-to points for all older people to enrol in active ageing programmes.

With the increase in AACs, 80% of older people will have access to the centres' activities near their homes.

In line with *Healthier SG* plans, the AACs also will serve as community connectors to help older people follow through with lifestyle interventions recommended by their family doctors (social prescriptions).

In addition, AACs (Care), provide care services including maintenance day care, dementia day care, and community rehabilitation.

A caregiver support action plan has been developed to help in informal caregiving.

Collectively, these services will enable older people to enjoy good health as they age in place, while remaining active and supported by a strong community.

2. Contribution: to enable older people to continue to contribute their knowledge and expertise and remain resilient, through an enhanced employment landscape. The statutory retirement and re-employment ages have been raised by one year to 63 and 68 years, respectively, from July 2022.

In my opinion, the retirement age should be abolished as ageing is very heterogeneous. There is no typical older person. Chronological age does not equate with capability, but the move to abolish retirement age is not welcomed by the government.

There is a Senior Employment Credit (SEC) scheme which provides wage offsets for employers who employ Singaporeans aged 60 and above who earn up to S$4000 a month.

There is another scheme to incentivise employers to offer part-time re-employment and flexible work arrangements and structured career planning for older workers.

The government plans to enact workplace fairness legislation to address age discrimination.

Life-long learning:
Ample provision been has made for older workers to be able to upgrade their skills through generous subsidies from the national *SkillsFuture* programme and to help them move into new occupations or sectors that have good opportunities for progression.

An important institution for older persons to continue life-long learning is the National Silver Academy. This is a network of post-secondary education institutions (i.e. Institute of Technical Education, polytechnics, universities, and arts institutions) and voluntary welfare organisations (VWOs) that offer learning opportunities for older people catering to their different interests and needs. More than 1000 courses are offered across a range of topics via a one-stop platform.

3. Connectedness: Older persons will be supported to age in place within an inclusive built environment while staying connected to their loved ones and society through support networks that embody the '*kampung*' (village in Malay) spirit and digital platforms.

With 99% of resident households here connected to the Internet, Singapore has one of the highest Internet penetration rates in the world. However, only 93% of older-person-only households have Internet access. The 7% gap is due largely to older persons' perceived lack of need, skills, and confidence in using the Internet. The Infocomm Media Development Authority and SG Digital Office launched the *Seniors Go Digital* programme in May 2020 to empower older people with the skills needed to go digital. There is also a provision for subsidised smartphone and mobile plans for lower-income older persons who want to go digital, but cannot afford it. Also, the organisation has recruited more than 1000 digital ambassadors to support over 200,000 older people. The ambassadors help older people use their digital devices to do everything from e-payment to booking transport.

Social Isolation

In 2021, the World Health Organization (WHO) stated that social isolation affects around 1 in 4 older adults worldwide. However, this number is higher in Singapore. The number of elderly living alone doubled to 63,800 in 2020 from a decade ago and is set to hit 83,000 by 2030.

A 2015 study by CARE, at the Duke-NUS Medical School, found that 2 in 5 Singaporeans aged 62 years and older are lonely. A more recent analysis from the long-running Singapore Chinese Health Study found that older Chinese are at higher risk of social disconnection than before. Social isolation or disconnection refers to the lack of physical, social, and emotional engagement with other people. Surprisingly, the most socially-disconnected individuals actually live with family members.

In the CARE brief (2018/04), it was reported that between 2000 and 2015 the percentage of older men living alone remained relatively constant while the percentage of older women living alone increased by 40%. This is likely due to women's longer life expectancy and higher chances of remaining single and being widowed. Living alone is associated with more depressive symptoms.

Some strategies to combat loneliness are evident in the refreshed *Action Plan for Successful Ageing*, but social isolation of older persons remains a big issue. These people are at increased risk of death, heart disease, stroke, dementia, and depression. It is hoped that social isolation and loneliness will be helped by another programme — *Age Well SG*.

Age Well SG

What is *Age Well SG*? It is a national programme announced by Mr Lee Hsien Loong, then Prime Minister of Singapore, in his National Day rally speech in August 2023 — it offers a comprehensive nation-wide transformation across the areas of transport, housing, active ageing, and care services to anchor ageing in the community.

This is a long-term programme that will be progressively implemented.

According to the Health Minister, *Age Well SG* will help seniors build social circles and live an active lifestyle in the community in order to fight loneliness. He said, "We hope to delay and avoid institutionalisation of as many seniors as possible. Living in a nursing home, their health deteriorates."

In a speech at the 15th Singapore Economic Policy Forum in November 2023, the Minster for Health said that the *Healthier SG* plan, a preventive care programme funded to the tune of S$400 million a year which helps people lead healthier lives, is Singapore's best bet to keep health care affordable but may not be enough for the country to achieve an elevated Blue Zone 3.0 status, where the gap between lifespan and health span narrows, without other measures. That is why Singapore is investing in *Age Well SG*.

This *Age Well SG* programme will complement the provision of senior-friendly features within HDB homes. Public housing flats, or HDB flats, are the most popular type of residential units in

Singapore offered by the Housing and Development Board. They are affordable homes that are available for purchase or rent at sub-sidised rates. These flats are conveniently located near amenities and public transportation. Currently, 80% of Singaporeans live in HDB housing, resulting in a high homeownership rate of 89.30%. Eligible citizens can purchase HDB properties at a lower price compared to private properties, but they must meet strict eligibility criteria, including specific monthly income ceilings and a 5-year minimum occupation period requirement.

The *Age Well SG* plan also oversees the built environment. The National Parks Board has plans to enhance its parks and gardens with more elder-friendly landscape features. There are initiatives to make streets more friendly for the elderly through features like wider footpaths, barrier-free pedestrian crossings, and lower speed limits for motorists.

Long-Term Care, LTC

Not only is our population ageing but those aged 75 and older form the most rapidly-growing segment of the older adult population in Singapore and globally.

One very important implication is the increasing demand for long-term care services for this group of the oldest old. More atten-tion needs to be paid to the heterogeneity in the nature of long-term care.

As of 2021, there were 639,000 senior citizens and permanent residents in Singapore. Most seniors age in place at home (97%). A minority reside in nursing homes (2.5%) and even fewer live in assisted facilities (0.1%) (*Assisted-Living Round Table Report*).

Singapore's approach to long-term care (LTC) focuses on home- and community-based care, nested within the overarching *Action Plan for Successful Ageing* and a policy shift towards a population health approach *(Healthier SG)*. To provide more assisted living options for older people to age in place, HDB will ramp up the supply of Community Care Apartments (CCAs). This is a public housing typology that pairs senior-friendly housing with on-site social activities and care services that can be customised according to the older person's care needs. Older people living in CCAs enjoy convenient access to various amenities.

However, the majority of LTC is provided informally, but the cost of informal care is ignored in official statistics.

We are also increasing nursing home capacity, with the number of beds set to double from 16,000 in 2020 to 31,000 in 2030, but most people in Singapore want to age in place.

Social Security System

There are four components of Singapore's social security system — CPF retirement income, home ownership, healthcare coverage, and Silver Support Scheme.

Central Provident Fund (CPF)

Singapore's pension system is based on defined contributions. Established in 1955, the Central Provident Fund (CPF) is a compulsory social security savings scheme and a crucial part of Singapore's social security system (Ministry of Manpower Singapore, 2022). Singaporeans and their employers pay into the accounts under the CPF. These funds can be withdrawn at older ages or used to finance a home, pay for medical expenses, or other approved investments (Haskins, 2011).

Launched in 2009, CPF LIFE is a national annuity scheme that provides Singaporeans with a monthly payout for life. The premium is deducted from the individual CPF accounts.

Those who are potentially not included in the CPF LIFE scheme include housewives, self-employed individuals, and business owners who do not contribute regularly to their CPF.

There is a very high rate of home ownership — 89.3% of Singaporean households own their own houses, and 90.9% of those staying in public housing own their flats as of 2022 (Singapore Department of Statistics, 2022b). Therefore, it is often said that Singaporeans are 'asset rich but cash poor'. The government has put into place a few housing monetisation options or schemes designed to offer older persons financial security into their twilight years.

Silver Support Scheme

For seniors with low incomes during their working years, resulting in lower retirement pensions, the government introduced the Silver Support Scheme in 2016. This scheme is meant to support the bottom one-third of Singaporeans aged 65+ with quarterly cash supplements. Eligible seniors will receive support per quarter depending on household income and type of housing, ranging from S$180 to S$900 (Silver Support Singapore, 2022). The quarterly cash supplements benefitted nearly 250,000 Singaporeans aged 65+. These payouts are low in amount and only augment other forms of retirement funds. More women than men are recipients of this scheme.

Gender Aspects of Ageing

In Singapore, the life expectancy of women is about 5 years longer than that of men. In 2022, the life expectancy for male residents in Singapore at birth was 80.7 years, while that for female residents was 85.2 years. Women live longer, but they are more likely than men to develop Alzheimer's disease, even when women's, on average, longer lifespans are taken into account. The reasons for this are unclear.[1]

Half of the women over 65 are single, because they never married, got divorced, or were widowed, making them more vulnerable to socioeconomic hardship and more handicapped by age discrimination. In fact, ageism can be more troubling for women than the ageing process itself.

An area with enormous gender implications is the realm of LTC in Singapore. As mentioned earlier, the code word for family is

---

[1] https://www.aic.sg/wp-content/uploads/2023/06/AIC_Living-With-Dementia_Booklet-1_Eng.pdf.

women. Today, the cost of caring for the substantial ageing population is falling disproportionately on women, many of them unmar-
ried, who have sacrificed careers and retirement savings to care for
their elders but have no children to do the same for them.

In 2021, the Centre for Ageing Research and Education (Care)
at the Duke-NUS Medical School reported a study of caregivers of
those aged 75 and older. In this study (TraCE), it was found that the
average age of caregivers is 62 years. Almost three in four caregivers are women. About one in three of the caregivers have never
been married. A significant proportion of caregivers to older adults
face health problems themselves and these issues may also make
them more vulnerable to the challenges and stresses that come
with caregiving.

The period of caregiving has also lengthened due to increasing
longevity, resulting in increased financial and emotional burdens
on caregivers. The average caregiver loses 63% of her income,
more than US$40,000, according to a 2019 study by AWARE, a
gender rights organisation.

Population ageing presents manifold and interrelated implications for societies but inevitably exacerbates gender inequity. The
simplest reason women are hardest hit by population ageing is that
gender inequality compounds over time and most older people are
women.

Silver Economy

Policies should not see older people just as a burden but instead
as a powerful human and social resource. Expenditure on older
adults is not a drain on societies but an investment in this economic
resource.

As the median population age increases, so do opportunities
for Singapore businesses to provide products and services for
older people.

Singapore's silver economy is booming from health care start-
ups using AI to treat elderly patients to platforms that curate their
lifestyle goods.

Singapore shows the largest market potential for an ageing population among 15 Asia-Pacific countries according to Ageing Asia's Silver Economy Index 2020, and is set to reach S$72.4 billion by 2025.

Conclusion

Successful ageing can be defined as older adults thriving in productive roles and having high levels of physical and mental well-being, social connectedness, and financial security (Chen *et al.*, 2018).

Successful ageing requires attention to physical, psychological, and social well-being. It necessitates a multi-stakeholder, whole-of-society effort to address this challenge and Singapore has done this with a multipronged approach to ageing, health, and care.

The reforms and plans for successful ageing in Singapore are relatively new, so smooth implementation will require continued effort to achieve and it will take time to assess the impact at the system and population levels in the medium and long term.

Blue Zone Status for Singapore

Since this essay was started on the Blue Zone status of Singapore, I will end on the same note. The Minister for Health has noted that Singapore is ageing successfully because we have infrastructure and programmes that nudge our people towards healthier behaviours. Ultimately, he said, healthier behaviours that were brought about by policies and programmes need to evolve into new lifestyles and habits over time. He added that it may take a generation to achieve this.

On a concluding note, he said, "Just like Singapore is a nation created by conviction and will, Singapore as a Blue Zone is constructed through policy."

A final thought for this essay — maybe we should all strive for 'successful living' and not 'successful ageing'. Ageing is what we do as soon as we are born. Living is what we do with our time.

Bibliography

Chen *et al.* (2018). Transitions in Health, Employment, Social Engagement and Intergenerational Transfers in Singapore (The SIGNS Study) — Descriptive Statistics and Analysis of Key aspects of Successful Ageing. Centre for Ageing Research and Education (CARE).

Chen C. *et al.* (2023). *Societal Aging and Its Impact on Singapore*. Singapore. https://www.nber.org/system/files/chapters/c14917/c14917.pdf. National Bureau of Economic Research (NBER) (Accessed 27 December 2023).

Haskins, R. (2011). Social policy in Singapore: A crucible of individual responsibility. *Ethos: Journal of the Society for Psychological Anthropology* Commentary in BROOKINGS (Singapore).

Soin, K. (2018). *Silver Shades of Grey: Memos for Successful Ageing in the 21st Century.* World Scientific, Singapore.

Chapter 25

We Need to Talk About Women: Retirement Policy and Practice in New Zealand

Jane Wrightson

New Zealand is generally regarded as a progressive country, the first country to give women the right to vote in 1893 and, in 1898, the first to offer a state pension fully funded by taxation.

As with many other countries, we have an ageing population (but not for Māori or Pacific peoples with their much younger demographic profile), and the policy development to address this tends to be sporadic. Our retirement policies are also only addressed infrequently, often with insufficient data and rarely a focus on women. This chapter will consider various retirement income issues through a gender lens.

There is remarkably little economic information on older women. Women's economic status can be tracked but less so for that of older women; some would say in a similar pattern to women's lessening visibility in society as they age. Women's contributions, as in most countries, are under-recognised and rarely accorded an economic value. In my lifetime, this has not changed very much — Dame Marilyn Waring's seminal work *Counting for Nothing* (Waring, 1988), asserting that as 'non-producers' women do not fairly receive the benefits of economic distribution, still rings true.

From the gender pay gap to the filtering out of women reaching higher-paid jobs, to career interruptions and caregiving, to unequal positions after divorce or other life shocks, majority of women will earn considerably less than their male counterparts during their life. And, their longevity means a longer retirement period to fund.

A comprehensive report on New Zealand's women and retirement (Morrissey, 2022, p. 18) provides a salutary summary that has barely changed over decades:

> *Women have lower income, with almost 50% of women (of pension age) receiving less than $30,000 p.a., compared to around a third of men. Women are more reliant on NZ Super (the government pension) than men because of their lower savings and investments. Women also live by themselves for longer, due to men's shorter life expectancy, and so have higher costs and a longer period to fund after the age of 65. Women who continue paid work after the age of 65 are more likely than men to identify financial reasons for their decision. Women perform 60% of all volunteer hours and many of these are performed by older women. On average, women have lower KiwiSaver (voluntary savings) balances than men, and lower overall wealth.*

So, nearly 50% of women aged 65–69 live on less than NZ$30,000 per annum.[1] These women are wholly reliant on the New Zealand Superannuation, compared to 30% of men of the same age (Morrissey, 2022, p. 65).

Yet, it is difficult to secure systemic improvement because the debate around retirement and its funding remains immature.

The New Zealand Retirement Savings System

The New Zealand retirement income system has just two tiers: the government age pension NZ Superannuation ('NZ Super') and voluntary retirement savings through KiwiSaver, an opt-out portable scheme with employer contributions. Unlike countries such as

---

[1] For the year that ended in June 2023, the median annual salary/wage was just over NZ$66,000 (Statistics NZ, 2023).

Australia and Singapore, there is no compulsory retirement savings scheme, and New Zealand's employer contributions are set at a low 3%, which can be folded into a 'total remuneration' package, meaning the employee in reality is paying the full contribution.

Unfortunately, there is no stated legislative purpose for the New Zealand system. The Retirement Commission has developed a purpose statement with which to assess policy changes:

Retirement Income Purpose Statement — New Zealand

A stable retirement income framework enables trust and confidence that older New Zealand residents can live with dignity and *mana*,[2] participate in and contribute to society, and enjoy a high level of belonging and connection to their whanau, community and country.

To help current and future retirees to achieve this, a sustainable retirement income framework's purpose is twofold:

1. To provide **NZ Superannuation** to ensure an adequate standard of living for New Zealanders of eligible age. NZ Super is the Government's primary contribution to financial security for the remainder of a person's life.
2. To actively support New Zealanders to build and manage **independent savings** that contribute to their ability to maintain their own relative standard of living.

The retirement income system sits within the broader government provision of infrastructure also needed to enable older New Zealanders to live well, such as health care, housing, and transport.

NZ Super

The good news is that NZ Super is a simple, gender-blind scheme with entitlement focused simply on reaching age 65 plus some

---

[2] A Māori word invoking concepts such as authority, respect, influence, and power.

residency requirements. NZ Super helps reduce elder poverty by providing a basic income, but is implicitly predicated on no significant housing costs, namely, that a pensioner has a freehold home or lives in suitable low-cost public housing. Both options are now under significant pressure for the foreseeable future: We are predicting a 100% increase in senior renters from 2018 to 2048.

In a comparative study of pension policies through a gender lens, Dale and St John (2020) note that NZ Super is a simple system compared to Australia and Ireland because of uncomplicated eligibility rules. However, the lack of quality data in all three countries obscures gender issues.

It is nigh impossible to develop efficient, effective policies without reliable data. New or improved policies that will lift retirement outcomes for women who will otherwise fall further behind should, where possible, reflect principles of simplification, adequacy, inclusion, and sustainability. Improved policies would acknowledge the value and range of the unpaid work, largely performed by women, that sustains our economies (Dale and St John, 2020, p. 57).

The bad news is that NZ Super, calculated as a percentage of median wage, is seen as generous by some and an unfair distribution of government resources by others since it relies solely on taxation funding. Most discussion is around its cost, with current gross expenditure around 4.7% of the GDP and projected to rise to 7.7% by 2060. This is unremarkable as NZ Super is the ninth least expensive pension in the OECD as a proportion of GDP (OECD, 2023).

New Zealand's expenditure on NZ Super will continue to be well below the OECD average in 40 years' time, without raising the age of eligibility.

However, debate seeking change tends to focus on the age of entitlement rather than, for instance, means or income testing (see, for example, Law, 2020). This debate is usually led by people with higher incomes and desk jobs and tends to ignore the inequity of such a move on Māori and Pacific peoples, those with lower life expectancies, and those with manual jobs.

A gender lens is rarely applied or taken seriously. If it were, and if there were better data, there would be useful conversations around, for example, the cost of the scheme versus the benefit it provides women. NZ Super, a strong and administratively simple scheme, comes under regular attack, often politically-driven, and with arguments focused purely on cost. New Zealanders themselves, when asked to consider the trade-offs in a University of Otago study, strongly opposed both means testing and raising the age of eligibility but were willing to consider taxation increases now rather than burden future generations (Te Ara Ahunga Ora Retirement Commission, 2022a).

Independent savings

NZ Super, in effect, is a universal basic income scheme. Additional savings are needed to provide a more comfortable retirement and especially to fund higher expenses such as health costs or household equipment. Here again, women are at a disadvantage as most earn less than their male counterparts throughout their working life due to the gender pay gap, time out of paid work, and high rates of part-time employment. The Ministry for Women estimates that, over their lifetimes, New Zealand women earn over NZ$880,000 less than men. (Ministry for Women, no date).

The KiwiSaver scheme is somewhat similar to Singapore's Central Provident Fund, in that it is an employment-based scheme that requires both employer and employee contributions. However, KiwiSaver is portable and focused on individual retirement savings using providers from the financial services industry. The scheme is just 17 years old and already shows troubling but predictable gender trends. The average KiwiSaver balance is NZ$27,379. There is a notable gap between males (NZ$31,496) and females (NZ$25,144) with the average balance for a male being 25% higher than the average balance for a female (Melville Jessup Weaver, 2023). This gap increased from 20% in just one year from 2022. There is a lack of data to confirm reasons and thus suggest policy improvements, but we expect the gender savings gap to continue to grow.

Outcomes for Māori and Pacific peoples, who also earn far less in their working lives, are even worse, so Māori and Pacific women are even more disadvantaged, as are women with disabilities (Te Ara Ahunga Ora Retirement Commission, 2022b).

Financial Capability

Financial capability or literacy is deeper than simply *knowing* what to do. Behavioural economics applied to financial capability (see, for example, OECD, 2018) shows there are other factors that diminish or build financial capability — cultural, psychological, social, and political. Figure 1 shows the influences (Te Ara Ahunga Ora Retirement Commission, 2023).

Figure 1.   What Influences Our Decisions?

Both professionally and personally, women's lesser economic status is compounded by their lower levels of financial literacy, even among better-educated women (Gamble, 2022). The gender gap in financial literacy is a global problem (Hasler and Lusardi, 2017). The reasons are complex, and solutions rely as much on better targeting of information and support from the financial services industry as on self-upskilling and simply being able to earn more money.

The truth remains that women on low incomes, with an interrupted work history, or who have experienced a significant life shock such as business failure or divorce, will simply not be able to save enough without intensive support and a genuine opportunity to increase their earning power. The portable retirement savings scheme KiwiSaver has been an excellent innovation, but it too has weaknesses — low mandatory contribution levels and a focus on salaried employment — that do not attract sufficient policy attention.

Politics and Change

Women comprise 53.2% of New Zealanders over 65, so the impact of any retirement income policy change on women should be a primary policy question. This is not currently the case.

A key issue is the difficulty in securing long-term agreements across different governments. With inadequate data, and gender aspects rarely being considered, it seems clear that women will be affected most by any regressive policy change.

The impact in the United Kingdom, which is in the process of raising its pension age from 65 to 66 then 67, has already revealed negative effects. Analysis conducted by the UK government's Department of Work and Pensions shows that after just a year with the pension age at 66, there has been a 13 percent increase in the number of 66-year-olds living in income poverty (i.e. having a household income that is 60 percent below the 2010/11 median UK household level after accounting for inflation). The impact of the age of eligibility change was even more pronounced for those who were single, those with low/no qualifications, and renters, with poverty rates increasing by between 17 and 25 percent for

66-year-olds falling into these groups[3] (Secretary of State for
Works and Pension, 2023, Annex).

Debates in New Zealand around other long-term issues, such
as infrastructure funding, public housing, and health provision, all
suffer from similar issues: an increasingly polarised political environment, increased abuse of politicians on all sides, binary arguments, and increased public mistrust of government and media.
This may be a temporary result of the COVID-19 intervention
years, but it is a difficult environment in which to moot and execute
good long-range policy. Particularly after the substantial cost of the
initial response to COVID-19, most countries including New
Zealand are facing significant fiscal challenges, and larger government expenditure items, such as NZ Super, are considered scepti-
cally in some quarters.

Long-term stability is a hallmark of a good retirement income
system, yet such stability is challenged by this fractious political
and media environment. A principled way to address the challenges would be a legislated, independent system review, reporting
to Parliament, say, every 7 or 10 years, looking at all aspects of the
retirement income system, including the impact on women and the
Māori, and making recommendations for improvement or adjustment as necessary.

A system review that was broad enough to consider gender
(and ethnicity) would start by assessing the strengths of the current
system and could formally propose a range of improvements or
alternatives, such as the following:

- Retaining the current eligibility age of 65 years.
- If government cost savings must be found, consider income
  testing for those who claim NZ Super (noting the case for
  Government savings remains unproven and that there are
  many types of expenditure reduction or revenue increases a
  government can choose). If income testing is introduced with a

---

[3] While there is no gender breakdown in this part of the report, we know that women tend to
be over-represented in these groups.

base of, say, twice the average wage, fewer women will be affected because they have lower incomes.
- Super-charging targeted, appealing, and long-running financial education initiatives for women.
- Financial recognition of unpaid work (for example, KiwiSaver contributions from the government for care or parental leave).

Trade-offs need to be balanced, the purpose of change clearly articulated, and discussion informed and inclusive. While the cost of the system is important to understand, it is not the only issue.

Retirement income policy is also about environmental and demographic change, political choices, and citizen welfare, with the circumstances of both current- and next-generation older women actively included. They are the largest group affected by any change, yet a gender lens is rarely used to understand and address the impact.

References

Dale, M. C. and St John, S. (2020). *Women and Retirement in a Post COVID-19 World*. Auckland: University of Auckland, Retirement Policy and Research Centre. Available at WP 2020-1 Women and Retirement FINAL.pdf (auckland.ac.nz). (Accessed 6 January 2024).

Gamble, J. (2022). *New Zealand Financial Capability: Focus on Women*. Te Ara Ahunga Ora Retirement Commission. Available at Deep-dive-on-womens-financial-capability.pdf (retirement.govt.nz). (Accessed 6 January 2024).

Hasler, A. and Lusardi, A. (2017). *The Gender Gap in Financial Literacy: A Global Perspective*. Washington D.C.: George Washington University School of Business, Global Financial Literacy Excellence Center. Available at Gender and Financial Literacy-A Global Perspective-06-28-17.indd (gflec.org). (Accessed 6 January 2024).

Law, D. (2020). *Policy Point: Borrowing to Save: Retirement Income Policy After COVID-19*. The New Zealand Initiative. Available at apo-nid306421.pdf. (Accessed 6 January 2024).

Melville Jessup Weaver (2023). *KiwiSaver Demographic Study*. Available at KiwiSaver Demographic Study (retirement.govt.nz). (Accessed 6 January 2024).

Ministry for Women (no date). *Women and Work*. Available at: https://women.govt.nz/women-and-work. (Accessed 6 January 2024).

Morrissey, S. (2022). *What Does Retirement Look Like For Women?* Te Ara Ahunga Ora Retirement Commission. Available at TAAO-What-does-retirement-look-like-for-women_2022.pdf. (Accessed 6 January 2024).

NZ History (undated). *Old Age Pensions Act becomes law.* Available at https://nzhistory.govt.nz/old-age-pensions-act-passes-into-law (Accessed 6 January 2024).

OECD (2018). *The Application of Behavioural Insights to Financial Literacy and Investor Education Programmes and Initiatives.* Available at https://www.oecd.org/finance/The-Application-of-Behavioural-Insights-to-Financial-Literacy-and-Investor-Education-Programmes-and-Initiatives.pdf. (Accessed 6 January 2024).

OECD (2023). *Pensions at a Glance: OECD and G20 Indicators.* Available at oecd-ilibrary.org. (Accessed 6 January 2024).

Secretary of State for Work and Pensions (2023). *Policy Paper: State Pension Age Review 2023.* London: Department for Work and Pensions. Available at https://www.gov.uk/government/publications/state-pension-age-review-2023-government-report/state-pension-age-review-2023. (Accessed 6 January 2024).

Statistics NZ (2023). Labour market statistics (income): June 2023 quarter. (Accessed 6 January 2024).

Te Ara Ahunga Ora Retirement Commission (2022a). *Policy and Research: NZ Super.* Available at https://retirement.govt.nz/policy-and-research/nz-super/. (Accessed 6 January 2024).

Te Ara Ahunga Ora Retirement Commission (2022b). *Review of Retirement Income Policies.* Available at RRIP_2022.pdf (retirement.govt.nz). (Accessed 6 January 2024).

Te Ara Ahunga Ora Retirement Commission (2023). *What is Financial Capability?* Available at https://retirement.govt.nz/financial-capability/what-is-financial-capability/ (Accessed 6 January 2024).

Waring, M. (1988). *Counting for Nothing: What Men Value and What Women Are Worth.* Bridget Williams Books. Wellington, New Zealand.